A TO Z

NOVEL IDEAS
FOR
READING TEACHERS

Kay Martin and Tina Willoughby

Cottonwood Press, Inc.
Fort Collins, Colorado

Requests for permission, other than personal classroom use, should be addressed to:

Cottonwood Press, Inc.
109-B Cameron Drive
Fort Collins, Colorado 80525

E-mail: cottonwood@cottonwoodpress.com
Web: www.cottonwoodpress.com
Phone: 1-800-864-4297
Fax: 970-204-0761

ISBN 13: 978-1-877673-42-0

Printed in the United States of America

The authors would like to thank students Sarah Jackson and Jaclyn Delgadillo for their art-work in the examples and answer keys. They would also like to thank the reading department at Driscoll Middle School for trying out ideas and offering current examples.

In loving memory, I dedicate this book to my best friend and co-author,
Tina Willoughby
December 10, 1953–September 27, 1999

Tina is fondly remembered as someone who enjoyed life to the fullest measure and impacted everyone she met. She taught those of us who knew her to live every minute, laugh every day and love unconditionally. She treasured reading, and she passed that legacy on to children and adults alike. Though she is missed terribly, her creative spirit lives on in the pages of this book and in the hearts of students whose lives she so positively and profoundly influenced.

Kay Martin

TABLE OF CONTENTS

CONTINUED

Using A to Z

A *to* Z activities give students the chance to explore their insights into literature in a variety of ways — through writing, poetry, art, research, and making personal connections to characters, quotations and events. The activities include easy-to-follow directions and, when appropriate, examples and sample answer keys. These teacher-tested, hands-on activities will engage students of all levels and learning styles.

We first presented some of our activities at the Texas Middle School Conference seven years ago. Over two hundred reading and English teachers crammed into a room, eager for fresh ideas related to the teaching of reading and literature. After our presentation, many in attendance told us that we should publish our materials. We decided to contact Cottonwood Press, which — happily — agreed. With the encouragement of the kind women there, the book is now a reality.

Kay Martin
Tina Willoughby

A TO Z

ACTIVITIES

AMAZING

With "Amazing," students respond to literature by completing open-ended statements. There are no right or wrong answers. The activity gives you, the teacher, insight as to how students are interpreting what they have read.

After they finish a reading assignment, have students complete any five of the following open-ended statements, relating the statements to what they have read:

- Isn't it amazing that . . .
- The most amazing part of the resolution was . . .
- Wasn't it amazing when . . .
- The most amazing description was . . .
- It is amazing how . . .
- The most amazing discovery was . . .
- _____ was amazing because . . .
- The turn of events that was most amazing was . . .
- The fact that was the most amazing to me was . . .
- The most amazing action by a character was . . .
- The most amazing lesson learned was . . .
- The most amazing quote was . . .
- The most amazing setting was . . .
- The most amazing conflict was . . .
- I am amazed that . . .

EXAMPLE

(Based on the book *The Invisible Thread*, by Yoshiko Uchida)

- Isn't it amazing that the United States government forced Japanese Americans into concentration camps?
- Tanforan was amazing because it didn't have doors on the toilets or showers, and people had to wash in long tin sinks like feeding troughs.
- The most amazing action by a character was Mama serving tea to the FBI agent.
- The most amazing lesson learned was that people can overcome terrible situations and still be happy.

ACROSTIC POEMS

"Acrostic Poems" are useful for checking students' understanding of character. Students base their poems on their favorite character — or the most interesting character — from their reading.

First, students complete a rough draft of their poem. Have them begin by writing the character's name down the page, vertically, in large, bold letters.

Next, have them use each letter in the character's name as the first letter in a line of poetry. Each line should make a statement about the character, suggested by the story's content.

EXAMPLE

(Based on the character Jesse from the novel *Bridge to Terabithia,* by Katherine Paterson)

Just a boy from the country who truly loved art . . .

Everyday, his mother had him do more than his part.

Sisters nagged him, except for Maybelle . . .

She "worshiped" him as anyone could tell.

Escape for him was being with Leslie.

Each line can say something independent of the other lines, or the whole poem can tell a story. The acrostic does not have to rhyme, but it should make perfect sense and use story content.

When students have polished their poems, have them make their final copies, adding drawings or illustrations that symbolize the character they have chosen. For example, for the character Jesse in the example above, a student might draw a piece of paper and colored pencils to represent Jesse's love of art.

SEE ALSO EXAMPLES IN ANSWER KEY, PAGE 65

APPENDIX

Completing an appendix can help clarify material for students. Depending on the circumstances, a class might complete one appendix as a group, or each student might prepare an individual appendix.

Explain that an appendix is a collection of supplementary material at the end of a book. It is used to provide information that may help readers better understand what they are reading. For example, some novels include names for objects, animals, colloquialisms, obsolete inventions, etc., which may be unfamiliar to readers. An appendix can be used as a reference to provide clarification.

Begin by having students collect words, terms and phrases for the appendix. Then have them alphabetize their collection and write a clear definition or explanation for each item. They should also include illustrations, when appropriate.

For *Savage Sam*, by Fred Gipson, one class made appendix pages for the following words and phrases:

adz
bobcats
buffalo
gray wolf
ruby-throated hummingbird
Indian healing
pronghorns
rattlesnakes
Apache Indians' religious beliefs
repeating rifles
tarantula
terrapins
water buffaloes

> **TIP**
> Save student-created appendix pages for use by future classes, or place them in the school library or media center for use by other students.

Books

At the end of a novel unit, have students create books of their own as a class project. Two ideas are "Class Chapter Book" and "ABC Book."

Class Chapter book

For a class chapter book, assign a chapter of a book to each student. On plain white paper, have students put the chapter number and title at the top of the page. Students should then draw a picture that represents the most important event in the chapter. The picture should be neat and colorful and fill most of the page.

At the bottom of the page, the student should write one or two sentences that clearly state the main idea(s) of the chapter. Encourage students to think carefully about how to best summarize the chapter in only a few words.

Example

**CHAPTER 15
HOMECOMING**

Gilly finally learns the truth about her mother and calls Trotter, crying and disappointed.

<u>**Tip**</u>
A contest for the cover design of the book always makes the finished product more interesting!

SEE ALSO EXAMPLES IN ANSWER KEY, PAGE 66

ABC BOOKS

For a class-generated ABC book, start by assigning a letter of the alphabet to each student. (If you have several classes, just start over until every student has a letter. If you wind up with three E's, include them all in the book, pick the best for the book, or make several books.)

Students must then connect the letter assigned to them with a concept from the novel they read. For example, they might choose a main character name, part of the setting, a symbol from the novel, a theme, or an object of significance in the story.

Have students follow this format at the top of each page:

A IS FOR ◆ ◆ ◆ **A**nnemarie, who bravely risked her life for her friend Ellen.	**B IS FOR ◆ ◆ ◆** **B**ravery, and all the times it was needed.

The rest of the page is reserved for an illustration. Ask students to use color and fill the page with the illustration, leaving a half inch or so on the left to allow for binding the pages.

EXAMPLE

Q IS FOR ◆ ◆ ◆

Quickly, which is how Annemarie ran on the path to give the basket to Uncle Henrik.

TIP

This project also works well with a unit of study such as the Civil War, Japan or ancient Egypt.

Another idea is to use the project for books students have been reading on their own, having each student complete an entire ABC Book project individually.

SEE ALSO EXAMPLES IN ANSWER KEY, PAGE 67

A to Z • Copyright © 2000 • Cottonwood Press, Inc. • Fort Collins, Colorado • 1-800-864-4297 • www.cottonwoodpress.com

CARTOON SUMMARY

"Cartoon Summaries" are useful for summarizing plot. You can photocopy the assignment on page 17 for your students, or simply have them draw the boxes themselves on white paper.

It is useful to review several comic strips with students before they begin working. Look at different styles of cartooning and different conventions used — like lines drawn next to the the feet to indicate running or a light bulb above a character's head to indicate an idea.

TIP

Limiting students to six cartoon frames forces them to review the plot carefully and select only the most important events.

EXAMPLE

(From *Cousins*, by Virginia Hamilton)

DIRECTIONS

Use the following squares to retell the story you read, in cartoon form. Pick the six most important events. Illustrate each event and add a caption that tells what is happening. You may also use thought or speech bubbles to convey what the characters are thinking or saying.

　　Taken together, your cartoons should summarize the story, and the sequence of events should be correct. Make your cartoon colorful! (Plan your work on another piece of paper before you begin drawing in the squares.)

CAST YOUR BALLOT

"Cast Your Ballot" allows students to express their opinions as they learn to support those opinions with examples.

Give students a list of categories and have them make nominations for "best" in each category, based upon the novel the group has read. Students should support their nominations by giving examples from the book or providing other explanations.

Make a class ballot based on the nominations and allow students to cast their ballots to come up with winners in each category.

EXAMPLE

NOMINATION FORM

1. Best female character: _____

2. Best male character: _____

3. Most descriptive paragraph: Page #: ____ Paragraph #: ____

4. Most humorous event: _____

5. Least favorite character: _____

6. Biggest surprise: _____

7. Saddest moment: _____

8. Most intense scene: _____

9. Most exciting chapter: _____

10. Most likely to happen in real life: _____

You will need to adapt the categories to fit whatever book the class has read. It's a good idea to limit the categories to no more than ten.

SEE ALSO EXAMPLES IN ANSWER KEY, PAGE 68

A to Z • Copyright © 2000 • Cottonwood Press, Inc. • Fort Collins, Colorado • 1-800-864-4297 • www.cottonwoodpress.com

Dot, Dot, Dot ◆ ◆ ◆

"Dot, Dot, Dot . . ." can be used with any type of reading material. The open-ended statements ending with ellipses can enhance discussion in the classroom.

After students have finished their reading, give them the entire list of incomplete sentences below. Then have them choose five items to "answer," completing each statement and providing examples from the reading selection to support their answers.

When they are finished, have students share with the class. Each student should read one statement. No one may share a statement that has already been read aloud (unless completed in a different way).

I think that . . .

The most surprising thing to me was . . .

I cannot believe that . . .

If I were (character's name), I would . . .

It made me angry when . . .

What I can relate to most is . . .

I did not understand why . . .

I wish . . .

I know that . . .

How could . . .

I was sad when . . .

I know someone just like . . .

I have . . .

Why did . . .

I wonder why . . .

The author . . .

The best thing . . .

I would like it if . . .

If . . .

When . . .

The beginning was . . .

It was exciting when . . .

Could it be that . . .

I loved it when . . .

Maybe . . .

Now . . .

My favorite character is . . .

It was great when . . .

I really laughed when . . .

I wanted to cry when . . .

I would never . . .

No wonder . . .

I agree with . . .

I predict . . .

I'm reminded of . . .

I would not . . .

TIP

"Dot, Dot, Dot . . ." also makes a great warm-up activity. As a warm-up, pick only one or two of the statements for the students to complete and share with the class.

SEE ALSO EXAMPLES IN ANSWER KEY, PAGE 69

EVIDENCE

"Evidence" helps students examine a work carefully in order to provide support for a statement or point of view.

After students have finished a chapter or short story, put a list of statements on the board about the plot, the setting, the characters, the mood, or other elements of the work. For example, you might use a list like this, from *Bridge to Terabithia*, by Katherine Paterson:

- Janice's friends were mean-spirited, just like her.

- The practical joke Jesse and Leslie played on Janice worked like a charm.

- Jesse's family didn't have much money.

- Jesse didn't want to disappoint his dad.

- Lark Creek was not a modern community.

Then have students locate sentences in the literature that will provide *evidence* for the statements. Have them write down the evidence, quoting exactly, and including the page number where the evidence can be found.

> **TIP**
>
> To give students a "stretch," you might select some statements that express totally opposite points of view. Students must then find support for each opposing viewpoint in the work itself.

SEE ALSO EXAMPLES IN ANSWER KEY, PAGE 70

Five Senses Contest

Students almost always enjoy a good competition. Use this contest after students have finished a novel or short story that is especially descriptive.

Begin by explaining that good writers appeal to the five senses when writing descriptions. By helping readers see, hear, feel, taste and/or smell what they describe, authors make descriptions seem vivid and real.

Start the "Five Senses Contest" by having students get into groups of two to four students each. Each group scans the literature, looking for specific examples of descriptive writing. Each tries to find as many examples as possible of writing that appeals to taste, smell, sound, sight and touch.

One student records for each group, using the chart on the following page. To receive credit for an example, the author's exact words must be put on the chart, along with the page number where the passage can be read.

At the end of the contest, have students count the number of specific examples found. Have the three top teams turn in their papers for a prize, or simply have them share their findings with the class.

EXAMPLE

(From the book, *Tuck Everlasting*, by Natalie Babbitt)

SOUNDS

"a creaking on the loft stairs," page 71

"a rich and pleasant voice," page 92

TOUCH

"The cushions of the sofa were remarkably lumpy," page 68

". . . her mouth went dry as paper," page 34

SMELLS

"smelled like old newspapers," page 68

"smelled agreeably damp" page 23

TASTES

"sweet, green velvet moss," page 24

"lick the maple syrup from your fingers," page 56

SIGHTS

". . . over the treetops, there was a flash of white," page 108

"bars of sunlight, a great many squirrels and birds," page 43

SEE ALSO EXAMPLES IN ANSWER KEY, PAGE 71

List specific examples of descriptive writing below. Don't forget to include page numbers for each example.

SOUNDS

TOUCH

SMELLS

TASTES

SIGHTS

FOOTnotes

With "'FOOTnotes," students study plot and practice summarizing at the same time. The activity can be used with a chapter, a short story, a nonfiction selection or an entire book.

Divide the class into pairs and give each pair of students a photocopy of a left or right foot (pages 24 and 25), as well as a selected section of the reading material — perhaps a chapter, a certain number of pages or several paragraphs. Students then summarize their selection, using only one or two sentences and writing directly on their "foot."

Arrange the feet on a bulletin board or around the room, the steps leading upward with the rising action to the climax of the story, and downward with the falling action to the resolution. (One way to make sure the feet alternate correctly is to assign Chapter One as a left foot, Chapter Two as right foot, and so on.)

EXAMPLE

(From *A Stranger Came Ashore*, by Mollie Hunter)

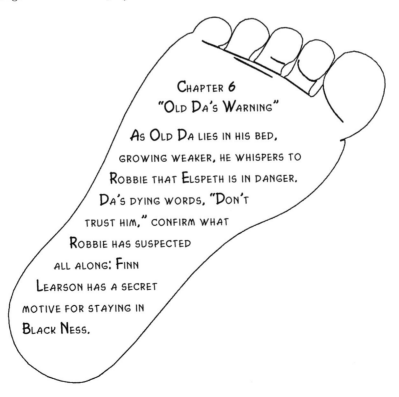

CHAPTER 6
"OLD DA'S WARNING"

As Old Da lies in his bed, growing weaker, he whispers to Robbie that Elspeth is in danger. Da's dying words, "Don't trust him," confirm what Robbie has suspected all along: Finn Learson has a secret motive for staying in Black Ness.

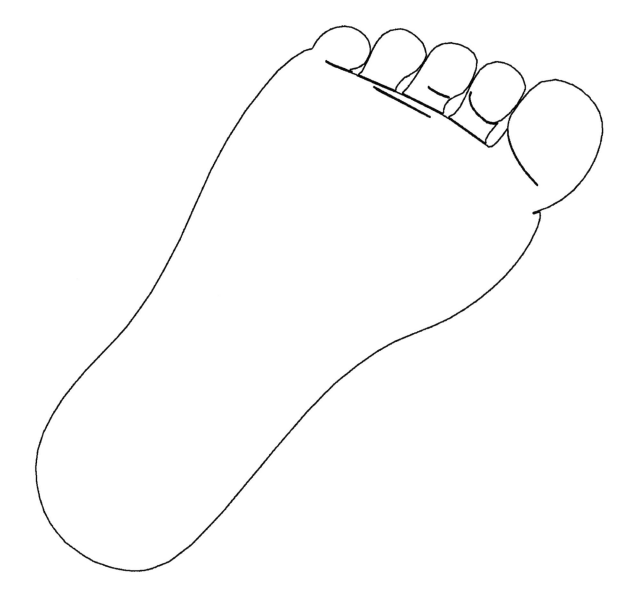

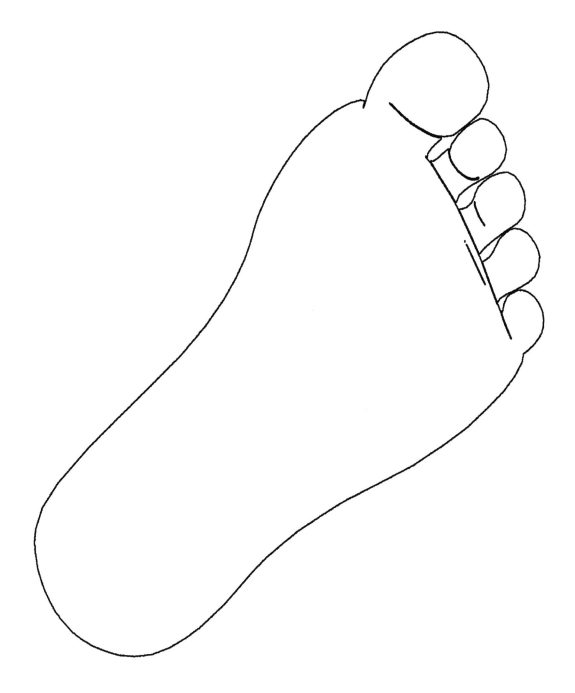

GARBAGE COLLECTOR

"Garbage Collector" promotes critical thinking and creativity. It is great fun, and students prove how clever they can be!

Begin "Garbage Collector" as a homework assignment. Ask students to come to class prepared to place an item in the trash — something that might be in the garbage of one of the characters in a novel. Students might draw something, cut a picture from a magazine, create a piece of mail or find some other way to contribute to the garbage. However, stress that they *must* use logic to connect the item with some event or detail from the book.

As students walk into class, they place their contributions in the trash. Later, as you pull each item out of the "garbage," one at a time, all students guess, in writing, which character's garbage it is and why they think so.

After each item, have a few students read their guesses. Finally, the person who brought the garbage explains his or her rationale for choosing the item.

EXAMPLE

(Based on the book *The Cartoonist,* by Betsy Cromer Byars)

Item #1:	Empty film box
Whose?	Lisbeth's
Rationale:	She is always taking pictures.
Item #2:	Wadded up drawings
Whose?	Alfie's
Rationale:	He is a perfectionist, so he often starts his cartoons over.
Item #3:	Last week's *TV Guide*
Whose?	Mrs. Mason's
Rationale:	She's a television junkie.
Item #4:	Paycheck stub
Whose?	Alma's
Rationale:	She's the only member of the family with a job.

HIT OR MISS • ◆ ◆

"Hit or Miss . . ." works with either nonfiction or fiction. It's great for a chapter review for social studies and science, too.

Ask students to prepare a list of statements about the events of a selected chapter. Some of these statements should be "hits" (true) and some of them "misses" (false). The object is to see how carefully the students have read, so tricky statements are encouraged. In addition, students should write statements that require drawing conclusions, making predictions and understanding cause and effect relationships — not just basic knowledge questions. Give them a few examples to get them started.

Later, as a review, start at the beginning of the row and have each student read a statement about the chapter. The class will say "hit" if the statement is accurate and "miss" if there is something wrong with the statement. If anyone responds incorrectly, the reader will explain why his statement is a hit or miss.

As the activity progresses, no statement can be repeated, so students must listen carefully and think quickly when it is their turn.

EXAMPLE
(Based on Chapter 1 of the book *The Cartoonist,* by Betsy Cromer Byars)

- *Alfie wants to make 12 super cartoons for a super calendar.* (Hit)
- *Alfie's mother threatens to pull him out of the attic by his ears.* (Hit)
- *Alfie would like the attic better if it had a window.* (Miss. He likes it just the way it is; his mom wants a window.)
- *When he was Alfie's age, Bubba was outside playing ball every day.* (Hit)
- *Alfie doesn't want to be on a team.* (Hit)
- *Pap approves of the President's actions.* (Miss. He thinks the president is wasting taxpayers' money.)
- *Pap underlines the important news stories in red ink.* (Miss. He uses a yellow magic marker.)
- *Pap's car only started once.* (Miss. It never started; they got one ride in it because it rolled downhill.)

HEADLINES

"Headlines" gives students practice in scanning. It also allows them the freedom to apply their imaginations.

Have students scan the newspaper in search of a headline that "fits" the story, chapter, event or novel they are reading. Explain that they are allowed to change only the nouns in the headline to fit their selection. They may either cut out the headline or write the original headline on the paper, with the changed nouns.

EXAMPLES

Original Headline: "Now all three convention bids in trouble"
New Headline: "Now all three boys in trouble"

Original Headline: "It's a no-go for Mojo"
New Headline: "It's a no-go for Kit"

Next, ask students to write a news or feature story, directly relating their reading to their selected headline.

> **TIP**
> After students share their articles, post the finished stories and headlines to make an interesting bulletin board.

EXAMPLE

(Based on the book *Tuck Everlasting,* by Natalie Babbitt)

Original Headline: "Census boss says answers required" (*San Antonio Express News,* 4-2-2000)
New Headline: "Sheriff's boss says answers required"

Sheriff's boss says answers required

Treegap's sheriff is in trouble again. Late last night, his only prisoner managed to escape while the sheriff dozed in the next room. Mae Tuck, arrested August 10th for the murder of the mysterious "Man in the Yellow Suit," slipped away sometime after midnight. Somehow, her accomplices managed to remove the bars from the jail cell window and slip her out. Meanwhile, Winifred Foster, a local ten-year-old, took Mae's place in the cell, covering up with a quilt to avoid detection. Mae Tuck had at least a four-hour head start before her absence was detected. Miss Foster offered no explanation for her part in the switch except to say that Mae Tuck was innocent. The sheriff replied, "No comment," when asked about the jailbreak, but sources say he was already on probation for other recent blunders. State officials will interrogate the sheriff this afternoon and decide whether a suspension is warranted.

I SAY ◆ ◆ ◆ YOU SAY ◆ ◆ ◆

"I Say . . . You Say . . ." is a review activity that provides a useful check to see if students are reading carefully.

First make a list of "I say . . ." statements (see below) that involve details about characters and their motives, cause and effect relationships, sequence, setting and plot, etc. Then go down the rows in your classroom, giving an "I say . . ." statement to each student and having the student respond with a "You say" statement. Here is how it works:

EXAMPLE

(Based on the book *Number the Stars*, by Lois Lowry)

From Chapter 5, "Who Is the Dark-Haired One?"

Teacher:	Mr. Rosen wants everyone to be this.
Student:	A teacher.
Teacher:	This happened just before Ellen and Annemarie awoke abruptly.
Student:	There was a pounding on the door.
Teacher:	Annemarie yanked it off and broke it.
Student:	Ellen's necklace.
Teacher:	This is the result of Annemarie holding Ellen's necklace so tightly.
Student:	It made the Star of David imprint on her hand.

Generally, students pay close attention to see if they would have had a response for each "I say" statement.

> **TIP**
>
> A variation of "I Say . . . You Say . . ." is to have students make up their own "I say" statements and take turns presenting them for responses.

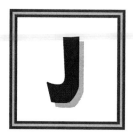

Journal of Facts and Statistics

"Journal of Facts and Statistics" is a project particularly suited to many nonfiction books. Just a few examples of topics that can work: space, dinosaurs, explorations, natural disasters, wars, pyramids, the Holocaust, the Hindenberg disaster, rain forest destruction, the Industrial Revolution, ancient civilizations.

To create a journal of facts and statistics, students collect and record information from the book they are reading. You might have the class create one large journal, or students can create separate, individual journals. They can also do further research to add more statistics and facts.

Here's one account of a teacher's use of "Journal of Facts and Statistics":

> After reading the nonfiction book Exploring the Titanic, by Robert D. Ballard, my students were fascinated by the statistics and facts. We decided to log all the measurements, dates, facts and statistics in a journal, and then we used them to do some practical comparisons. We went to the football field to get an idea of the length of the Titanic, the size of the hole the iceberg made in the side, the size of the anchors, etc.
>
> This book was one that the students talked about to their friends and parents. By logging the stats and facts, the students had a quick reference when they were explaining the enormity of the ship and the amazing feat of discovering it on the ocean's bottom some 2½ miles down.
>
> The students were competitive about the journals because they would often brag about the number of facts and statistics they recorded as they finished reading the chapters.

SEE ALSO EXAMPLES IN ANSWER KEY, PAGE 72

KINFOLK

"Kinfolk" provides a way for students to personalize reading material and relate it to their own lives.

Discuss the meaning of the word "kinfolk." Be sure to mention that, for this activity, "kin" can refer to either blood relatives or people students choose to *treat* as kin. Have students write about "kinfolk," choosing one of the following topics:

- Choose a character from the reading and describe how that character is similar to one of your own relatives or "kinfolk."

- Choose an incident from the reading that reminds you of something that once happened to one of your relatives or "kinfolk."

EXAMPLE

(Based on the book *The Egypt Game*, by Zilpha Keatley Snyder)

Character: April

The description of April in the first part of *The Egypt Game* reminds me of my younger cousin, Valerie. In the story, April tries to act sophisticated because she's from Hollywood. She tries to arrange her hair in an "upsweep," wears false eyelashes and carries a big plastic purse, and if that's not bad enough, she wears some kind of fur stole. My cousin, Valerie, also likes to wear anything that I call "glitzy." She loves that glitter gel that some kids wear but hasn't learned that a little goes a long way. Also, she wears huge, clog-type shoes with four inch thick soles, usually black patent leather. She's only ten, but has a real disco-thing going. She's so much like April in the book — someone trying too hard to be cool.

LIFE-SIZED CHARACTERS

"Life-Sized Characters" is a cooperative learning assignment for a short story or novel.

Begin by breaking the class into small groups. Assign each group a different character from the reading material. Then have someone from each group lie on a large piece of butcher paper or newsprint while others in the group trace around him or her with a pencil (great fun!).

Students then use a marker to make the lines more defined. Each group follows the instructions below.

- Put the name of the character boldly at the top of the paper.

- Decorate the character in the clothes she might wear, and show physical features described in the story.

- Use the five senses to explain what the character feels, hears, tastes, smells, sees. Also include other categories, like what the character does, thinks, says. (All details must be specific to the story.) Write these explanations right beside your character drawing.

Variations of the assignment include listing the thoughts of the character by his brain, putting significant quotes of the character by his mouth, listing what he does beside his hands, listing where he goes beside his feet, listing his emotions by his heart, etc. Give the students a chance to come up with their own ideas as well.

> **TIP**
> To avoid problems, it's a good idea to make each group all boys or all girls. At the very least, have a boy draw around a boy, a girl draw around a girl.

SEE ALSO EXAMPLES IN ANSWER KEY, PAGE 73

A to Z • Copyright © 2000 • Cottonwood Press, Inc. • Fort Collins, Colorado • 1-800-864-4297 • www.cottonwoodpress.com

MOVIE CASTING

Students become the casting director for a movie about the novel or short story that they have completed reading. They cast students, teachers and famous people as the actors in an upcoming movie based on the book or story. (They do only the casting — no actual directing!)

DIRECTIONS

- Students should make a list of characters in their reading.

- Students then choose a student, teacher or well-known person to play each role in the movie, basing the selection on character traits held by each. Explain that only famous people should be cast as the unpleasant or unpopular characters. After all, the point of the assignment is not to hurt anyone's feelings by saying he is "just as mean as Jake" or "as stupid as Frank." This activity is not meant to be a forum where students have permission to ridicule others.

- Students must explain why a particular student was assigned a part — what characteristics they have in common. Again, remind students that if they are using student or teacher names, comments as to why someone was cast in a certain role are to be *positive* statements only.

- Students then write their choices on the casting boards (poster board or newsprint) that are displayed around the room.

- Discussion should focus on comparing and contrasting choices and character traits.

SEE ALSO EXAMPLES IN ANSWER KEY, PAGE 74

MATCHING REVIEW

"Matching Review" works well as a review for a test or as a discussion technique.

To prepare, write enough questions/answers so that each student in the class has either a question *or* an answer. Put each question on one strip of paper and the corresponding answer on another. (An easy method is to type out all the questions and answers and then cut them apart into strips for each class.)

As the students walk into class, hand each a strip of paper with either a question or an answer. Students are to hold onto the strips until you give the class instructions.

When everyone has a strip, explain that each student is to match what is on his strip with either a question or answer. This is to be done silently and as quickly as possible. When a student finds her match, she is to stand or sit beside that person. When everyone is matched, each pair stands and reads aloud the question and the answer.

EXAMPLES

(Based on the book *Down a Dark Hall*, by Lois Duncan)

Question strips:
- What physical sensation is Kit aware of when she enters Sandy's room at night?
- What is Kit's first reaction to the grounds and the school building?
- What does Kit see in the mirror at the end of the hall?
- Who is Ellis?
- What abilities does Kit possess when she's "dreaming"?

Answer strips:
- A gust of freezing cold air
- She thought they were evil.
- A man
- The "person" helping Sandy write poetry
- She can play piano beautifully

> **TIP**
>
> If you are using "Matching Review" as a test review, you may want to have several matching activities during the class period. If you are using it as a review of the previous night's reading, one round is probably just right.

Mystery Box

"Mystery Box" is designed as a week long activity, but it can be shortened to fit any time span. It is designed to enhance thinking skills. Because the object of the activity is to guess what is hidden in a box, the activity also works well as part of a mystery unit.

Directions

- Choose a small item represented in a book the class has read. For example, you might choose a needle and thread to represent Boo sewing up Jem's ripped pants in *To Kill a Mockingbird*, by Harper Lee. Place the object in a closed box or container. Leave the box where students can see it. (If you are doing a mystery unit, you may want to simply hide *any* object in the box. It might be something ordinary — a twist tie, a small salt package, a catsup packet, a shoestring, for example.)

> **Tip**
>
> It's a good idea to have a different item and box for each class. The activity takes about 5–7 minutes of class time per day.

- Each day, give every student the opportunity, in front of the entire class, to ask *one* yes or no question about the object. Each question and answer should take no more than about 30 seconds. Students may want to keep track of questions asked.

- On Friday, after the last question has been asked, each student guesses what is in the box, writing down the guess on a piece of paper.

- Go through the slips of paper and place all correct guesses in a box. Then draw one name for a small prize of your choice.

SEE ALSO EXAMPLES IN ANSWER KEY, PAGE 74

Newspaper Page

By creating a newspaper page for the "Top Story Gazette," students gain practice summarizing and communicating the main ideas from their reading. At the same time, they are given the freedom to be creative.

DIRECTIONS

- Photocopy the page layout for the *Top Story Gazette*, page 37, and give each student a copy. Explain that students are to create the front page for the new *Top Story Gazette*, based on material from the book they have read.

- The "Top Story" column is where the students will summarize what they feel is the most important story related to the book they read. They should write the material for this column in the form of a news story, beginning with a topic sentence that grabs the attention of the audience and answers most of the "5 W" questions: *Who? What? When? Where? Why?*

- Students can use the box in the center of the page to illustrate a memorable moment of the book, complete with a caption.

- With the "Critic's Corner," students can express their opinion about the book, or a part of the book. However, their opinions should be substantiated with solid reasons and examples from the reading.

- The remaining space can be used for one or two feature articles inspired by the book. For example, in the book *Number the Stars*, by Lois Lowry, Denmark's Navy destroys its ships to prevent the Nazis from using them. This event from the book could be turned into a newsworthy story for the *Top Story Gazette*.

SEE ALSO EXAMPLES IN ANSWER KEY, PAGE 75

Top Story Gazette

Volume 1 Issue 1   Date:

_____ Top Story _____

Critic's Corner _____

ONE SIGNIFICANT QUOTATION

With "One Significant Quotation," students gain practice in scanning material and looking carefully at the element of *plot*.

Photocopy the quotation bubble and instructions on page 39. Go over the instructions with students, making sure they understand what they are to do.

EXAMPLE

(Based on the book *Izzy, Willy-Nilly*, by Cynthia Voigt)

> THE TROUBLE IS, YOU'RE USED TO PEOPLE LOOKING AT YOU AND ENVYING YOU, WISHING THEY WERE YOU. YOU'RE NOT USED TO PEOPLE LOOKING AT YOU AND PITYING YOU AND BEING GLAD THEY AREN'T YOU. BUT IF YOU LOOK AT IT FROM ANOTHER ANGLE, THEY'RE BOTH THE SAME MISTAKE BECAUSE PEOPLE AREN'T EVER SEEING YOU.

ROSEMUND, PAGE **224**

After Izzy loses her leg in a car accident, she fears going back to school. Before she had been a cheerleader, admired by girls and boys alike. Now, with her physical disability, she realizes that many people will see only her "flaw," and the reaction will be so different from what she is used to. Rosemund, Izzy's new friend, points out that many people never knew the real Izzy before the accident — they only saw the beautiful, blonde cheerleader. Rosemund understands what it's like to be judged by appearance alone because she's not one of the beautiful people at school. Now Izzy must fight to get people, including herself, to see who she really is.

DIRECTIONS

Scan the chapters of the book, looking for a turning point in the novel. Isolate one significant quotation that you believe had an important effect on the plot. In the speech bubble below, neatly write down the quotation. (The bubble takes the place of quotation marks.) Below the bubble, note the page number of the quotation and who said it. On the back of this page or on another piece of paper, write a brief paragraph explaining your choice. Tell why you chose this quotation and explain how it contributed to the turning point in the book. Be prepared to share your response with the class.

PROVE IT IN PICTURES

"Prove It in Pictures" is a quiz that gives right-brained individuals a chance to shine. However, it is also a good activity for everyone because it forces left-brained students to stretch their thinking and approach things in a different way.

DIRECTIONS

- Have the students divide their papers into quadrants by folding them twice.
- Explain that they are to use only symbols and pictures on this quiz — absolutely no words.
- Choose four mental images that are really significant in a chapter. Write a question that requires students to draw these images. The drawing should show that they have read and understand the chapter.

Here are some examples:

From *Savage Sam*, by Fred Gipson
- Draw the position Travis was in when the Indians punished him in this chapter.
- Draw the transformation Arliss underwent in this chapter.

From *Bridge to Terabithia*, by Katherine Paterson
- Draw Jesse's Christmas gift from his father.
- Draw the tool used most often in this chapter.

From *Tuck Everlasting,* by Natalie Babbitt
- Draw a picture of the animal that did not drink from the spring.
- Draw what Winnie did to the toad in this chapter.

From the book *The Serpent Never Sleeps*, by Scott O'Dell
- Draw what Anthony did for Serena on the first few days of the voyage.
- Draw what Serena received from the admiral because of the ring.
- Draw what happened to the ships after the storm.
- Draw the person who knew about the ring without being told.

You will find this quiz easy to grade and a great change of pace. Your students will probably feel the same way!

QUOTATIONS FROM THE PAST

With "Quotations from the Past," students make connections between familiar sayings and what they have read.

Give students the list of quotations and sayings on the next page. Ask them to choose one that they feel is in some way representative of their reading. Students are to copy the chosen quotation and then explain why or how the saying relates to the reading. Remind them to give specific reasons justifying their choice. Have students share their responses with the class. (Note: Their finished papers can also make an effective bulletin board.)

EXAMPLE

(Based on the book *Tangerine*, by Edward Bloor, as it applies to the character Paul)

"The pessimist sees the difficulty in every opportunity;
the optimist, the opportunity in every difficulty."

The quotation, "The pessimist sees the difficulty in every opportunity; the optimist, the opportunity in every difficulty" applies to Paul Fisher in the book *Tangerine*. An accident in Paul's life leaves him legally blind, yet he refuses to let his disability stifle his dreams. He works hard to be the best soccer goalie imaginable. Though Paul's father spends all his energies promoting his older brother's football career, Paul refuses to be discouraged. When Paul literally watches his middle school disappear into a "sink-hole" he turns this misfortune into an opportunity by enrolling in a different middle school notorious for its gangs. Oddly, Paul fits in with this tough crowd and gets a chance to prove his skills as a soccer player. Throughout the book, Paul welcomes difficult challenges and sees the opportunities rather than the difficulties.

The early bird gets the worm.

He that would have fruit must climb the tree.

The pessimist sees the difficulty in every opportunity;
the optimist, the opportunity in every difficulty.

Waste not, want not.

Behold the turtle; he only makes progress when he sticks his neck out.

If at first you don't succeed, try, try again.

Character is power.

Don't put all your eggs in one basket.

A penny saved is a penny earned.

You can't teach an old dog new tricks.

What is a friend? A single soul dwelling in two bodies.

What we anticipate seldom occurs; what we least expect generally happens.

Don't put the cart before the horse.

Actions speak louder than words.

History repeats itself.

Be wiser than other people if you can, but do not tell them so.

Imagination is more important than knowledge.

A life without cause is a life without effect.

Beauty is in the eye of the beholder.

You can run but you can't hide.

QUESTION ROTATION

"Question Rotation" makes an excellent review for students following a long reading assignment.

Begin by assigning each student a page from which to write a good comprehension question. Explain that "Why?" or "How do you know?" questions are better than "What?" questions. In other words, students should ask questions that require some explanation, rather than just a simple one or two word answer.

The next class period, hand students Post-It™ notes as they enter the classroom. Have each student write his or her question on a note, along with the page on which the answer can be found. The student then attaches the note to the upper right hand corner of the desk and leaves the book on the desk, clearing off all other materials.

Students then move back one desk from their own and answer the question from the note that is on top of their "new" desk. They should write their answers on their own paper, leaving the Post-It ™ note in place.

The activity is timed. Give students only a minute to read the question, look up the answer (if necessary), answer the question and be ready to move to the next desk. By the end of the activity, students should be back at their own desks. If time allows, have each student read his or her own question and give the correct answer.

> **TIP**
> You may want to allow students to check their own work. Allow them to miss 4–5 questions and still make a 100 because sometimes the time limit is too restrictive. Also, there are always a few students whose questions are awkwardly worded and thus difficult to answer.

RAP IT UP

"Rap It Up" allows students to play with language as they search for rhymes, prepare a performance and, at the same time, demonstrate their understanding of what they have read.

Ask students to retell a story, article, chapter or book by creating a rap number. Of course, have them perform their number for their class.

EXAMPLE

(Based on chapters 1–3, *Switching Well*, by Peni R. Griffin)

> Amber was unhappy in 1991.
> She found out her parents' marriage had come undone.
> Ada felt trapped in 1891.
> The weight placed on women hit her like a ton.
> Both found a well.
> Both made a wish.
> And before they knew it, the switch was done!

> **TIP**
> You might want to introduce students to rhyming dictionaries. They are very helpful in creating lines that rhyme.

SYMBOLIZE IT

With "Symbolize It," students take a look at symbols and their meaning, as well as review characterization.

Assign each student a character from the reading. Then have students decide on a symbol that might represent their character.

Students draw their symbols on unlined paper, using the format below. Below the symbol, they should explain the reasons for their choice.

EXAMPLE

(Based on the book *Tangerine*, by Edward Bloor)

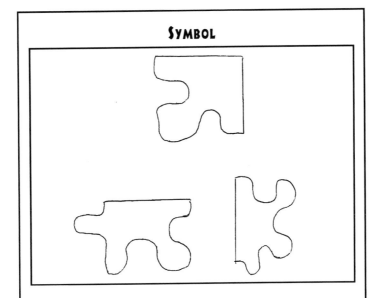

SYMBOL

Character: Paul Fisher
Explanation: Throughout the book, Paul remembers bits and pieces about his "accident," which caused his vision problems. It takes time and constantly trying to figure it out to put all the pieces together. The puzzle is complete at the end when he remembers the details of the accident.

SCRAPBOOK PAGE

With "Scrapbook Page," students reinforce their reading while contributing to the creation of a group project.

Have the class make a scrapbook of a novel or short story students have finished reading. Make each student responsible for creating one page for the scrapbook.

Assign each student a character from the book. (Some students may have the same character, if necessary.) Ask students to think about the items the character might keep as souvenirs of his or her life. Then have them create a scrapbook page for that character.

Each scrapbook page should include the following:

- Three items related to individuals the character had contact with or shared something with in the book

- Three items connected to places relevant to the character

- Three items that were significant to the character

- One picture of the character

Items for the scrapbook may be drawn or cut out of magazines or newspapers. They should be glued neatly on an 11" × 14" piece of construction paper. When students are finished, collect all the pages and put them together to form a scrapbook.

STUMP THE TEACHER

"Stump the Teacher" is a contest that gives students the opportunity to quiz the teacher about the story or chapter they have just read.

At the beginning of class, have the students pair up. Assign different pages of the story to each set of partners. Students then write five questions that they hope will stump the teacher.

To play the game, one set of partners begins by asking you, the teacher, a question. If you answer correctly, you receive a point. If you are stumped, the class gets a point. (To be fair, if students ask a question that stumped you earlier in the day, give the class the point.)

Different classes compete with one another, seeing who can stump the teacher most often. The class with the most points, of course, wins.

EXAMPLE

(Based on chapter seven of the book *The Great Gilly Hopkins*, by Katherine Paterson)

Question (students)	Answer (teacher)
What had Gilly's short life taught her?	That a person must be tough.
What was Agnes' grandmother's full name?	You stumped me! . . . It's Gertrude something! (*Gertrude Berkheimer*)
How many times did it seem to Gilly that William Ernest said, "I don't understand"?	Thirty.
How did Mr. Randolf's house feel, according to Gilly?	I don't know . . . creepy? OK, you stumped me again. (*Dark and damp*)
What did Gilly tell William Ernest that Mr. Randolph said about him?	She said Mr. Randolph thinks William Ernest is just like a grandson to him.

TIP

"Stump the Teacher" works well when you are teaching a book or story for the first time. Tell students that you are going to read the assignment they have been given only once, to make it harder for you to get the answers correct. However, explain that, since you know they will ask difficult questions, you are going to read carefully and adjust your reading rate so that you remember as much as possible about the events, details and characters.

TRINKET QUIZ

"Trinket Quiz" is a quick and effective means of assessing comprehension. It can be done upon completion of a chapter, novel or short story.

Collect five to ten items or pictures related to the material the class has been reading. Place the items in a paper sack or "trinket bag." Students number their papers. As you pull out one trinket at a time, students write down an explanation of how the trinket relates to the reading.

EXAMPLE

(Based on the book *A Stranger Came Ashore,* by Mollie Hunter)

Fiddle: Found in every Shetlander's home; Peter played it for the drowned sailors. It was also played during "Up Helly Aa," a Celtic winter festival that started in the Shetland Islands.

Candle: Yarl Corbie took one with him to the cave to look for Finn's skin.

Gold coin: Finn gave one to the Hendersons for his room and board. He compared the color to Elspeth's hair.

Charm: Elspeth hung it over the barn door to protect the cattle from the crows during "Up Helly Aa."

Wand: Held in the Skuddler's hand to lead the guisers in the traditional dances of "Up Helly Aa."

Red ribbons: Given to Elspeth by Nicol. She wore them during "Up Helly Aa" and, therefore, Robbie was able to locate her more easily in the crowd.

White handkerchief: Worn over the faces of the Skuddler and guisers during "Up Helly Aa" to conceal their identities.

TIE IT IN

With "Tie It In," students use critical thinking to relate a news story to the book or story they are reading in class.

Pass out copies of a daily newspaper and ask students to find an article containing an issue they can connect to their reading. Ask them to summarize the article and explain how they associate it with the story.

Another approach is to have students find articles and share their connections in a class discussion.

If the assignment is done properly, students will have to skim many articles and read portions of others in order to find one that will work. They will have to make predictions about a newspaper story, based on the headline.

EXAMPLE

(Based on the book *Exploring the Titanic*, by Robert D. Ballard)

> "*Monster iceberg drifts near cruise ship path*" by Laurie Goering, Chicago Tribune, cited in San Antonio Express News, 10/10/99

The article, "Monster iceberg drifts near cruise ship path" ties in perfectly with Robert D. Ballard's *Exploring the Titanic*. The newspaper article is about an iceberg that drifted away from Antarctica and is now in the waters off Tierra del Fuego. It measures 38 miles long and 13 miles wide. Unfortunately, it has drifted into the direct path used by cruise ships heading to Antarctica. Scientists don't believe there is any danger that this huge floating county could sink a ship, but they are worried about the problem of "calving." That's when chunks about the size of football fields come off the iceberg. Collisions with icebergs can cause serious structural damage.

Ballard's book contains the chapter "That Fateful Night," which explains the Titanic's impact with a monstrous iceberg. He points out the contrasts between the technology of 1912 and the modern, sophisticated radar systems used today. He also talks about how the heavily reinforced, steel-hulled ships today are made to withstand arctic ice.

TRASHKETBALL

Games can be used for any type of reading review — vocabulary, comprehension, recall of facts, end of unit tests, etc. Trashketball is a game that many students enjoy.

MATERIALS

- Trash can

- Recycled paper wadded into a ball about the size of a baseball (You may want two or three of these.)

- Numbered squares, equal to the number of students in class. Half the squares should be red, half blue. Each half should be numbered separately. (A class of 30 students would have 15 red squares numbered 1-15, and 15 blue squares numbered 1-15.)

- 2 masking tape strips, taped to the floor as "throw lines"
    1 strip about 5 feet from the trash can (5 point line)
    1 strip about 8 feet from the trash can (10 point line)

- A study guide, with review questions

DIRECTIONS

- Give students a study guide. Allow them some time to answer the questions.

- Divide the class into teams by handing students either a red numbered card or a blue numbered card. Have students memorize their card number and color. Then collect the cards and place them in two containers, one for red cards and one for blue cards.

- Pull a "contestant" number out of one of the containers. Ask the contestant a question from the study guide. If the contestant answers correctly, he or she tries to make a basket, choosing to attempt the throw from either the 5 point or the 10 point line.

- Pull a "contestant" number out of the alternate container, and the game continues. The winner is the team with the most points made in the designated time for the game.

UPDATE THE LYRICS

"Update the Lyrics" works especially well for biographies. It can also be used with fiction as a summarizing activity for a chapter, short story or novel.

Have students get into small groups and think of old familiar songs that everyone seems to know — "On Top of Old Smokey," "My Bonnie Lies Over the Ocean," "Itsy-Bitsy Spider," "The Addams Family," the theme song from "The Beverly Hillbillies," etc. Then ask them to brainstorm all the ideas possible about the person whose biography they have just read.

Students pick one tune and rewrite the lyrics so that they tell about the subject of the biography. On the day the assignment is due, they turn in a copy of the lyrics and sing their song for the class.

EXAMPLE

(Based on the book *Izzy, Willy-Nilly*, by Cynthia Voigt)

To the tune of *My Bonnie Lies Over the Ocean.*

Oh, Izzy went out to a party,
The kids there were drinking some beer.
Her date who was too drunk to drive her
Insisted that he could still steer.

Chorus

Oh, take back, take back,
Take back this wrong choice for her, for her.
Take back, take back,
Take back this wrong choice for her!

He swerved and ran into a tree trunk,
And Izzy woke up in a bed.
She didn't remember what happened.
The girl must have hit her poor head.

Repeat chorus.

Her leg suffered way too much damage,
And save it the doctors could not.
Her life as she knew it is over.
A new one she'll now have to plot.

VIDEOS, VAN GOGHS AND VIRTUOSOS

"Videos, Van Goghs and Virtuosos" has students making connections between what they have read and other art forms.

Ask students to bring to class a painting, an art print, a piece of music, a clip from a movie video or some other piece of art that either reminds them of something from the book they read or that represents a feeling or attitude from the book. Students then make short (five minute or less) presentations to the class, explaining how their particular piece of art relates to the book. Students should also summarize their views, in writing.

EXAMPLE

The novel *There's a Girl in My Hammerlock,* by Jerry Spinelli, deals with the topic of discrimination. A student might show a five-minute clip of *G.I. Jane,* a movie about the first woman to join the Navy Seals, or *Pistol,* a movie about the problems of a short person wanting to play basketball. The student would then draw a parallel between the discrimination in the movies and the discrimination in the book.

Or a student might bring in a print of a women's suffrage poster and talk about how the problems of the suffragettes were similar to the problems faced by the characters in *There's a Girl in My Hammerlock.*

Or a student might play a tape of the song "Don't Take the Girl," about a boy who would rather his dad take *anyone* fishing than a particular girl. By the end of the song, the boy has grown and is in love with the girl. The song depicts how people can change their minds about other people as they grow older. The student would explain how the boy's growth is similar to the growth shown by a character in the book.

WRITE IT WITH ALLITERATION

When studying literary terms such as alliteration, students will often understand a technique better if they try it themselves. "Write It with Alliteration" is one example.

Have each student pick a descriptive passage from the novel or story the class is reading. Using a thesaurus when necessary, students then rewrite their passages, putting in as much alliteration as possible.

At the end of class, students share their work. Since they are familiar with the original passages, they will enjoy and even be amused by the transformations.

EXAMPLES

Original (from *The Egypt Game*, by Zilpha Keatley Snyder)

And so while Toby staggered around the altar, beating his chest with wild-eyed abandon, sprinkling real ashes . . . in his hair . . . April and Melanie did more or less the same thing.

Alliterative version

And so while Toby traipsed around the temple, thumping his torso with terrified and terribly tortured style, tossing ashes in his tresses, April and Melanie together tried to copy him.

Original (from *Number the Stars*, by Lois Lowry , page 22)

Annemarie was almost asleep when there was a light knock on the bedroom door. Candlelight appeared as the door opened, and her mother stepped in.

"Are you asleep, Annemarie?"

"No. Why? Is something wrong?"

"Nothing's wrong. But I'd like you to get up and come out to the living room. Peter's here. Papa and I want to talk to you."

Alliterative version

Annemarie would soon slumber, but suddenly someone slightly knocked, shedding candlelight as she stepped in softly.

"Annemarie, are you sleeping so soon?" Mother sweetly solicited.

"Certainly not. Is something upsetting you?"

"Certainly not. So sit up, please; you're summoned to the center room. Peter is here, and we should settle some serious subjects."

eXtra Chapter

Students often talk about the events that "should have happened" in a book they have just finished. Why not use the opportunity to have them write creatively? Ask them to make up an "eXtra Chapter" for the book.

Give each student a copy of the eXtra Chapter Organizer on page 55, or something similar. The organizer will help them plan what they will write and make decisions ahead of time about what to include in the chapter.

When students have finished the organizer, have them write a rough draft and then a final copy of their chapter. Students will enjoy hearing what others have written, so allow time for sharing at the end of the project.

SEE ALSO EXAMPLES IN ANSWER KEY, PAGE 76

NAME _____

eXtra Chapter Organizer

Name of extra chapter:

Where is the chapter located in the book? (The extra chapter does not have to come at the end!)

Description of the major action or "event" that will take place:

Characters in the chapter:

Mood of the chapter:

Setting:

Problem(s) or conflict(s) that occur in the chapter:

List descriptive words — adjectives and adverbs — you might use to describe characters or the setting:

List vivid action verbs you might use to describe action taking place in your chapter:

What dialogue will need to take place?

How will the chapter end?

eXpress Yourself

"Express Yourself" focuses on paraphrasing. There are several variations to the activity.

PROCEDURE

- Using classroom reading material, locate examples for the students to rewrite in everyday language. (Novels, short stories, newspaper clippings, etc., can be used.) Students should copy down the sentence exactly as written in the original source.

- Students then rewrite the sentence, updating it and using modern language.

EXAMPLE

(Based on the book *The Witch of Blackbird Pond*, by Elizabeth George Speare)

Original:

"*A very excellent dinner, Mistress Wood. I warrant there's not a housewife in the colonies can duplicate your apple tarts.*"

He had just better compliment that dinner, thought Kit. The preparation of it had taken the better part of four days. Every inch of the great kitchen had been turned inside out. The floor had been fresh-sanded, the hearthstone polished, the pewter scoured.

Rewritten in today's vernacular:

"Great meal! Miss Wood. I bet no one around here makes better apple pie."

Yeah, you better say that, Kit thought. I've been working almost four days to get this kitchen ready for company. I refinished the floors, cleaned the oven and hand washed all the dishes.

A variation of this activity is to turn something written in today's teenage language into something that their parents or grandparents could relate to. For example, just write down, verbatim, a dialogue between a couple of students. Then have the students rewrite it in language that might go in a book.

EXAMPLE

Original:

"Yo, dude! What's up?"

"Nothin'. Just chillin'. Hey, have you seen Jeff? He's all, like, mad or something."

"He's bummin' because he, like, totally bombed his history test."

"That's totally lame, man."

Rewritten in parent or grandparent language:

"Hi, Sam. What are you doing?"

"I'm not really busy right now. I'm just relaxing. By the way, have you seen Jeff? He seems to be perturbed or upset."

"I think he's depressed because he performed so poorly on his history test."

"That's unfortunate."

> **TIP**
> Use the activity to create a bulletin board. Type or print the original work on a large square of paper. Have the students write their modern versions on strips of colored paper and post the new versions around the original.

You Ask It!

"You Ask It!" is a great activity for a study review before a test or a comprehension check over a reading. Students write questions for others, using question starters like "Who could . . ." or "Why is . . ."

The wording of many of the question starters encourages students to write questions involving higher level thinking. Answering the questions involves more than just recall.

Procedure

- Give each student five or six question starters. (See box below.)
- Have students write questions that begin with each of the question starters they have been given, based on the particular pages or chapters you have designated.
  They should also answer their own questions, using a separate piece of paper. Allow about 20 minutes for students to write the questions and the answers.
- Students then exchange papers with a partner, and the partner answers the questions written by another student.
- Upon completion, papers are traded back and each student "grades" the partner's paper.

Question Starters		
Who can . . . ?	What will . . . ?	When might . . . ?
Who should . . . ?	Where would . . . ?	Which did . . . ?
Who will . . . ?	How might . . . ?	Which is . . . ?
What did . . . ?	Why might . . . ?	How can . . . ?
What should . . . ?	Why did . . . ?	How could . . . ?

Variation

After students have their original questions back, have them place a star by their "best" two questions. Make a review sheet, using the starred questions, to be used the following day for review by the whole class.

SEE ALSO EXAMPLES IN ANSWER KEY, PAGE 77

ZERO IN

Use "Zero In" as a creative way for students to explore the thesaurus while making connections to literature.

Students work in pairs. Give each pair a copy of pages 60 and 61. Each student should also have a thesaurus.

For each letter of the alphabet, students scan the thesaurus entries and select the best word to describe a character in their book. Partners must agree on word choices and be ready to defend their choices.

At the end of the activity, randomly call on students to share their word choice and describe why a word fits a particular character.

Variations of the activity include searching for words that describe the setting, mood and/or actions that have occurred in the book.

EXAMPLES

(Based on the book *Tuck Everlasting*, by Natalie Babbitt)

A is for AFFABLE. Jesse Tuck is playful, easy-going and extremely likeable in *Tuck Everlasting*. He enjoys life and shows it with his carefree manner.

B is for BEWILDERED. Angus Tuck is bewildered when the man in the yellow suit says he wants to make Winnie drink from the spring so he can use her for his "demonstrations."

SEE ALSO EXAMPLES IN ANSWER KEY, PAGE 78

A _____

_____

B _____

_____

C _____

_____

D _____

_____

E _____

_____

F _____

_____

G _____

_____

H _____

_____

I _____

_____

J _____

_____

K _____

_____

L _____

_____

M _____

_____

N _____

_____

O _____

_____

P _____

_____

Q _____

_____

R _____

_____

S _____

_____

T _____

_____

U _____

_____

V _____

_____

W _____

_____

X _____

_____

Y _____

_____

Z _____

_____

A TO Z

ANSWER KEYS

ACROSTIC POEMS, PAGE 12

The following examples are based on the book *The Cartoonist*, by Betsy Cromer Byars.

ALFIE MASON

All he wants is a quiet place to sketch his cartoons.
Lies to his mother about activities in the afternoon.
Football is how Mom wants him to spend his time.
If only she understood him, that would be sublime.
Even Alma knows he needs his space.

Maureen and Bubba are moving back.
Alfie will lose the attic, so he's on the attack.
Securing the door, he won't come down.
Old Pap says, "Come down Alfie," with an angry frown.
No way will Alfie give up HIS place.

BOOKS: CLASS CHAPTER BOOK, PAGE 14

The following statements, with illustrations added, form the pages of a chapter book based on the book *The Great Gilly Hopkins*, by Katherine Paterson.

CHAPTER 1 "Welcome to Thomson Park." After moving from foster home to foster home, Gilly arrives at the home of Mamie Trotter, a mammoth woman!	**CHAPTER 2** "The Man Who Comes to Supper." Arriving next door to get Mr. Randolph for dinner, Gilly is shocked to learn he is black, so she runs off.	**CHAPTER 3** "More Unpleasant Surprises." Gilly has another unexpected surprise. She meets her new black teacher.
CHAPTER 4 "Sarsaparilla to Sorcery." While Gilly is at Mr. Randolph's, she stumbles across some money hidden in one of his old books called *Sarsaparilla to Sorcery*, and she steals it.	**CHAPTER 5** "William Ernest and Other Mean Flowers." Gilly helps William Ernest with flying his paper airplane while Trotter watches in awe. (She plans to make William Ernest an accomplice!)	**CHAPTER 6** "Harassing Miss Harris." Gilly makes a card for Miss Harris. Gilly thinks the card is hilarious because it insults Miss Harris' race and will make her furious. (She has another think coming!)
CHAPTER 7 "Dust and Desperation." While she's cleaning, Gilly finds out there's no more money left in Mr. Randoph's house.	**CHAPTER 8** "One Way Ticket." Gilly plans to get a ticket to go to see her mom, but she gets caught instead and has to return to Trotter.	**CHAPTER 9** "Pow!" Gilly teaches William Ernest how to fight.
CHAPTER 10 "The Visitor." Mrs. Hopkins, Gilly's grandmother, comes to visit Gilly and can't believe what kind of family Gilly is stuck living with. She promises to get her out.	**CHAPTER 11** "Never and Other Canceled Promises." Gilly's grandmother comes for Gilly who now wants to stay. Gilly reminds Trotter that she told Gilly she would never have to leave.	**CHAPTER 12** "The Going." Gilly leaves to go and live with her grandmother. She tells Trotter she loves her.
CHAPTER 13 "Jackson, Virginia." Gilly wonders if her mother was everything she imagined she was.	**CHAPTER 14** "She'll Be Riding Six White Horses (When She Comes)." Gilly writes to William Ernest from her new place in Virginia and tells him she's rich and owns horses. She has been keeping in touch with Trotter often.	**CHAPTER 15** "Homecoming." Gilly sees her mother for the first time and has a bitter disappointment: her mother was paid to come see her! She calls Trotter, who convinces her that things will work out, even though it isn't what Gilly expected.

BOOKS: ABC BOOK, PAGE 15

The statements below, with illustrations added, form the pages of an ABC book for the book *Number the Stars*, by Lois Lowry.

A IS FOR ◆◆◆ **A**nnemarie, who bravely risked her life for her friend Ellen.	**B IS FOR ◆◆◆** **B**ravery, all the times it was needed.	**C IS FOR ◆◆◆** **C**asket that contained warm clothing for the Jews.	**D IS FOR ◆◆◆** **D**anes of Denmark, who dared to resist the Nazis.	**E IS FOR ◆◆◆** **E**llen, a Jewish girl forced into hiding.
F IS FOR ◆◆◆ **F**ish skin, which replaced leather for shoes.	**G IS FOR ◆◆◆** **G**illeleje, from where Uncle Henrik's boat sailed.	**H IS FOR ◆◆◆** **H**enrik, who hid the Jews below the deck of his boat.	**I IS FOR ◆◆◆** **I**llegal newspaper, delivered by Peter.	**J IS FOR ◆◆◆** **J**ohansens, Protestant Danes who loved their Jewish friends.
K IS FOR ◆◆◆ **K**irsti, a five-year-old chatterbox.	**L IS FOR ◆◆◆** **L**ying about Great Aunt Birte.	**M IS FOR ◆◆◆** **M**rs. Hirsh, whose button shop was closed by Nazis.	**N IS FOR ◆◆◆** **N**azis who occupied every corner of Copenhagen.	**O IS FOR ◆◆◆** **Ø**sterbrogade, the street where Annemarie and Ellen lived.
P IS FOR ◆◆◆ **P**eter, a brave resistance fighter who sacrificed his life.	**Q IS FOR ◆◆◆** **Q**uestioning endlessly done by the Nazis.	**R IS FOR ◆◆◆** **R**osens, who had to go to Sweden.	**S IS FOR ◆◆◆** **S**tar of David, proudly worn by Ellen.	**T IS FOR ◆◆◆** **T**ivoli, the Danish amusement park closed by Nazis.

U IS FOR ◆◆◆ **U**nknown contents of the packet Henrik must have.	**V IS FOR ◆◆◆** **V**ictory, two years after the Rosens left Denmark.	**W IS FOR ◆◆◆** **W**orld War II, a tragic time in history.	**X IS FOR ◆◆◆** **X** (the Roman numeral) for King Christian X of Denmark	**Y IS FOR ◆◆◆** **Y**ears of Nazis occupying Denmark.	**Z IS FOR ◆◆◆** **Z**any Kirsti, who almost told the soldiers about Ellen.

CAST YOUR BALLOT, PAGE 18

Answers will vary. The following answers are based on the book *The Witch of Blackbird Pond*, by Elizabeth George Speare. *(Need justification for each)*

NOMINATION FORM

1. Best female character:
   KIT, BECAUSE OF HER BOLD SPIRIT AND WILLINGNESS TO SUFFER FOR HER BELIEFS. SHE RISKED HER LIFE TO HELP HANNAH.

2. Best male character:
   NAT, BECAUSE OF HIS GALLANT NATURE, SENSE OF HUMOR, AND HOW HE RISKED PRISON TO STAND UP FOR KIT.

3. Most descriptive paragraph: Page #: __133-134__ Paragraph #: __4__
   THE MOST DESCRIPTIVE PARAGRAPH IS THE AUTUMN VIEW FROM KIT'S UNCLE'S PORCH. SPEARE MAKES US SEE THE AUTUMN VIEW WITH VIVID DESCRIPTIONS OF COLOR AND LIGHT.

4. Most humorous event:
   KIT MAKING CORN STUFFING, BECAUSE SHE WAS CLUELESS ABOUT COOKING, AND THE PRODUCT WAS AWFUL.

5. Least favorite character:
   GOOD WIFE CRUFF, BECAUSE OF HER COLD, INSENSITIVE NATURE AND ABUSIVE TREATMENT OF HER DAUGHTER, PRUDENCE.

6. Biggest surprise:
   WHEN KIT FULLY CLOTHED, JUMPED OUT OF THE BOAT TO RETRIEVE THE DOLL (PURITAN WOMEN WERE FORBIDDEN TO SWIM BECAUSE THEY THOUGHT THEY WOULD DROWN).

7. Saddest moment:
   WHEN HANNAH TUPPER'S CABIN BURNS DOWN. SHE WAS BURNED OUT OF HER HOUSE AND HAD TO RUN FOR HER LIFE BECAUSE SHE WAS "DIFFERENT."

8. Most intense scene:
   WHEN KIT WAS LOCKED IN THE SHED. SHE WAS UTTERLY ALONE IN HER MOST DESPERATE TIME. SHE FEARED NO ONE WOULD HELP HER.

9. Most exciting chapter:
   THE TRIAL, BECAUSE PEOPLE LIED AND IT LOOKED AS THOUGH KIT WOULD BE CONVICTED AND EXECUTED.

10. Most likely to happen in real life:
    SOMEONE BEING FALSELY ACCUSED, THE "PROVERBIAL" WITCH HUNT

Dot, Dot, Dot ♦ ♦ ♦, Page 19

Answers will vary. The following answers are based on the book *The Invisible Thread*, by Yoshiko Uchida.

I think that the future will be awful if we don't start doing more to protect the environment.

If I were Keiko I would be so bitter!

It made me angry when they were forced to live in horse stables.

What I can relate to most is not fitting in at school.

I did not understand why the citizens allowed the Japanese Americans to be incarcerated.

I wish we knew then what we know now.

I know that the Japanese Americans were victims.

How could Pearl Harbor have gotten bombed without warning?

I was sad when they had to leave their dog.

I know someone just like the sister when she's driving.

I have friends that it would be hard to say good-bye to.

Why did Papa just let them take his house without a fight?

I wonder why they didn't move inland to avoid an internment camp.

The author speaks from an unforgettable experience.

The best thing was when they were finally released from camp.

I would like it if I could talk to someone who lived through this experience.

If I had the power, I'd see that the government paid them lots of money.

When I am older, I hope to be like Mama — strong.

The beginning was slow; there were parts I couldn't relate to.

It was exciting when they took their cruise and stayed with their relatives for the first time.

Could it be that some were really spies after all?

I loved it when they bathed under the stars.

Maybe there were other things the U.S. did to people that we don't even know.

Now, this could never happen.

My favorite character is Keiko, who's incredibly "gutsy."

It was great when their neighbors came to help them pack and store their belongings.

EVIDENCE, PAGE 20

Journal entries will vary. The following answers are based on chapter 14 from the book *Izzy, Willy-Nilly*, by Cynthia Voigt.

1. *Izzy realizes that her friends aren't the same since she lost her leg in the car accident.*

    Page 174. "I didn't pay any attention because I was realizing that Suzy had just said to me what you said when you wanted someone to go away, get out. I was realizing, watching them get up and put on their down vests, that of my three best friends, only one of them seemed to want to continue our friendship."

2. *Suzy didn't really want to visit Izzy.*

    Page 173. "After about an hour, Suzy started looking at her watch and trying to catch Lisa's eye while Lisa ignored her."

3. *Francie needs attention.*

    Page 175. "Once Francie had made her point about how great she was, she'd go back and watch TV or something. 'Do you do gymnastics?' Francie asked, with all the subtlety of a sledgehammer.
        'Listen, kid,' Rosamunde said. 'Your sister and I have work to do. Why don't you beat it?'
        'I do,' Francie went on. 'I'm on a team and we have meets and —'
        'You're not listening . . . now scoot. We've got stuff to do.'
        'I'm going to tell, Izzy. It's everybody's kitchen, not just yours.'"

4. *Izzy and her twin brothers share a mutual love and respect, a special relationship.*

    Page 179. "I didn't want anything more than just to be in the same room with them for a while. They were talking back and forth and laughing; they brought sunlight into the room and they filled it with words in their rough voices . . . They had come home to see me. They hadn't told anybody . . . They had decided, even though it wasn't long at all until Thanksgiving, that they wanted to see me right away."

5. *Rosamunde's family doesn't have much money.*

    Page 181. "'Although, none of you seem to have a realistic sense of money — those games cost thirty dollars, or thirty-five.'
        That wasn't much money, I thought, then I thought that it clearly was to Rosamunde, and I wanted to drop the subject."

FIVE SENSES CONTEST, PAGE 21

Answers will vary. The following answers are based on the book *Number the Stars*, by Lois Lowry .

SOUNDS

"The soldier laughed and dropped the bruised apple to the ground," page 116. "Bombs exploded in the factories," page 8. "The wooden wheels creaked and clattered on the street," page 20. "Awakened by the sounds of explosions," page 33. "She chattered and giggled during dinner," page 35.

TOUCH

"The kitten lay purring in her lap," page 63. "She stroked Kirsti's cheek," page 9. "Mrs. Rosen feared the width, depth and cold of the sea," page 94. "The winter nights were terribly cold," page 18. "She clutched Ellen's necklace and imprinted the Star of David into her palm," page 49. "Wet whiskers," page 67.

SMELL

"My dogs smell meat," page 116.
"The sharp, not unpleasant smell of salt and fish," page 56.

TASTES

"Oatmeal and cream," page 68.
"Hot water, flavored with herbs," page 6.

SIGHTS

"Metal helmets," page 10. "Gold trimmed gowns," page 12. "Sunlit kitchen," page 69. "Nets filled with shiny silver fish," page 69. "Tabletops crowded with bouquets," page 70. "Four tall, shiny boots planted firmly," page 2. "Huge colored splashes and burst of lights," page 31. "Norway was pink on the school map," page 15. "The yellow dress with its full skirt flying as she danced," page 16.

JOURNAL OF FACTS AND STATISTICS, PAGE 30

Journal entries below are based on Chapter Two, "The Biggest Ship in the World," from *Exploring the Titanic*, by Robert D. Ballard.

DATES

1907: plans made to build the Titanic and two other luxury liners

May 31, 1911: the hull of the Titanic is launched at the Harland Wolff Shipyards in Belfast, Ireland

April 10, 1912: passengers arrive at Southampton for boarding and departure

MEASUREMENTS

Titanic length: 882 feet

Nine decks: eleven stories high

Three anchors weight: 31 tons

Boilers: 15 feet high

Middle propeller: 16 feet across

Two other propellers: 23 feet across

OTHER STATISTICS

Rivets used: over three million

Lubrication used to slide hull into water: 22 tons

Whistles on the funnels: largest ever made

Swimming pool: first ever on a passenger ship

Captain Smith: 38 years with White Star; no accidents

People who witnessed the launching of the hull: over 100,000

LIFE-SIZED CHARACTERS, PAGE 32

This is a description of Clara Driscoll, From *Clara Driscoll: Savior of the Alamo – Her Life Story*, by Nelda Patteson.

"Savior of the Alamo"
~ Clara Driscoll ~

- Civic-minded Clara served as a committeewoman through 4 presidential elections.

She saw the decline of the shrine, The Alamo, so she campaigned to save it!

- She spoke about our duty to preserve historic sites, decades before it was popular!

Her heart was broken when her mother died on her birthday trip to Europe.

- Though she traveled the world, she loved her Texas ranch best!

She gave thousands of $$$ to the Alamo project.

- She donated her home, "Laguna Gloria," to serve as an art gallery in Austin.

She wrote short stories, novels, and Mexicana, a Broadway musical

Clara left her entire estate to build and operate a children's hospital for the poor families of Corpus Christi.

She petitioned the state legislator to appropriate funds for the Alamo project.

Clara and husband Hal went to Chile to serve as U.S. Ambassadors.

She traveled around the world for her eighteeth birthday.

– SARAH JACKSON

MOVIE CASTING, PAGE 33

For the book *Just Like Martin*, by Ossie Davis:

Samuel L. Jackson should play the part of Isaac Stone, Sr. In the book, Isaac forbids Isaac Jr. to march on Washington with Martin Luther King. His anger and ability to speak his mind with passion need a strong character like Jackson. The author portrays Isaac Sr. with an edginess that I think only Samuel Jackson could duplicate.

Jaleel White (Steve Erkle) would make a perfect Pee Wee because he's an annoying, pesky character! In the book when Pee Wee encourages Hookie Fenster to fight Stone, and he locks the two in the bathroom stall, his "Erkle-ish" quality is really apparent.

A young Will Smith would make a believable Stone. As the junior assistant pastor, Stone is respected by the kids in the book. They often look to Stone for answers about life. Will Smith comes across as a determined young man, respected, admired, and suitable for the character Stone in *Just Like Martin*.

MYSTERY BOX, PAGE 35

On Monday, a box wrapped in red and covered with question marks was placed at the front of the classroom. Each day, students were allowed to ask one "yes-no" question. The final day, the students made their guesses.

Object inside: a pebble. In the book, *Tuck Everlasting*, Winnie is tossing pebbles in the direction of a toad at the beginning of the book. Also, the Tucks had piled pebbles on the "everlasting" spring to conceal it.

SAMPLE QUESTIONS FROM THE WEEK

Is it edible?

Does it have an odor?

Is it breakable?

Is it plastic?

Is it wooden?

Is it metal?

Is it organic?

Is it smooth?

Was it ever alive?

Does it weigh less than a pound?

Does it weigh less than an ounce?

Do teachers use it more than students?

Is it square?

Can you buy it at the grocery store?

Is it round?

Would you find it in a school?

Is it found out of doors?

Does it have round edges?

Can it roll?

Is it useful?

Can it be found in this area of the state?

Is it smaller than a Band-aid box?

Is it smaller than a stick of gum?

Is it smaller than a marble?

The final day, students submitted their guesses.

NEWSPAPER PAGE, PAGE 36

Answers will vary. The following answers are based on the book *Number the Stars*, by Lois Lowry.

De frie Danske

The Free Danes: An underground publication of the Danish Resistance

December 13, 1941

Nazis raid secret meeting

Lise Johansen, 18

Two nights ago, Nazi's learned of the United Danish Resistance secret meeting. Local leader, young Peter Nielson narrowly escaped with only a gunshot wound to his left shoulder. However, his fiancé, Lise Johansen, spotted and run down by a Nazi patrol car, met her death on Tuesday at 1:51 AM. Services for Miss Johanson are scheduled for Friday.

"I am devastated," said Nielson, "but I promise Lise's death shall not be in vain." The secret meeting's agenda, getting Danish Jews out of Denmark safely, yielded several feasible plans as reported by Peter Nielson.

All Danes wish them God's speed.

Danish naval fleet destroyed

Attribute the loud explosions heard throughout Copenhagen late last night to Denmark's not so dormant Navy destroying its own ships. As Nazi threats to use the ships intensified, Admiral Bode gave the order to sabotage the Nazis with this supreme sacrifice—the entire Danish fleet. *(Story continued on page 3)*

Critic's Corner

by Kevin Brown

I enjoyed reading *Number the Stars* immensely. The story, based on real events of Nazi occupied Denmark, kept my attention from the early pages to the "Afterword," which explained how clever Danish scientists and fishermen fooled expertly trained Nazi dogs. I learned so much history!

I rate this book ☺☺☺☺☺

eXtra Chapter, page 54

The following epilogue is based on the book *Scorpions*, by Walter Dean Myers.

It was cold and rainy as Jamal climbed out of his new car. He opened his umbrella and headed towards the cold metal gate of Upstate New York Prison. UNY was the newest prison built in 2013, just a year ago.

The gates parted slowly, and Jamal entered a lobby. "Name. Purpose," a deep, hoarse voice said over the intercom.

"Jamal Hicks. I'm here to see Randy Hicks, inmate 40772." The second door opened, and Jamal entered a third, computerized terminal where he placed his hand on the screen and stated his name. Jamal was led into a small room with two chairs and several surveillance cameras. He sat anxiously for several minutes.

"Yo! My main man. What's happening?" Randy called out to Jamal. He coolly strutted over and sat in a chair. The door closed and locked.

"Uh, fine. It's just been so long, " Jamal stammered. He stared at Randy's face. It was aged and badly scarred. His long beard went down to his chest.

"Twenty some years! You never were able to get me out on parole. I've got six more years. So, what's your life been like?"

"Well, you know about Tito saving me and all. Mack told that to you when he came back to visit you."

"Man, that dude put up a cover for you and that Tee-you!" Randy exclaimed.

"It's Ti-to. Well, the gang still bugged me, so Mama, Sassy, and I moved to Virginia. It's the only place Mama could get a job. I studied hard, and didn't get too involved socially," Jamal said almost regretfully.

"So you were a dweeb!" Randy snickered. Jamal was getting quite annoyed with his older, more immature brother.

Jamal continued, slightly miffed, "Then I attended a local college and got a degree in architecture. Boy, the structure of this building is very poor. You see the walls . . . "

"Man! You come in here to flaunt yourself; I want to know about the family!" Randy barked angrily.

"OK, OK. I got married after that. I think that's when the Scorpions disbanded. Well, that's what Mama told me. Mama's in such good health for a woman of her age. Sassy is very beautiful. She even got a modeling contract with Cosmo. She's quite a girl. She just seemed to forget the tough times here in New York."

"Not any tougher than my time in the slammer!" Randy still only thought of himself. He yawned and brushed his fingernails on his shirt. The fingernails were filthy.

"Look. I have to be at a school recital for my daughter in an hour. I live about an hour from here."

"OK, dude! Thanks for coming."

The doors unlocked and Randy was escorted out.

Later that evening, a postcard arrived for Jamal. He carefully turned it over and read,

Dear Jamal,

How are you? It's me, Tito. I never could write back to you because Abuela and Mother would intercept the letters. I live in France with my wife, Elaine, and son, Jamal. I'm an engineer. Please keep in touch. I have a great boat now. I'll race you when I can get to America! I hope you are doing great.

Your pal, Tito

That night, for the first time in twenty years, Jamal fell asleep assured that every obstacle was overturned, every road to success open. He was satisfied and happy. "We all lived happily ever after," he said under his breath before he drifted off.

YOU ASK IT! PAGE 58

Answers will vary. The following questions and answers are based on the book *Bridge to Terabithia*, by Katherine Paterson.

Who can explain Jesse's Christmas present to Leslie?

He gave her a puppy. He saw a sign that said "Free Puppies" on his way home from school, and so he got off the bus and got one for Leslie.

What did Jesse's father give to him?

He gave him a cheap race car set that seemed to be too young for him.

Where would Jesse get enough money to buy Maybelle's present?

He would save (or rob) some of the money from Brenda and Ellie's gifts so that he could afford a Barbie for Maybelle.

Which is more appropriate for Jesse: Leslie's gift to him or his father's gift to him? Why?

Leslie's gift was far more appropriate; he loved his art and she gave him supplies he could never afford for himself. His dad's gift was cheap and intended for a younger child, but Jesse knew his dad paid more than he should and he tried to act pleased about it.

What should you do when you don't have enough money to buy a gift for someone you love?

You might make the gift or give something you have that you would like to pass on to the person. Maybe, like Jesse, you might find something that's free.

How can you tell that Leslie was pleased with her gift? Be specific.

Leslie expressed strong emotions about the dog. She had never had a pet before, and she immediately suggested that they make him part of their imaginary kingdom.

ZERO IN, PAGE 59

Answers will vary. The following answers are based on the book *A Stranger Came Ashore*, by Mollie Hunter

Character: Finn

Attentive — He noticed Old Da talking to Robbie.

Bold — He flirted with Elspeth right in front of Nicol, her "young man."

Cruel — He lured young maidens from their homes and they eventually drowned.

Deceitful — He made the Hendersons believe he was from a shipwreck.

Eager — He was always willing to offer his help in order to win favor from Robbie's parents.

Fearless — He offered to distract the Press Gang while the men of Black Ness escaped.

Gallant — He carried Elspeth to the house after she fainted.

Handsome — Everyone noticed his strong build, even white teeth and rugged good looks.

Intriguing — He told of his travels and life on the sea.

Jaunty — He danced as though he had grown up in Black Ness.

Keen — He waited until the most opportune moment to step in with a solution to a problem.

Light-footed — He could dance.

Magical — He transformed from a seal to a man.

Notorious — Legends of Black Ness warned of his return.

Observant — He saw Robbie near the cave even though Finn was way above him on the cliff.

Powerful — He put Elspeth and Tam under his "spell."

Quiet — He listened to others and offered little information about himself.

Ruthless — He would kill Nicol to achieve his goal.

Suspicious — Something in his smile made Robbie not trust him.

Tempting — He promised Elspeth riches, servants and life in a castle.

Unpredictable — He saved Robbie when Robbie fell out of his boat.

Violent — He fought the Skuddler with the intent to kill.

Wondrous — The way he tricked the Press Gang was incredible.

Xanthous — His complexion was unusual.

Youthful — Though he was ancient, he looked young and strong.

Zealous — He would stop at nothing to get Elspeth.

BOOKS FOR MIDDLE SCHOOL STUDENTS

Among the Hidden, Margaret Peterson Haddix

Armageddon Summer, Jane Yolen and Bruce Coville

Brian's Return, Gary Paulsen

Bridge To Terabithia, Katherine Paterson

Bud, Not Buddy, Christopher Paul Curtis

Catherine, Called Birdy, Karen Cushman

Cousins, Virginia Hamilton

Dark Side of Nowhere, Neal Shusterman

The Devil's Arithmetic, Jane Yolen

The Face on the Milk Carton, Caroline Cooney

The Girl Death Left Behind, Lurlene McDaniel

The Giver, Lois Lowry

The Great Gilly Hopkins, Katherine Paterson

Harry Potter and the Sorcerer's Stone, J.K. Rowling

Harry Potter and the Chamber of Secrets, J.K. Rowling

Harry Potter and the Prisoner of Azkaban, J.K. Rowling

Holes, Louis Sachar

Into Thin Air, Jon Krakauer

The Invisible Thread, Yoshiko Uchida

Invitation to the Game, Monica Hughes

Kissing Doorknobs, Terry Spencer Hesser

The Last Silk Dress, Ann Rinaldi

The Lion, the Witch and the Wardrobe, C.S. Lewis

Maniac Magee, Jerry Spinelli

Maze, Will Hobbs

My Louisiana Sky, Kimberly Willis Holt

Nothing But the Truth, Avi

Number the Stars, Lois Lowry

October Sky, Homer H. Hickam, Jr.

The Only Alien on the Planet, Kristen D. Randle

Out of the Dust, Karen Hesse

The Outsiders, S.E. Hinton

Petey, Ben Mikaelsen

Scorpions, Walter Dean Myers

A Stranger Came Ashore, Mollie Hunter

Shiloh, Phyllis Reynolds Naylor

Swallowing Stones, Joyce McDonald

Tangerine, Edward Bloor

Tuck Everlasting, Natalie Babbitt

Walk Two Moons, Sharon Creech

The Watsons Go to Birmingham, 1963, Christopher Paul Curtis

The Westing Game, Ellen Raskin

What Child Is This? Caroline B. Cooney

Where the Red Fern Grows, Wilson Rawls

Wringer, Jerry Spinelli

A Wrinkle in Time, Madeleine L'Engle

MORE GREAT BOOKS FROM COTTONWOOD PRESS

CLASSROOM MATERIALS THAT REALLY WORK!

 **A SENTENCE A DAY**—Short, playful proofreading exercises to help students avoid tripping up when they write. This book focuses on short, playful, interesting sentences with a sense of humor. Order #SD-B. $9.95

 DOWN*WRITE* FUNNY—Using student's love of the ridiculous to build serious writing skills. The entertaining activities and illustrations in this book help teach all kinds of useful writing skills. Order #DWF-B. $19.95

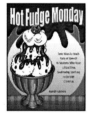 **HOT FUDGE MONDAY**—Tasty Ways to Teach Parts of Speech to Students Who Have a Hard Time Swallowing Anything To Do With Grammar. This new edition includes quirky quizzes, extended writing activities, and Internet enrichment activities that reinforce new skills. Order #HOT-B. $21.95

 **IF THEY'RE LAUGHING THEY JUST MIGHT BE LISTENING**—Ideas for using HUMOR effectively in the classroom—even if you're NOT funny yourself. Discover ways to lighten up, encourage humor from others, and have fun with your students. Order #IF-B. $12.95

 **RELUCTANT DISCIPLINARIAN**—Advice on classroom management from a softy who became (eventually) a successful teacher. Author Gary Rubinstein offers clear and specific advice for classroom management. Order #RD-B. $12.95

 **PHUNNY STUFF**—Your students will smile *and* sharpen their prooreading skills as they correct the jokes and urban legends in this handy book of 100 reproducible proofreading exercises. A great way to start class each day! Order #PHS-B. $21.95

 SINGUINI—Even kids who think they don't like to sing can't resist the goofy songs in *SINGuini*. The songs vary widely, everything from warm-ups and rounds to parodies and partner songs. Order #SING-B. $18.95

 **TWISTING ARMS**—Teaching students how to write to persuade. This book is full of easy-to-use activities that will really sharpen students' writing and organizational skills. Order #TA-B. $16.95

 **UNJOURNALING**—Some people just don't want to share intimate details about their thoughts, feelings and lives—at least not with others in a class or group. That's where *UnJournaling* comes in. Order #UNJ-B. $12.95

 **YOGA FOR THE BRAIN**—Far too many people think of writing as a chore. *Yoga for the Brain* quickly helps dispel that notion with 365 daily writing prompts that are interesting, playful, lighthearted, challenging, quirky—or all of the above! Order #YOGA-WB. $14.95

COTTONWOODPRESS INC.

www.cottonwoodpress.com

Family Literacy Experiences

Creating reading and writing opportunities
that support classroom learning

Jennifer Rowsell

FOREWORD BY
Dorothy Strickland

Stenhouse Publishers
PORTLAND, MAINE

Pembroke Publishers Limited
MARKHAM, ONTARIO

Dedication:
For Madeleine, our meaning-maker

For all the images that speak as loud as words, thanks to the following:

Oliver and Simon; Paris and Aengus; Aidan and Anne; Lisa, Rowan, and Maggie; Kierra, Madeleine, and Theo; Andrew, Liam, Eric, Laura, Kaitlin, and Franklin; Aric, Olivia, Ryan, Sara, Dom, Leigh, Chelsea, Cody, Tom, and Louise; Jason and Sarah; and Hugh, Claire, Olivia, Maxine, Jason, Angela, Chris, Carolyn, Elva, Collin, Kathryn, and Lienne.

© 2006 Pembroke Publishers
538 Hood Road
Markham, Ontario, Canada L3R 3K9
www.pembrokepublishers.com

Published in the U.S. by Stenhouse Publishers
480 Congress Street
Portland, ME 04101-3400
www.stenhouse.com
ISBN 13: 9781-57110-491-7
ISBN 10: 1-557110-491-5

Thanks for permission to use cover of *Captain Underpants Extra Crunchy Book of Fun* by Dav Pilkey. Published by Scholastic Inc./Blue Sky Press. Copyright © 2001 by Dav Pilkey. Used by Permission.

Thanks to Simone Dublin for photos used in cover image.

We acknowledge the financial support of the Government of Canada through the Book Publishing Industry Development Program (BPIDP) for our publishing activities.

We acknowledge the assistance of the OMDC Book Fund, an initiative of the Ontario Media Development Corporation.

Library and Archives Canada Cataloguing in Publication

Rowsell, Jennifer
    Family literacy experiences / Jennifer Rowsell.

Includes bibliographical references and index.
ISBN 13: 9781-55138-207-4
ISBN 10: 1-55138-207-5

1. Family literacy programs. 2. Reading—Parent participation. 3. Language arts (Elementary). 4. English language—Study and teaching (Elementary). I. Title.

LC149.R69 2006   372.6'044   C2006-902676-9

Editor: Kat Mototsune
Cover design: John Zehethofer
Cover photography: Ajay Photographics
Typesetting: Jay Tee Graphics

Printed and bound in Canada
9 8 7 6 5 4 3 2 1

Contents

Foreword

My first response to Jennifer Rowsell's excellent book was, "Why didn't I think of that?!" Although I had written and talked about family literacy for many years, I had never approached the topic in quite the way it is done in the extraordinarily useful volume you hold in your hands. The book is grounded in the well-known research linking strong home literacy environments and student achievement. However, rather than building on this research in typical ways, suggesting that educators work to change homes in order to fit school expectations, Rowsell turns these findings in a different direction. She and her colleagues creatively explore the use of the evidence to explore how schools can learn from homes and from the out-of-school experiences that children seek and enjoy. Perhaps most important is that the information is applicable across many grade levels and demographic groups. There is something here for every educator who is willing to listen and use it. The message will serve them well and, of course, benefit the children and families with whom they work.

Family Literacy Experiences taps into what is known about the broader range of literacy activity and engagement that helps make children successful, literate human beings both within and beyond the classroom. Most research on family literacy has focused on young children and their families, where the evidence regarding the link between supportive home literacy environments and children's literacy development is well-established. Efforts to get books into the hands of parents of very young children and to get them to read to their children have worked to some extent, increasing parent–child literacy activities among many families. Unfortunately, the increases among families whose children were considered to be at risk for failure have often lagged behind that of other families. As a result, researchers began to recommend that efforts to promote shared reading with children go beyond giving books to families and include suggestions for how parents might engage in these activities to promote conversation and dialogue. Today, researchers go even farther to suggest that it is not the frequency of book reading nor even the quality of the talk that accompanies book reading *alone* that is related to children's language and literacy abilities, but the broader pattern of parent–child activities and interactions inside and outside the home that supports children's literacy achievement.

Recommendations such as these are particularly salient at the middle- and high-school levels, where problems associated with low motivation among students perplex teachers and administrators trying desperately to cover the required curriculum. At the same time, their pre-adolescent and adolescent students find it difficult to reconcile school literacy with the reading and writing they engage in outside of school. Students may fail the standardized literacy curriculum, yet demonstrate proficiency outside the classroom environment. Even the most successful readers may perceive different reasons for reading and writing in school and out of school. For instance, in school they may read and write simply to complete assignments, whereas outside of school they read and write to communicate, create, and participate.

Rowsell and her colleagues offer a multitude of excellent and highly doable suggestions for making use of what already excites and motivates students. Making use of movies, music, video games, and print media of a variety of genres are just a few of the possibilities explored. The media become both tools and texts for exploration and learning. The traditional curriculum is neither neglected nor subjugated to a lesser status; rather, the suggestions offered serve as entry points and support for the knowledge base for which teachers and students are held accountable.

Family Literacy Experiences: Creating reading and writing opportunities that support student achievement reminds us that the educational community in which students live extends well beyond the walls of the school. Indeed, for many students, what is learned outside of school may be more salient to them than what they experience in the classroom. Certainly, schools have the responsibility to educate students with a solid foundation that reflects the prescribed curriculum. The use of materials and activities that students find engaging outside of school may be precisely the way to get the job done. Rowsell and her contributors provide an abundance of suggestions that make learning inside and outside of school mutually supportive in ways that allow students to extend and demonstrate new understanding, knowledge, and skills with a sense of purpose and satisfaction.

Dorothy S. Strickland
Samuel DeWitt Proctor Professor of Education
Rutgers, The State University of New Jersey

Introduction

Our first memories of making meaning with words, images, and objects occur in our homes. Children's early development lay the foundation for later learning. It follows that early environmental influences have a strong impact on young children's meaning-making and early notions of what it means to be literate. Children have cultural experiences that they carry with them from their homes. We have reached a point in the history of literacy teaching and learning at which we need to build a bridge between the domains of home and school, because the gap is ever-widening (Hull & Schultz, 2001). The aim in writing this book is to issue an invitation: to invite home into school, to bridge a gap between the rich diversity of literacy that takes place in homes and the purposeful, meaningful literacy that takes place in our classrooms. Family literacy takes account of how parents and children engage in literacy—at home and together at school.

In this book, there is a variation on this concept—we look at the texts from which we make meaning outside of school, with families and friends, and feature how they make us literate. That is, we focus on the skills that "outside texts" imbue and how we can harness these skills to our teaching of literacy. Texts that children use are a window into their minds and their habits of mind, and many of these texts derive from popular culture. In a study of more than 90 children, Janet Evans asked them what their out-of-school and home interests were; their answers were wide-ranging and fell into categories such as film, video, TV programs, and computer games. These kinds of texts are the driving force of the book—their purpose, their language, their visuals, and their skills.

As a result, in *Family Literacy Experiences*, I present the communicational and cultural landscape of children, adolescents, and teenagers so that we can speak to skills that are not necessarily incorporated in literacy teaching.

Family Literacy Experiences is organized around texts and how to use texts from home at school. Although there is much more to family literacy than simply using texts, texts guide the process and are an artifact of meaning making. The book sets out to look at how to bring family literacy from home to school through texts. To explore the nature of all types of texts allows us to appreciate how important it is to draw on our students' cultural resources.

"As educators, we are in urgent need of a newly conceived language and literacy curriculum, in which we start where children are, in a media-filled world that is increasingly diverse and interconnected. We may begin by using children's experiences with varied media resources as bridges to a more traditional curriculum."
— Anne Haas Dyson

Using this Book

Structured around text genres in the home, *Family Literacy Experiences* foregrounds skills that emerge from these genres and ways of building on new genre skills in your planning, teaching, and assessment of literacy. The first section of this book—Bridging Home and School—ties family literacy practice to new theories of literacy education in the fields of New Literacy Studies and multiliteracies. The second section of the book—New Texts, New Skills—is divided into genres of texts. Each genre chapter includes

Words tied to new theories of literacy education are defined in the Glossary on page 147.

- moments of the genre's use
- the skills each genre offers and how to build them into your program
- activities you can build into your planning
- as assessment frame to correspond to the particularities of the genre

Throughout the book, I present snapshots of theorists, of literacy memories, of practical applications, and of school-wide approaches to give you a comprehensive program for incorporating family literacy into your school. I rely on gifted teachers, researchers and scholars, and inspired administrators in schools to present ways of bringing those outside worlds in

- Meaning-Makers: Profiles of meaning-makers feature actual learners and their outside literacy practices.
- Literacy Moments: These are memories of literacy events, literacy traditions, or unique literacy practices that inform the way people understand literacy.
- Voices from the Field: Literacy scholars and researchers in the book profile their work to place theory within practice.

Part 1

Bridging Home and School

> "We cannot understand how children find their way into print unless we understand the principles of their meaning-making."
> — Gunther Kress

We now know a great deal about literacy. We know that words are rendered more meaningful when they are taught within context and in relation to context. We know that students should have a balance of language skills coupled with an appreciation and understanding of the meaning and message of texts. We know that boys' literacy needs do not always accord with girls' literacy needs. We know that students need to learn language in contexts. We know that language development is cognitively *and* socially constructed. We know that we should read to children every day. We know that text form is tied to text function. Yet, there is still an achievement gap.

There is a quiet, insistent undercurrent to literacy teaching—that literacy is riven with values. We carry values about literacy that guide our teaching and our students' understandings of literacy. Literacy is tied to who we are as teachers and as people, where we come from, and, to a great extent, where we are going. Literacy teaching is a deliberate, symbolic engagement with the world and, however we choose to approach it, our literacy teaching shapes our students' understanding of how to make meaning out in the world. In this way, we carry our own funds of knowledge that overlay our planning and assessing. To plan in terms of our students' funds of knowledge, we need to open our teaching to other views of language learning and to find ways of including them. Parents will have opinions about literacy and discussions about your program; its aims and objectives will pave the way to mediating them with the community in which you work, and with the needs and capacities of your students.

There are two good reasons why we need to think about literacy values:
• to appreciate that our values beget student values
• to be aware that our students come into our classrooms with values that need to be acknowledged.

CHAPTER 1 — What Is Family Literacy?

The term "family" is used broadly to define intergenerational learning that encompasses siblings, caregivers, guardians, mothers, fathers, grandparents, and extended family. There is a danger in viewing the home as an isolated domain or container that we enter and exit. Instead, I prefer to see the relationship between home and school—or, more broadly, out-of-school and in-school—as fluid. These contexts move in and out of each other and bear traces of the other all the time. In a discussion of literacy out-of-school, we want to avoid the temptation to oversimplify the differences; rather, we need to emphasize the similarities.

Invitations to Bridge Home and School

Inviting Home into School

In the years before schooling, children are, for the most part, left to their own devices, their own cultures, their family rituals and practices, and their own spaces in which to learn. This is a magical time in a child's development, when a formative picture of how to make meaning in the world occurs. Early forms of literacy represent a medley of play, modeling, and using the materials and means at hand to make meaning.

Homes are intimate spaces. What separates home from school is the tremendous variability of homes, each complex of such factors as socio-economic background, race, religion, traditions, tastes, interests, family composition, etc. Objects, books, furniture, and spatial arrangements are meaningful to the people who occupy a home space. As teachers, we may pause to think about what our students do when they are at home, but we seldom think about a student's home and meanings within the home that take on relevance and are rendered meaningful by a child.

Inviting School into Home

We need to critically frame texts so that children look at the messages of popular culture in ways that do not undermine their pleasure.

Family literacy emphasizes using the pleasure and comfort children experience with texts they use at home and out in the community to motivate them and offer opportunities to develop as readers and writers. Popular culture can be used to motivate children, and is particularly helpful to boys who show less interest in "schooled literacy practices" (Street, 1995) or literacy traditionally associated with school, such as choral reading from a basal reader, that is unlikely to take place at home. Family literacy, however, involves much more than popular culture. Family literacy involves the tacit things that we do within our home space that cast an impression of what it means to be a reader or writer.

These rites and practices strongly inform our children's understanding of language, meaning-making, and, importantly, feeling at ease in a setting so that learning can take place. As teachers, we should know the kinds of texts and practices our students have and perform at home, honor them, and plan around them.

Inviting Meaning-Making

Family Literacy Experiences has an agenda: to open up what we mean by literacy. Reading and writing have shifted dramatically over the past decades. The screen has transformed literacy as we know it. Although we cannot assume all children have access to computers at home or at school, they increasingly think in terms of the screen. The shift from language to highly designed visual texts and interface may seem at odds with what we think of as texts, but it is the reality of our children's worlds. I deliberately use the term "meaning-maker" instead of "reader" to signal a shift from solely written, printed texts to texts of all shapes, sizes, and dimensions.

Meaning-making is about constructing individual interpretations of our students' experiences.

Inviting New Texts and New Skills

Different text genres fill our students' worlds. There are texts that play a part in family rituals. There are texts that serve as a historical centrepiece, as mementos to remind us of our past. There are more universal texts, such as dictionaries and religious texts, that occupy a sacred place in a home. There is a sea of picturebooks of all kinds. There are interactive texts, such as video games on a computer. There are comics and graphic stories that can be read on cushions or in a comfy chair. There are movies on television or on DVD; there are cartoons. In short, there are endless texts at home, on the street, on the Internet, in places of worship, at the mall, and at school—we are surrounded by texts.

Texts are our bridge between home and school.

We may not be comfortable with the amount of time our children spend engaging in new media and technology; nevertheless, we need to understand new skills that emerge from use of them so that we can build on the affordances of their worlds.

With new curricula taking account of literacy skills our students have developed from computer use and exposure to multiple genres of texts, we have some way to go in bridging the gap between the sophisticated set of skills our students have and what actually takes place in school.

Literacy is everywhere and is shaped by the spaces we enter and exit. This is particularly helpful when we think about students who are experts in gaming, texting, surfing, blogging, and working with hypertext.

A PICTURE OF CHILDREN'S LITERACIES

School Literacy	Literacy Dealing with Technology	Literacy Dealing with Culture	Literacy Dealing with Family	Adolescent Social/Cultural World
Reading	Internet	Cultural practices in the home	Family heirlooms	Music
Writing	Multimedia	Cultural texts	Children's artifacts	Movies
Speaking	E-learning	Religious and sacred texts	Communicational texts	Youth culture
Listening	Texting	Dual- and single-language texts	Configurations of space	Posters

School Literacy	Literacy Dealing with Technology	Literacy Dealing with Culture	Literacy Dealing with Family	Adolescent Social/Cultural World
Grammar	DVDs	Religious icons	Furniture	Magazines
Visual communication	Console games	Cultural practices	Posters, art	Peer group areas in the home
Representing	Blogs	Artifacts signaling culture	Clothes, bedspreads, and objects tied to interests and popular characters	Clothes signaling interests
Drama	Web pages	Generational texts tied to culture	Books	
Essay writing	E-mailing			

Voices from the Field

....

Home and School Working Together

by Lesley M. Morrow

I have the wonderful opportunity to watch literacy development with my two grandchildren, three- year-old James and six-month-old Natalie. My daughter, her husband, and grandparents have read to James and Natalie daily from the time they were born. We look at books, talk about the pictures, and read stories. Books are all around my daughter's home. There are accessible bookshelves in their rooms. There are books in the kitchen, the bathroom, and play areas. James sees his parents reading frequently—professional literature as well as novels, magazines, and newspapers—and at times they join them with their own books. In addition to books there are magnetic letters and numbers, paper and pencils, markers and crayons. Playing with these and books bring as much joy as playing with dolls and trucks.

Family literacy encompasses the ways family members use literacy at home and in their community. Family literacy occurs naturally during the routines of daily living and helps adults and children "get things done." Examples include using writing or drawing to share ideas, composing notes or letters to communicate messages, keeping records, making lists, following written directions, or sharing stories and ideas through conversation, reading, and writing.

Although literacy activity is present in one form or another in most families, the particular kinds of events that some families share with children may have a great deal of influence on school success. Conversely, the kinds of literacy practised in classrooms may not be meaningful for some children outside school. Family literacy must be approached to avoid cultural bias, and activities must be supportive rather than intrusive.

Schools need to view families as partners in the development of literacy. Because no two communities are the same, family literacy programs need to be tailored to the needs of the individuals they serve:

• Hold meetings at varied times of the day and days of the week, in accessible locations that are friendly and nonthreatening. Provide transportation if no public transportation is available or if parents do not have a way of getting to meetings.

- Provide child care and refreshments at meetings.
- Work with parents alone, and with family members and children together. There should be sharing times when family members and children work together.
- Provide support groups for families to talk about helping their children and to find out what they want to know.
- Provide families with ideas and materials to use at home, including easy literacy activities that family members consider useful, such as talking and reading about childrearing concerns, about community life problems, etc.
- Include the opportunity for parental participation in school activities during school hours.

Likewise, teachers should help promote parental involvement in children's education: informing families on a regular basis what is happening in scool and how they can help their children; involving families in school activities during the day and providing activities for families to do at home. Families need to feel that they are welcome in the classroom:

- At the beginning of the school year, send home the literacy development goals to be achieved for the grade level you teach, in a format that can be understood by all.
- With each new unit of instruction or literacy concept, send home a letter to let families know what you are studying and what they can do to help.
- Invite families to school for parent conferences and school programs.
- Invite families to help with literacy activities in the classroom, such as reading to children, helping with bookbinding, taking written dictation of stories, and supervising independent activities while teachers work with small groups and individual children.
- Send home activities for families and children to do together.
- Require some feedback from the parents or child about working together.
- Suggest home activities such as writing in journals together, reading together, visiting the library, recording print in the environment, writing notes to each other, cooking together and following recipes, following directions to put together toys or household items, and watching and talking about specific programs on television.
- Participate in homework assignments together.
- Invite families to school to share special skills they may have, to talk about their cultural heritage, hobbies, jobs, etc.
- Send home notes when a child is doing well. Do not send notes only for problems.
- Provide lists of literature for families to share with their children.
- Hold meetings for family members and children about progress and projects.

We need the help of families to support the work done in school to promote literacy. All parents can help in some way, and schools need to be persistent in involving them in the literacy curriculum and finding how they can help in a way that is comfortable for them.

CHAPTER 2 **Rethinking Literacy**

Over the past decade, there has been heightened attention paid to literacy as it occurs outside of school. Some of the major concerns identified are recognizing that students today have new sets of skills from their use of media and technology; that there are more texts than there ever have been; and that these need to resolve a gender gap in literacy, so that we invite texts and practices that both boys and girls enjoy and find meaningful.

Things we know about literacy:

- Literacy is embedded in the things that we do and where we do them. (Street, 1995)
- Policies for literacy curricula must be based on a wide range of evidence, and look forward to future needs for literacy in globalized and technologically evolving societies. (Allan Luke)
- New multimedia technologies can serve the learning needs of particular learner groups, such as literacy development for immigrant or at-risk students. (Jim Cummins)
- Early literacy policy is social policy. Educational and social support services for preschool need to be coordinated across local and provincial agencies. (Dorothy Strickland)
- Boys and men are readers, and we need to open up our notions of literacy so that we recognize, respect, and include texts that they use, understand, and enjoy. (David Booth)
- Children behave early on as their parents do. (Margaret Meek)
- Children possess an expertise about their own popular culture that is theirs by virtue of being the intended audience and/or customer, but is also theirs by their willing and sometimes passionate engagement with the show, book, or toy. (Claudia Mitchell and Jacqueline Reid-Walsh)
- Children have agency in the construction of their own imaginations. They appropriate cultural material to participate in and explore their worlds, especially through narrative play and story. (Anne Haas Dyson)
- At the heart of many studies about the semiotics of children is an understanding that all children's writing, drawing, play, and symbolizing is shaped by the context in which they are produced and that this then shapes the form of the sign. (Kate Pahl)
- If we lay a grid across the curriculum we can see that teachers tend to privilege particular versions of literacy during the primary years. (Barbara Comber)
- Boys in Grades 4–6 think multimodally in their use of texts—particularly non-fiction texts. (Gemma Moss)
- Teachers need to be sure of the possibilities each new medium offers—the choices to be made between words and pictures, and so on—and how these

The New Theories of Literacy Development chart on pages 25–26 features age ranges and relates ways of teaching to new theories of literacy development.

can be best adapted for children's meaning-making. (Jackie Marsh and Elaine Millard)

- Literacy programs need to start by listening to parents and need to acknowledge that parents are experts on their own children, for professionals cannot be expected to know individual children as well as parents do. (Peter Hannon)
- The growth of understanding is accomplished while doing things with tools (including symbolic systems) available to the child. (Lev Vygotski)
- Children are active and purposeful meaning-makers, drawing upon the cultural resources made available to them in their society. (Julia Gillen)

The field of New Literacy Studies has emerged from three fields of thought:

1. New Literacy Studies argues that literacy takes place everywhere, and that context shapes literacy development.
2. Multiliteracies argues that the screen has changed the way we learn literacy, and that our teaching must teach overtly and critically to new skills from new technologies.
3. Multimodal literacy argues for an expansion of our understanding of texts, and an equal account of modalities that are visual, written, and have sound and movement.

New Literacy Studies invite us to think about and plan around literacies outside of school.

Distilled down to their essence, these relatively new fields of research show us that reading and writing are no longer about sitting and reading written texts in a comfy chair (although it is still a lovely thing to do): most books and other media are presented through images of varying sizes, shapes, textures; they are designed with particular users in mind; they use color, diversify fonts, and more often than not, have sound, movement, and animation. We read these texts differently and we simultaneously make choices about how we will read them. Children are abundantly aware of choice and of the physicality, or materiality, of the kinds of texts that they use (Burke & Rowsell, 2006).

New Literacy Studies emerged to better encompass what our students are doing outside of school. It has become evident that our students' skills are quite different from those that we older generations possessed at their age—not better or worse, but different in nature and intent. In the history of reading, we were schooled predominantly in print-based models of literacy that regarded reading and writing as a continuum, equally weighted in terms of their importance. Our means of communication shifted from primarily written script with letter writing, to oral communication with the telephone, to typing on a keyboard through e-mail and chatrooms. Our students are writing all the time—online, playing video games, texting friends, updating blogs—and the writing is slightly different with each genre. Typically, this kind of writing is not governed by accurate spelling and punctuation, but it has its own grammar. As literacy teachers, we need to think through what this means as we plan our programs.

Gemma Moss (2001) traces the changes in design information texts. Moss talks about how text design positions the reader, and affects both likely reading behavior and the reader's subjectivity towards the individual text. Among other things, Moss suggests that some texts, such as I Spy books, orientate the reader towards reading as play rather than reading as work.

"We must learn who our children are—their lived culture, their interest, and their intellectual, political, and historical legacies… we must create Perry's 'intentional communities,' designed around a counternarrative—one that affirms Black brilliance both to the students themselves and to their communities. Then, we begin to educate the inheritors of the planet."
— Lisa Delpit

	Classroom Activities	At-home Activities
Communicative Skills	• Problem-solving in teams • Give PowerPoint™ oral presentations	• Engage in online communities • Use class or personal blogs to discuss homework or classroom/school events • Use technology as a form of communication
Cultural Literacies	• Examine cultural interpretations of historical events • Study a range of texts that tell the same story but from a different cultural perspective	• Read texts from different perspectives, either taking on characters from a given culture or imposing a cultural interpretation as a writing assignment
Curriculum Literacies	• Write for different purposes • Hybrid texts; i.e., use different genres of texts at once, like hypertext on the computer • Underscore the role of spelling and grammar, and tools to support them, in formal writing; less emphasis on conventions in informal writing	• Be discerning about web content • Consult a variety of Internet sources • Take a cross-curricular approach to reading and writing • Critique canonical texts in light of contemporary ones and vice versa • Explore literature through movies
Multimodal Literacies	• Think about visual aspects of texts as well as written features • Observe visuals, audio, words, movement, gestural aspects of texts	• Recognize limitations of some modalities and the sort of possibilities they offer • In writing assignments, think in terms of different modalities

The task of looking critically at literacy can be upheld if we take account of a disparity between present practices and what students are doing in their lifeworlds. Literacy is not a stable, immutable thing—it shifts as we enter and exit contexts. We leave school and go home or out in the community and we interact with people in different ways with varying degrees of familiarity. Similarly, people from different cultures inhabit different roles as they leave their home, where they engage with their own cultures and cultural texts, and enter work or school, with its own culture and sets of texts. We have always had variety in our language use and interactions, we just have more of it today and in more media and dimensions.

We arrive at these new perspectives on literacy:

• Literacy is not simply a set of skills we acquire and use, but instead it is a way of making meaning as we cross sites (e.g., from home to school).
• Literacy is a social practice that we acquire by using language in different settings.
• Literacy events occur when we use language in a particular situation at a particular time (e.g., writing anecdotal notes about a student's literacy development). (Barton & Hamilton, 1998)

- Literacy practices are different types of speech acts (e.g., developing a hook for a lesson).
- Literacy can be broken down into four essential components: the meaning-maker, the text, the context, and the practice.
- Literacy practices take place within communities and a community's way of being. (Wenger, 1992)
- Communities of practice are communities where we do things and act in a certain way—at home, at school, at work, out in the community. We can belong to several communities of practice at once (e.g., teacher, writer, tango dancer, etc.).
- Language shifts as we enter and exit situations and experiences.
- We use multiple Discourses in situated speech (Gee). We bring with us different parts of our identity that influence the way we communicate with others as, for example, a mother or father, or a quilter, or someone passionate about cooking.
- Students should understand that they move between and among discourse communities, and that these communities inform the way they understand experiences and conversations.
- When we make meaning we do so in multiple modes that can be written or oral, performative or artistic.
- We draw on multiple senses when we make meaning, and at times privilege one sense over another (e.g., we are more visual than we are oral learners).
- Students today work in three dimensions more than they ever have, and their capacity to scan multiple texts and write hypertext and code script has given them different kinds of skills.
- Students work interchangeably and simultaneously in multiple modes which are animated, gestural, visual, and written.
- Student reading paths have shifted; they are more comfortable with hybridity and moving to multiple texts onscreen, and they expect some form of movement or animation in their use of electronic texts. That is, instead of movement being limited to front-to-back, as it is in static printed texts, they use the ability to move into the text and use other texts to inform the way they understand it.
- Our histories in person—where we come from, our culture, our background, our pedagogical preferences (Holland, 1998)—inform the way we teach and how we teach (Rowsell & Rajaratnam, 2005).
- Culture is a lens through which we see, hear, visualize things.

Gunther Kress offers a way of seeing texts and meaning-making as more open to this heterogeneity in our worlds, and he sees "individual speakers and writers not as language users but as language makers" (1997). It is the "making" bit that is key. If we concede that speech and writing give rise to particular forms of thinking, then we know our teaching needs to model these genres. If we also concede that the surfeit of texts inhabiting children's worlds are cultural and multimodal (using visual means of representing and communicating as much as written and aural), we admit that children have both choice and new skills.

You can use the Popular Culture Inventory on page 27 to keep track of students' use of different genres of texts.

"The task, then, is to engage in dialogues which will help children recognize the different representational demands made by different texts. They—and we—need to have a vocabulary for the several dimensions of texts, including movement, the sound, the dynamic, implicit in print texts—both visual and verbal."
— Eve Bearne

Text (genre, author, illustrator, language, etc.)	Text Summary (plot, characters, etc.)	Skills (reading abridged text, compositional awareness, etc.)	Potential Problems with Text (e.g., subversive material not suitable for classroom)
Sponge Bob Squarepants: Battle for Bikini Bottom video game (2003)	"The evil Plankton has set in motion his most diabolical plot ever to take over the world and the Fate of Bikini Bottom has been put in your hands."	Solve puzzles; answer trivia questions about plot of story; solve games.	Too much potty humor.

Voices from the Field

Implicit Understanding in the Reading Classroom

by Margaret Mackey

By definition, we do not readily articulate what we understand implicitly. Our tacit assumptions operate silently without conscious attention. Thus, it is easy for teachers to overlook radical changes in the kinds of implicit assumptions about books, reading, and other forms of media literacy that many contemporary children are bringing with them to school.

If you are an even moderately privileged Western child of the 21st century, there are many things you may take for granted. Some of your assumptions may lead you to question why the printed word should automatically be valued more highly than other media, as many teachers tacitly assume it will be. For example, if you are used to a family web site where your personal photographs are regularly uploaded and updated, you may assume that updates are an essential component in the recording of meaning; the unchanging stolidity of the book may be a source of perplexity to you.

If you play interactive games where characters address players from the screen, you may wonder why the book is so silent and perceive the absence of even artificial communication between characters and readers as a deficiency. If you have encountered interactive stories on CD-ROM or DVD, you may find the unyielding surface of the paper page to be rather unsatisfactory; you may instinctively want to click on the picture for further information, or tour the landscape. A ten-year-old once remarked to me that, after exploring a digital scene, she was annoyed when she looked at a paper version of the same image and couldn't check out what was behind the tree.

Children who arrive at school equipped with such tacit understandings of the mediated world may be mismatched with teachers who prize the printed word above all other forms of media—a bias that is often equally implicit, unarticulated, and unquestioned. There are many advantages to print on paper, and teachers should not feel defensive in promulgating the positive virtues of the book. Books do indeed do some things better than anything else. Print is abstract, and enables us to import our own private images and understandings to the vivification and interpretation of the page. Print is silent and enables us to merge our own voice with the voice of the author as we shape the cadence of the words in our own minds. Print, laid out in unobtrusive rectangles on a page, is often designed to efface itself and allow us to merge our own thinking with that of another human being. Print is excellent at yielding control over pace and repetition to a reader. These are unique and important qualities, and it is natural that teachers should be eager, even anxious, to teach children how to engage with this powerful medium.

Today's children are growing up in a world where print operates as one among many media. Acknowledging what print can do very well and, equally importantly, what it does not do as well as other media, is a much more productive way of engaging the understanding of even little children today. Drawing on ways in which other media can support and scaffold print reading is a productive way forward, but it is probably a mistake to consider that support for print reading is the main virtue of the scaffold. An audio book may support a reader who is struggling with how to achieve overall coherence rather than "barking at print," but it is also a worthwhile experience in its own right. An interactive story may allow for pleasurable exploring that enhances a child's awareness of the setting of a fictional world, but it is also a pleasing and engaging activity that stands on its own merits.

A TV program such as *Sesame Street* may foster awareness of character and setting that transfers helpfully to the decipherment of the printed page, but *Sesame Street* does not simply exist to make better print readers; it has its own dynamic rhythms and purposes *as television*.

Multiple Modes and Literacies

Meaning Makers

Flyers Under a Sofa

Ahmed likes to read, create, and organize flyers. He gets the habit from his dad, who is forever seen at home looking through flyers from everywhere from WalMart to Home Depot, and placing them under the sofa. During a conversation with his mom, she spoke at some length about Ahmed's keen interest in flyers, which he finds in different places:

> "On the cars, yes, in the newspapers. But then come Friday evening, every Friday evening he's looking forward to the flyers. I don't know why. Toy 'R' Us, Zellers, WalMart and Future Shop, you name it." Ahmed is a struggling reader and his mother finds it difficult to spark any interest in reading or writing. However, he enjoys reading and creating flyers at home, like his dad, and puts them in different places in his home space. (Broad, Diiorio, Rowsell, & Tessaro, 2006)

Imagine for a minute that you are a Grade 2 teacher who has planned a language arts lesson wherein children work at multiple stations: a drama station; an arts and crafts station; a writing station; educational software on the computer to help with putting words together to make a sentence; a reading corner; and word work on the word wall or with magnetic letters. Each station includes color, texture, some movement, some talk, gesture; some require dimensions; some have sounds; etc. Go one step farther and think about how different each child is, why the children respond to certain activities more than others, and why there is such a buzz of activity. Each text, each rite, each practice is deeply entrenched in multimodality. Multimodality is not a new phenomenon, it has been around for the longest time. The key difference today, however, is that multimodality has become more sophisticated and more complex in the face of increasing media, technology, texts of all kinds, and popular culture. The other

Modes: features in texts from which we make meaning, such as a dominant color in a web site's interface.

Literacies: different kinds of literacy events, texts, and practices.

Genres: different styles and formats for texts that fit their form and function, such as computer manuals with a reader-friendly format for quick reference information.

Concepts that emerge from multimodality:
• Sensory Awareness
• Reading Path
• Materiality
• Affordances and Constraints

key difference is that students think in terms of multimodality and not, necessarily, in terms of the written word.

Multiliteracies pedagogy (Cope & Kalantzis, 2000) is built on the principles of multimodality, contending that students exist within multimodal, multi-dimensional spaces and that their habits of mind are very much based on principles of design, as opposed to language/linguistic principles. The screen has transformed the way we conceive, understand, read, and write "language," and we need to think more in terms of design and design principles in our language work.

With Anne Burke, I have conducted studies with elementary and secondary students (Burke & Rowsell, 2006a; Burke & Rowsell, 2006b), tracing how they navigate through web spaces. The data shows a definite shift in reading and writing practices from the way texts are read (hybridity in reading patterns, using multiple texts at once); to awareness of the potential or affordance of texts and equally on their constraints; to appreciating available designs and how they can be redesigned.

The significance of increased multimodality in our students' texts is that they are a means of representing and foregrounding identity. The way in which our students choose a font and format for their writing manifest identities and priorities that they place on their communication of ideas. The interests of our students are therefore mirrored in the manner in which they create text and use multimodality to send across particular messages in a particular way.

Sensory Awareness

With the emergence of multimodality in technology and in the kinds of texts that our students use, there are more choices in how we produce and receive/read texts. Texts today have a diverse visual landscape that can have movement/sound/image, or that have their own grammar of visual design (Kress & Van Leeuwen, 1996). Our natural inclination towards certain modes over others has been called synaesthesia, and planning with multisensory responses in mind makes our classrooms more inclusive.

> One of my relatives started [my daughter] on a postcard collection. So for Christmas this year she asked for a big huge wall map, a laminated wall map so that she could actually mark where every postcard had come from, and it came in handy the other night because she taught her dad something from a postcard. They were watching a show and he didn't know where Mackinaw Island was. Grandma had just been there and she pulled out the postcard and she said, "It's in Michigan, Dad." I think with her it's the getting of the mail. She gets postcards from everybody… So most of the neighbors now know that when they go, they just send her a postcard and she's collecting them and alphabetizing them.

The above excerpt (from research I have done with colleagues) shows how Angela's daughter, Sophie, is a natural, tactile learner. Sophie consolidates and appreciates geography and a sense of place by identifying locations around the world on a map. For a young girl who struggles with reading and writing, meaning-making comes alive when she can find places on a map and cross-reference them with a family artifact—a postcard collection from her aunt. The example unites synaesthetic awareness of visuals with an innate capacity for tactile learning. In the example, Sophie's pathway into literacy rests on collecting, alphabetizing, and locating places on a map, and the cluster of skills grows out of a family practice.

Reading Path

In their use of computers, students have changed how they move through texts. When reading a book, we can skim, scan, and read it in a different order; but, generally speaking, we follow a relatively predictable trajectory of reading a text. However, in using computers, we can move almost anywhere while working onscreen. We can not only move to multiple texts within a document, but also read hypertext, move to endless web pages, send e-mails, and buy an item online. In the following excerpt from an interview by Anne Burke, a young man at a computer at his school discusses a BBC science and nature web site:

Anne: Okay, so click into that. Let's go into that, we can have a look. Do you interact with the text; do you do the test yourself sometimes?

Tony: Oh yeah, I've done it like numerous times and I know all the gross things about it.

Anne: All right. So this is quite interactive. You look at a picture and your selecting on a scale of one to ten how disgusted you would be to touch that.

Tony: Like this one is a dirty soccer ball.

Anne: A dirty soccer ball, so we're looking at sensitivity. So do you like the idea that the graphics in pictures ask you how you feel?

Tony: Oh yeah, but some of these pictures are really gross, you have to have a strong stomach.

This excerpt illustrates a movement through an electronic text, goverened by the reader's interest and leading him in sundry directions.

Materiality

Texts are made of different modes that are chosen because they best suit a text, or because someone feels that they should look that way. Materiality guides the content and design of texts. We see materiality in the types of illustrations and the trim size in picturebooks. We see it in animation and color schemes chosen for interface. And we see materiality in three-dimensional artifacts that students make at home and at school. An example of materiality emerges from the following conversation with a young mother of three, who took note of materiality within texts for a tween and adolescent readership.

I was just noticing the other day in a bookstore in the airport that books are even color-coded, like, gender coded. You'll see all these girls books for my daughter's age group are pink, and then it's clear that they want the boys to read this chunk of bookshelf and the girls should be looking at this chunk of bookshelf. And I suppose when you think about what I read as a child it may well have been that I was reading books that were read more by girls. It's very much marketing now.

In this example, a parent notes how color and font signal gender and developmental stages.

Affordances and Constraints

Affordances: the ability to use materials that enhance a text
Constraints: aspects of a text that holds it back from being functional

Some texts carry with them more purposes and prominence than others. For example, in a schooling context, printed textbooks sometimes carry more affordances than comic books; there are constraints on text on a web page when visuals, color, and movement are far more appealing. There are times when a text carries privileges because of the way it looks and sounds, and there are times when a text is constrained by its design and content. Our students are as aware of affordances and constraints as we are, and we need to take this into account in our teaching of literacy.

In the following focus group excerpt, you see evidence of the affordances of certain kinds of texts over others. Within the represented family, it was a ritual to read encyclopedias and hover over them to read definitions. With the proliferation of information available on the Internet, encyclopedias lend an investigative aspect to the reading process; it is the joy of finding a word and discussing the definition that lies at the heart of the literacy event.

Professional and personal experience or familiarity with visual communication can make a difference for students. (Pahl & Rowsell, 2006)

> I was going to say something just as it occurs to me—we're talking about computers and books and things, and one of the things that I'm sort of struggling with is the Internet makes everything so available, this whole idea of Internet research and so on, and yet I love reference books and so does my husband, so we have these great dictionaries and stuff like that. What's better because everything is online. There's nothing like sitting down with an encyclopedia in front of you and sort of looking at it. So that's something that we'll probably do for Christmas or something… I'm sort of conscious that I think that [using the Internet is] a different set of skills to have than a big book in front of you, because you can also find a lot more things incidentally. Obviously, the way you read, I think, is very different, reading a book than if you're reading online, and that kind of thing.

The simplicity of looking up words in a book is lost in the face of reference books online. The act of sitting down in front of an encyclopedia brings this family together and has become a family rite during holiday times.

Assessing Multimodality and New Literacy Studies

To assess based on New Literacy Studies and multimodality, students need to think in terms of making appropriate choices. Students today need to be helped to make appropriate choices to suit their purposes of communication. Teachers can respond to and value the kinds of evidence they get from multimodal texts. The assessment framework on page 28 underpins the assessment presented at the end of the chapters in section II: New Texts, New Skills.

Voices from the Field

What Will Teachers and Parents Continue to Do?

by David Booth

No one could have predicted the thousands of changes that have occurred in the teaching profession over the last thirty years, in every English-speaking country. I can't even count the educational thrusts experienced in the name of helping our youngsters learn—the institutes, workshops, seminars, speeches, in-service sessions, and courses. I have a wall of books and articles full of techniques, strategies, programs, and stories, chronicling our history in educational change. But one factor remains constant: every weekday morning, children arrive at the school's doorstep, waiting (and even hoping) to enter. I am heartened and strengthened by the continuing existence of the place we call school, and would like to celebrate those components of literacy that seem to have survived the years of turmoil. And I need to say how sweet it is to see in each new educational movement those teaching/learning events that remain significant staples of all-powerful literacy classrooms, and that connect to and are nourished by home life. Together, home and school circle the child, and the literacy potential of each individual is allowed to flourish and deepen.

1. We will continue to help our children experience what successful literacy events feel like at school and at home, so they will know they are supported in their struggle towards independence as readers and writers. They will need to make choices in their literacy lives, to feel ownership of their reading and writing selves, by selecting some of the books they read, the topics they write about, and the projects they research.

2. We will make certain that learners with different strengths and challenges find themselves sitting alongside those who are involved in and excited about learning, so they have role models for what a literacy life could be, and so they can begin to sense how successful readers and writers function.

3. When students arrive at school in the morning, we will talk about their home reading and their life events. They may come to realize that we care about who they are and that we want to be involved in their literacy learning. We will recognize the home culture and the multitude of literacy experiences they bring with them, from comics to video, from street games to music. They will see that, in our literacy classrooms, everyone and everything matters.

4. We will continue to read aloud to our students at home and at school—to increase the satisfaction and joy that quality children's literature can offer, to increase their background knowledge, and to challenge their minds with ideas and constructs they may not yet find in their own reading.

5. We will continue to find techniques for having the students read aloud, to highlight fluency and interpretive reading using shared oral reading. Choral work involves and supports the whole community of readers and writers: no one is excluded.

6. We will continue to ensure that our homes, libraries, and classrooms are full of a variety of books, including extensive selections for special-needs children, so they can come to see reading as a welcome and engaging activity. We should look for the best books we can find, so that the artistry of the author can help influence the competency of the reader.

7. We will create time for children to spend writing—actually composing, drawing, and arranging their ideas. For many, talking about what they may write is a prerequisite for the process of writing, getting them prepared and confident to begin to compose their thoughts. Webs, lists, brainstormed ideas, and computers can help them move immediately into the act of writing instead of worrying and stalling for time.

8. We will continue to take time to respond to students' writing, as we encourage them to develop and expand their jottings and recollections.

9. We will continue to build word power with young readers and writers, so that they have an ever-increasing word bank of immediately recognizable words, effective ways to discover unknown words in their reading texts, and useful strategies for spelling words in their writing. Word power is cumulative and lifelong, so we must aim for significant individual growth from year to year.

10. We will continue to help children acquire handwriting skills that promote an easy flow of ideas and support communication with others. Children often are defeated

by the mechanics of creating written text. Continuous writing through the years will support handwriting improvement, and that maturity will have an effect on how they form their words.

11. Children will need successful experiences with literature circles, where they focus on the themes and issues as well as the words and structures of the best books for young people. We need to model for these children the way we take part in literary discussions, encouraging their participation through prompts and questions, modeling appropriate behavior with our own responses, and inviting students into the conversation.

12. We will continue to offer special support with information texts, helping children recognize the features of different genres of writing and how to make sense of content effectively and efficiently

13. By collaborating with and listening to parents, we will discover a great deal about their family literacy, and incorporate that knowledge into the programs we develop for their children. We can increase communication, making them aware of how our program functions and able to give appropriate support. We need to value parents as partners in the education of their children.

14. We will continue to read professionally, onscreen and in books and articles; to engage in meaningful conversations with our colleagues about the multitexts we are sharing; to welcome meaningful progress as professionals; and to feel connected to all of those who share their lives with children.

New Theories of Literacy Development

Age Ranges	Social Contexts	Critical Literacy	Multimodality	Multiliteracies
2–4	Home and early childhood environments	• Highlight who characters are—their cultures—what different texts do, say, look like. • Environmental print walks. • Daily talk during child-initiated activities. • Ask students to retell a familiar story from another perspective.	• Encourage all kinds of play; tactile picturebooks; emphasis on cultural resources in the home. • Environmental print displayed. • Display and honor children's artwork and three-dimensional figures.	• Interaction with print and with moving images that are slow-moving and repetitive. • Have students move from reading a text to making their own rendition of text.
5–8	Home, school, out in community with parents and friends	• Explore the nature of settings and characters (how they are unique; what makes them that way); look at power issues (comparing and contrasting power in fiction and non-fiction texts; why certain characters have more power than others); account for different cultures and multiple interpretations of them. • Explore different approaches that peers have to texts. • Ask students to make intertextual connections.	• Develop awareness of different genres of texts and *choices* used in the making of texts (why does a text look this way? who is the audience? what kinds of texts students are making and why?). • Encourage and analyze children's three-dimensional figures. • Ask students to describe why a text falls into a genre based on the way it looks and sounds (e.g., fantasy books vs. magazines).	• Explore different and varied genres of texts. • Demonstrate different kinds of reading. • Students begin to understand and appreciate different kinds of visuals, talk, and vocabulary. • Increased use of new media and technology; harness teaching to understanding of different texts to move from one genre to the next. • Ask students to make inter-genre connections (e.g., something online and moving to a piece of art you can hold in your hand).

New Theories of Literacy Development (cont.)

Age Ranges	Social Contexts	Critical Literacy	Multimodality	Multiliteracies
9–11	Exploring home, school, out in community with parents, friends, and web spaces	• Enhance students' skills as text decoders. • Have students peel away layers in texts in terms of content and design. • Encourage students to analyze and be critical of different traits a character can possess (e.g., having physical power vs. having wisdom). • Balance stories with strong male characters and strong female characters.	• Be aware and plan around different genres of texts; foster an understanding of what certain text genres offer over others. • Create assignments that tap into students' awareness of different modalities (what can one text do that another cannot; and vice versa?)	• Develop using understanding of one genre (e.g., a web page) to move into another genre (e.g., an essay discussing an issue) in teaching and planning. • Interview students about what they do at home and out in the community. • Incorporate technology as much as possible, being aware of its issues of access.
Adolescence	Home, school, community, out in the world	• Content and design of texts represent messages, people, and institutions that affect how we understand them. • Incorporate questioning and critical framing of texts to get at deeper meanings and their relevance/ implications. • Acknowledge students' lifeworlds (e.g., rap) but acknowledge that content is often inappropriate for the classroom, and why this is so. • Ask students to think about positioning in their reading, writing, listening, and talking.	• Students should use, understand, and engage with all sorts of texts; know that texts can be widely perceived; see that each carries different designs, content, voices, ideas; recognize that these factors affect how we read them. • Different modes carry different potentials we can use in our reading and our writing. • Look at classic modalities and media and how they became modern modalities and media.	• When planning and assessing, acknowledge and take account of contemporary skills (e.g., how students use abridged text in their electronic correspondence that they should not use in more formal writing). • Assess based on composition and structure of texts, thereby building on their tacit understanding of multimodality.

Popular Culture Inventory

Text (genre, author, illustrator, language, etc.)	Text Summary (plot, characters, etc.)	Skills (using abridged text, compositional awareness, etc.)	Potential Problems with Text (e.g., subversive material not suitable for classroom)

Assessment Framework

1. Grammar, Punctuation, and Register

- Assess how students use a varied range of sentence structures depending on the nature of the text.
- Assess how grammatical structure and punctuation enhances meaning.
- Assess ability to write with technical accuracy of syntax and punctuation in phrases, clauses, and sentences; to vary sentences for clarity, purpose, and effect.

2. Structure and Organization

- Assess ability to select and use structural devices in texts.
- Assess organizational devices that students use in their writing— such as subheadings, bullets, speech bubbles—to separate information.
- Assess ability to balance modalities in texts (e.g., how to find an appropriate visual for written text).

3. Multimodality, Discourse and Narrative

- Assess ability to write imaginative and thoughtful texts that are appropriate to the task/practice, reader, and purpose.
- Assess how ideas and themes are conveyed in appropriate styles.
- Assess whether the design of the text suits its content.
- Assess ability to select and choose a format that matches the viewpoint and reader.

(adapted from Qualifications and Curriculum Authority, UKLA, 2004)

CHAPTER 3 **Texts**

Literacy Moment

Uncle Larry's Books
by Larry Swartz

I am a great-uncle. My niece is married and they have two sons—Matthew who is six and Zachary who is three—and so a good uncle became a great-uncle. As someone who is immersed in the field of literacy, I find my niece turning to me for expert advice on how to turn her boys on to books. I knew that establishing a committed ritual of reading aloud to Matthew and Zachary might prove a significant factor to make books matter in their lives. Of course, I also wanted to play a part in encouraging their love of books, and decided that I would contribute to building the bookshelves of their childhood.

When Matthew was born, I bought several picturebooks with his name in the title. My first gift to him was a bag of books that included *Matthew and the Midnight Tow Truck, Matthew's Meadow,* and *Reading to Matthew.* I knew that Matthew wouldn't experience some of these titles for several years, but I wanted him to know that Uncle Larry was there to plant the seeds of a garden grown with books.

When Matthew was three years old, he wore an elephant costume for Halloween. Matthew loved animals and was especially enamored with elephants. I sent Matthew picturebooks about elephants for several months, until I ran out of titles. I told Matthew that it was time to explore a new animal. "Pandas!" he declared, and so I sent him stories and information books about pandas. From elephants and pandas, Matthew went on to enjoy books about space, Garfield comics, and detective adventures. Recently, Matthew called me to say, "Uncle Larry, I think I'm ready for chapter books." So for his sixth birthday, I sent him the first three titles in *The Magic Treehouse* and *Cam Jansen* series.

When great-nephew #2 came along, his parents named him Zachary. I wanted to give Zachary some picturebooks with his name in the title, just as I had done with Matthew, but I was a bit stumped about appropriate titles. Lo and behold, Amazon.com provided me with six picturebooks (and two novels) featuring characters named Zachary (or Zack)— including *Zack's Alligator* and *Hairy Maclary and Zachary Quack.*

Books matter to both Matthew and Zachary. The bags have been packed for their journey as readers. As the two boys continue to learn to break the reading code and engage with texts of all kinds, as they develop their tastes and interests, as they become surrounded with the world of media and technology, as they swim in the sea of school reading, they might continue to have books as part of their lives. If this should happen, it might be because of those bedtime read-alouds, library visits, trips to bookstores, books offered by grandparents, teachers, friends, grandparents, aunts, uncles—or a great-uncle who hoped that, book by book, he was building a ladder to help his nephews climb higher into the literacy sky.

In this book, the word "text" is used loosely. Much of teaching is about mixing and melding sundry texts within our practice from policy documents, reading programs, picturebooks, graphic stories, etc. Texts can range from family artifacts, such as a rug or an old train set, to non-fiction books used during a guided reading session. As discussed in the last chapter, what is common to all texts we are looking at is that they are multimodal—made up of a variety of modes that influence how and when they are used (sometimes even who uses them). The argument is not simply to bring these texts into school, but to identify skills in using—understanding, reading, and writing/creating—them, and to build on these skills in our teaching. To teach every text, from a standardized test to a graphic story, as a multimodal discourse, and to pull back the layers of ideas, form, and function should be our goal as language teachers.

> "A text is not just a form of visual and verbal representation but also a material object with distinct physical features which are, in themselves, semiotic and which, at the same time, interact with verbal and visual semiosis in multi-modal meaning making."
> —Fiona Omerod & Roz Ivanic

Shifts in Cueing Systems

Texts are valuable learning tools, they are artifacts of practices and a part of meaning-making processes we need to plan for our students. Texts are anything children use to make meaning and, as such, they cannot be confined to printed texts. For example, early texts for small children can be oral language. We must teach all sorts of texts because our students have more choice in the kinds of texts they hear, see, read, and write than they ever have.

Texts can have dimensionality or not, they can be visual or written, they can be in HTML or abbreviated text. Students today have greater latitude for embedding their identities into texts. Visual and written texts can sparkle and move and dance around on a screen. Readers not only adapt a visual to suit words, but also transform it to suit their purposes. Through pioneer work by thinkers like Gunther Kress, we are able to appreciate that texts are windows into a child's pathway to literacy (Kress, 1997).

There are prescribed practices, or embedded rules, that accompany texts. For example, there are certain blogging practices; when playing video games, gamers have codes of behavior; when dueling with collector cards, you need to follow strict rules as they are set out. Although cueing systems have not changed, they have taken on different, expanded roles in how students master them, as we can see from these examples:

- Semantic Cues: the meaning governing a web site relies equally on visual and written codes in the interface
- Syntactic Cues: the layout of texts combines the grammar of visual design (Kress & Van Leeuwen, 1996) with the written grammar
- Graphophonic Cues: words are choreographed with sound/music and movement
- Pragmatic Cues: modalities work together in texts, and certain genres have dominant modes (e.g., a newspaper has more written text than magazines)

We are contemporizing the way that we use and apply cueing systems. It is worth noting that rethinking literacy to align more with contemporary texts does not mean abandoning what we know, but rather building on it. After all, today it is less about understanding written text than about mastering multiple media and the practices implied in each one. If we look at the skills that good

readers traditionally exhibit, they transfer to many of the genres spotlighted in this book:

- Oral Language: Examples include cultural practices in the home around oral retellings of stories; interactive media such as speaking during *Dora The Explorer*; creating video clips with oral language to put on blogs
- Prior Knowledge and Experience: The notion of building on students' cultural backgrounds is premised on prior knowledge—teaching to what students know; prior knowledge is also tied to skills exhibited in the use of video games, and knowing the rules of the game and mastering them
- Concepts about Print: Students have a tacit understanding of genres—what genres can and cannot do, and how to use the affordances of genres to the greatest benefit. For example, a handheld computer can be transported, but you cannot work on it with several people at once.
- Vocabulary: Some game cards have very sophisticated vocabulary that students master, even if they are struggling readers and writers.
- Metacognition: Joining chatrooms or creating blogs enhances students' awareness of language and linguistic and figurative devices; it invites them to reflect on their writing and mediate them with visuals (e.g., a photograph from an event, or, to represent a thought)
- Higher-Order Thinking Skills: Video and interactive games hone students' problem-solving skills and higher-order thinking about character, settings, plot in stories

Text Selection

Maxine Greene (1995) suggests that multimodal expressions encourage students to think alternatively about fictional worlds of literature and the contexts around them. With expression of all kinds crossing into different modes—for example, having Walt Whitman's poems online narrated with visuals—educators must begin to think differently about literacy and language. Teachers should have knowledge about the various modes of expression, and how to research, design and develop projects that are complex, modally interesting, and reveal a deeper understanding of ideologies manifested through these modalities. As Gunther Kress noted in *Writing the Future,* a text is "a microcosm of the social world in which it was made" (1995). It chronicles a form of cultural truth about individuals who produced it—be it film, letter, or work of art.

When selecting texts, keep these key points in mind:

- Use a variety of genres.
- Look for strong visuals, sounds, animation.
- Look at the length of texts.
- Think about form in terms of function and function in terms of form.
- Always consider cultural representations.
- Think about language or discourse.
- Ask yourself if the texts you use resemble the ones your students use. If not, why or how are they different?
- Think about how to mediate New Literacy Studies texts with the curriculum.
- Consider why modes are dominant in a given medium.

> "In the (social semiotic) theory of writing which I put forward here, reading is the process whereby new materials can be 'assimilated,' can be transformed, and become transformative in terms of an individual's existent set of resources, and thereby of her or his subjectivity."
> — Gunther Kress

- Plan for bridging New Literacy Studies with assessment measures.
- Reflect on how a text reflects social, cultural, economic, and political reality.

Our students' reading, writing, creating, and enjoyment of texts influences their individuality and their understanding of language. This is integral, and must be taken account of in our teaching. Teaching based on multimodality and student texts encourages curiosity about how things have come to be as they are; a view of students as active, creative, and innovators.

Meaning-Maker

Paris's Art

When a child makes a text like the drawing below, it is totally precise and how it should be. Every night, the 14-year-old who drew these pictures spends hours drawing creatures from mythical places inspired by a love of Digimon© and Pokemon© cards. No two are exactly alike because they are exactly as they should be.

New Literacy Studies in the Classroom

Use the New Literacy Studies Checklist on page 35 as you set up a program, or simply pick up some of the ideas in the book. Over the course of a school year, ask yourself the questions and, interview a student each day with these questions in mind.

Voices from the Field

Cultural Artifacts

In her work, Vivian Vasquez speaks of an "audit trail" of constructing curriculum and monitoring students. In order to represent connections between texts and themes, Vasquez gathers artifacts and contrives such themes about rain forests and environmentalism as environmental issues; different people and different places; girls and boys; TV and newspapers; strength and power; thinking alike. Artifacts from home and school can be used to elucidate these themes, which are tied to a more critical framing of literacy and meaning-making (Vasquez, 2004).

Given that we are using a loose definition of texts, the acts involved in rendering texts meaningful are as diverse and variable as the learners who use them. In the following list, I provide some ways of using texts as a bridge from home to school and back.

- Plot meaning-making: In an early-years classroom, have students chart objects they have made to reveal how different children are making meaning in the classroom.
- Play and writing: Let children value their writing and see its relationship to play. For example, Madeleine dictated written text to accompany her drawing of her soccer coaches and her improvised hut made of blankets, cushions, and a chair. Play and writing can be symbiotic and one can build on the other.
- Understand their internal signs: As noted, children each have their own unique pathway into literacy. To foster this pathway, have students use whatever mode they like (visual, written, three-dimensional, dramatic play) to complete a task, such as creating a summary of the story just read.
- Gallery walk: Set up your room like a gallery and have students walk around, looking at each other's works of art and talking about how they made them.
- Listening to children: Listening to children's talk while they are making meaning can tell you a great deal about what interests them, how they learn, and what modes they prefer or privilege over others.
- Making links: It is essential to make links between artifacts that children create in your classroom and how they are progressing with their reading and writing broadly, and how the same skills they have used in production cross over into their reading and writing specifically.
- Works-in-progress: As formative assessment, keep track of what students are working on and how they change as they get closer to completion.
- Bringing home into school: As Kate Pahl expresses it, "be aware that models made at home may have deep significance for the child" (Pahl, 1999). As a result, have students talk about their model-making at home and help them see the tie between work they do at school and the kinds of activities that they do at home.
- Diversify texts: After reading a story, have students use cultural resources to extend story ideas. For example, for a story about a girl who lives in a hotel and who is very naughty and rides the elevator, have students create a diorama of a scene in *Eloise*.

• Parents as a cultural resource: Have a parent come to class to discuss why a particular artifact is important to their family.

As Barbara Comber sagely advises, "the local and specific nature of children's lives will always influence what teachers of critical literacy believe is needed and is possible" (Comber & Nixon, 2005). What is needed and certainly possible is an acknowledgment of the stuff that presides over our students' meaning-making. Using such resources as family literacy practices or popular culture as hooks will open up our teaching to our students' worlds.

New Literacy Studies Checklist

☐ I have situated my literacy teaching within the lifeworlds of the students.

☐ I have mediated New Literacy Studies with the curriculum in the following ways:

- _____
- _____
- _____

☐ I am speaking to skills students possess (e.g., a different reading path; an understanding of multiple texts used at the same time).

☐ I have accounted for issues of gender in my teaching in my choice of texts and the ways in which we use these texts.

☐ I have thought about the funds of knowledge that my students bring to the classroom. (Who are my students? What do they like in terms of texts and practices with texts? When do they engage in these practices? With whom?)

☐ These skills are implicit in each text that I use (e.g., non-fiction provides facts and often carry a seemingly objective voice):

☐ I have accounted for multimodality in the texts that I use.

☐ I have thought about the benefits certain texts afford over others (e.g., a pop-up book gives students a sense of three-dimensionality and offers more materiality to the story).

☐ I have critically framed the material that I teach.

☐ I am aware of my own identity and biases in my literacy teaching as I plan and assess.

CHAPTER 4 **Funds of Knowledge and Culture**

Literacy Moment

Why is this night...?

by Larry Swartz

When might family members gather in their homes to read texts aloud together? In the Jewish tradition, the Passover holiday provides a context for parents and children, relatives and friends to join and spend time lingering over a text. It is a celebration that provides an authentic shared reading experience in the home.

The first two nights of the holiday are celebrated with rich meals called Seders, in which the history of Passover is recalled. Special foods, plates, and silverware are all part of the Seder service. The word *seder* means "order," and the events of the evening follow a particular order to relate the story of the Jewish people's escape from slavery by the Egyptian Pharaoh more than 3000 years ago. This order is laid out in a small booklet called the Haggadah, usually in both Hebrew and English. The word *haggadah* means "tell or to relate." Each participant at a Seder is offered a copy of the Haggadah to follow the narrative, a narrative set in the context of a parent–child dialogue.

Early in the service, it is required that the youngest at the table ask the Four Questions that are answered in the Haggadah: Why is this night different from all other nights? Why do we eat bitter herbs at our Seder? Why do we dip foods twice tonight? Why do we lean on a pillow tonight? The youngest was usually the shyest and the most nervous at the table and often needed to be persuaded to stand up in front of all and "just give the questions a try!" After the mumbling of the words the child had practised for days, everyone would "ooh" and "aah" and say, "That's terrific!" Sometimes, a volunteer would be called upon to recite the questions and show off what was learned in Hebrew School classes. Cousin Terry would always read the questions quickly in Hebrew. Cousins Marcia and Zelda would attempt to read the questions in unison. I usually chose to sing the Four Questions, using the tune every child learned.

After the Four Questions were asked, we would follow the order of the service to tell the story, to say prayers, to sip wine and taste small bits of food, each with its own significance in reminding us of the struggle of the Israelites in their quest and journey to freedom. For example, we would each taste Haroseth—a mixture of chopped walnuts, wine, cinnamon, and apples—that is intended to remind us of the mortar the Jewish slaves used to assemble the Pharoah's bricks.

Each Passover, my father, would lead us through the Haggadah storytelling, spontaneously assigning each of us at the table to read a part of the story aloud. We never knew when we would be called upon, but every one of us needed to be ready to read our assigned portion in Hebrew or English as everyone at the table followed along in his or her own copy of the booklet.

My father passed away many years ago. In our family, the Seders have been carried on at my brother Stan's house. Over the years I have listened to my nieces and nephews as they have become part of the Four Question tradition. Now, my grand-nephews are responsible for carrying on the tradition, for reciting the Four Questions just as millions of Jewish boys and girls throughout the world have done for centuries. I am aware that every Jewish family customizes the Seder rituals in their own fashion, drawing from traditions that are thousands of years old and shaped from practices realized from generation to generation. Some may celebrate Passover for one night, some for two, but for a tiny fraction of the year, it is an occasion to read text aloud, to listen to stories about the past, to pray and sing, to eat and drink, to laugh and gossip, to reunite, and to give life to authentic family literacy.

Family literacy is a way of viewing teaching that builds on the communities in which you teach. Family literacy is a way of describing how parents and children read and write together or alone during everyday interactions. Families in your community represent a tremendous range of living arrangements, and we can build on the strengths and resources of households. To do so, we need to view our students' literate lives outside of school as funds of knowledge (Moll et al, 1992) that we can draw on and harness to our teaching. As observable interactions involving print or "talk over texts" (Barton & Hamilton, 1998), literacy practices are distinctive because they draw on people's lives.

"Reading is something you do with your whole self ... We have come to understand much more about the role of the reader in reading, the way in which different readers bring different things to texts and all readers bring themselves ... their identity as a man or woman, a black or white person, a person from a particular social background or class—their social identity."
—Myra Barrs

Culture is central, as a resource we need to pull on to meet student needs. Culture relies on tools, beliefs, and rituals that mediate our thinking. From birth, there are ways of being and belief systems that surround us and inform the way we see the world, interact with others, and mediate thoughts. What is more, we are socialized into ways of speaking, viewing, writing, and understanding through our cultures.

Teachers can elicit funds of knowledge in their teaching and build on cultural resources in their planning. Children are not passive bystanders, but instead active participants in the home, and we need to acknowledge and draw on these interactions in our activities and our lessons. As a teacher, you can access funds of knowledge in several ways:

- Go on home visits to your students' households to learn about families and their literacy practices.
- Regularly speak with students about what they do at home.
- Have students bring in and present family artifacts.
- Have students interview family members about their experiences. For example, if you are doing a unit on biography, have students interview members of their family about their biography and migrations from one place to another.
- Build a family component into open houses and parent-teacher nights. Have parents chat with each other and create an open, friendly forum about what goes on in the home.
- Incorporate vocations of parents into teaching and units.
- Find out where parents work and arrange field trips to their workplaces.

The Literate Lives of Urban Children

by Catherine Compton-Lilly

My 18 years of teaching suggested to me that students' learning was not only determined by methods, materials, programs, or pedagogy but by the social, cultural, and economic contexts in which children live and learn. As an urban teacher, I felt the need to understand the literate lives of my students and their families.

The ten children who were involved in my longitudinal study were my first-grade students during the 1996–1997 school year. They attended a large urban school that served children from the lowest socio-economic section of a mid-sized northeastern city. Every three years I have returned to interview the students and their families. The data from the initial study included four semi-structured interviews with each of the ten parents and children. Interviews focused on people's experiences with learning to read, self-assessment of their reading abilities, critical events in their lives as readers, and their feelings about reading over time. Student portfolios, audiotapes of class discussions, lesson plans, and daily field notes were collected. In the second and third phases of the study, interviews were conducted with each parent and child. Student writing was collected and student reading ability was assessed. Field notes documented each interview and case studies were constructed for each family.

The study reveals unquestioned dominant discourses that surround reading and explores contradictions and complexities that surround reading practices in urban households. A major finding of the research suggests that poor urban families are often more literate than is generally assumed, and that much needs to be done to confront the myths that surround urban families and literacy. Later phases of the study explored various discourses that surround reading and urban families:

- While parents were highly critical of urban parents in the abstract, when they described their own neighbors and acquaintances a much more positive picture emerged. It appeared the parents often subscribed to the same negative assumptions about urban parents that are often voiced by the larger community.
- Parents and children often described sounding out words when reading, yet running records revealed that children rarely sounded out words sequentially.
- Although parents placed great faith in computers and technological toys, the actual computer experiences of children generally involved playing low-level games or were nonexistent.
- While parents praised the recent high-stakes testing movement for documenting children's progress, few of the parents in this study actually knew how their child performed on these state tests.
- Children's designations as successful or unsuccessful readers often involve forms of capital that extend beyond reading ability.

Home Literacies

Within families, there are many different ways in which we read and write, and make meaning more generally. For example, we create bulletin boards with tasks we need to do and notes to ourselves; we write personal letters, e-mails, and cards to people close to us; we manifest our identities in the home through the placement of furniture, posters on walls, photographs on display, objects children create, etc.; there are manuals and reference materials on display, not to mention books, newspapers, and magazines.

We have rituals in the home associated with literacy, such as reading excerpts from the newspaper. Sometimes, as Barton and Hamilton have noted (1998), our ideas, beliefs, and values we display in the home are as much a form of social participation as protesting with placards.

Over the 2004–2005 academic year, Broad, Diiorio, Rowsell, and Tessaro conducted a series of focus groups in an inner-city school in Toronto on how to bridge home and school literacies. The following themes emerged strongly from their study:

1. Familial Literacy Patterns: Six out of ten parents in one focus group made a direct link between literacy practices (Heath, 1983) that take place at home and their understanding of literacy at school. One mother claimed that it was a family tradition to read books together at night, and vestiges of this tradition have been noted by classroom teachers in the child. This same mother has three children at the school and each one prefers spoken or oral literacy activities over silent reading or writing activities. Another parent has a boy who struggles with literacy.
2. Crossing Generations: Three out of ten parents talked about literacy practices in the home being carried over generations, becoming a generational literacy practice. One talked about the tradition of writing thank-you letters crossing generations.
3. Emotional Literacy: Three out of ten parents mentioned that literacy can be tied to emotions. For example, they each talked about how their children write letters after having a disagreement with a friend or parents to resolve the issue.
4. Choosing Parental Literacy Mentors: Several focus group participants noted that their children chose a parent as a literacy mentor and modeled their literacy habits. One parent spoke about how her child at a very young age read books in bed just as the mother had. Early on, her son saw his mom as literate and a reader because she reads novels. His father, an academic, reads all the time, but somehow did not seem as literate.

A large body of literature indicates that parent–child interactions in the home are associated with school readiness. It has been shown in research that parent-and-child book reading is associated with language skills, reading ability, and school achievement. Interactions around problem-solving and playing with toys also are associated with school readiness. However, we do not know if these associations are stronger for some teaching situations than others.

In Britto et al (2006) two distinct groups emerged: storyreaders and storytellers. Surprisingly, it was not the storyreaders, as they anticipated, who talked moved around the text and made real-world connections, but it was the storytellers who clearly demonstrated a more interactive pattern, interspersing their discussion around the book. Mothers who treated book-reading interaction as an opportunity to have a conversation with their children beyond the pages facilitated more language use and understanding. As a result, children's vocabulary development appears to be associated with more interactive maternal book reading patterns. What emerges is the integral role of talk in literacy in the home, and more broadly in literacy learning. Preschoolers whose mothers provide them with high levels of support and guided participation have greater school readiness and expressive language.

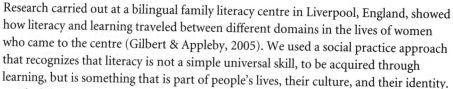

Literacy and Learning on the Move

by Yvon Appleby

Research carried out at a bilingual family literacy centre in Liverpool, England, showed how literacy and learning traveled between different domains in the lives of women who came to the centre (Gilbert & Appleby, 2005). We used a social practice approach that recognizes that literacy is not a simple universal skill, to be acquired through learning, but is something that is part of people's lives, their culture, and their identity.

The bilingual centre works with people from many language communities, some recently arrived and some from settled communities. Most of the women want to learn English to be able to support their families, particularly children at school, and to be able to become more independent themselves. The centre recognizes that where learning is connected to what learners want to learn, as part of their lives, it is more meaningful and relevant. In their everyday lives some of the women spoke, read, and wrote in different languages, within and outside their families. For example, several women spoke but were unable to write Arabic, and were learning to speak, read, and write in English. Many were teaching their children how to speak Arabic, giving them quizzes and using games, while their children supported their mothers' spoken and written English.

We found much intergenerational learning between adults and children at home as well as within wider support networks and communities—what Denny Taylor calls family strength and community practices (Taylor, 1991). Everyday objects like the television, shopping lists, junk mail, and letters were used to teach and learn language and literacy skills. Sometimes these were for everyday practical purposes, like dealing with the school or buying material, and sometimes these were to make links with families and communities from "the old country." The centre developed a large resource of bilingual storybooks, including nursery rhymes with character puppets, for the women to use when practising with each other. This crossed the language divide in the classroom and created a fun way to learn, which the women took home and used with their children. Traveling into the home domain, these resources enabled them to practise and gain confidence in reading and speaking to their younger children, who also benefited from this early language and literacy experience.

The women's everyday experience also traveled into the centre and became embedded in the teaching materials, which became part of their everyday lives. This is clearly shown in the example of the Notebook. Women were each given a small blank notebook with separate reference and contents pages to be glued in when completed: names, addresses, children's names, birth dates, names of schools, and telephone numbers. The Notebook also included spaces for practical topics, such as Hospital, School, Pregnancy, Money, and Time, with relevant vocabulary and language structure. It contained general and local information, including maps and language pages showing things like letter writing. As each woman completed her Notebook, it became not just a learning tool but also a useful personal reference. Having information—often required for forms at school or the hospital—written in the Notebook provided the women with a sense of security and independence.

The women carried their Notebooks everywhere, in their bags or pockets. Several of the books wore out and had to be replaced—they had become part of the women's lives and supported their increased literacy and language social practices. The Notebooks, embedded in the concrete existence of each learner, provided language, grammar, and expressions from the real world, connecting lives and learning. Unlike the graded course primer, the Notebooks connected the purposes and uses of language and literacy from everyday life, family, and home to learning at the centre. Traveling between these domains, they were valuable to and were valued by the women.

Culture

Literacy Moment

Writing Letters to Loved Ones
by Barbara Bolyi, Limpopo Province, South Africa
(shared with the kindness of Pippa Stein, University of Witswatersand)

In 1968, I was ten years old and in Standard 1 (Grade 3) when I came to Petanenge (Put Leg) village in Limpopo Province, so named because of the river one has to cross to reach the place. The community in Petanenge was illiterate, if I may use the word in its traditional sense. It was without a single school, teacher, or doctor. Our house, like many houses surrounding us, was mud built. The fathers worked on mines in Johannesburg and Pietersburg—many never came back to their families, and left them destitute. There was little or no motivation to learning. My two sisters and I were among the few who stuck to school. Since the place did not have any electricity or telephones, communication was limited to letter writing. Many people would come to us every week to ask us to read or write letters for them. The majority would be women who wanted to communicate with their husbands, children, or boyfriends.

These were the most humbling moments I could remember from my youth, humbling because many of the old people would entrust me with the most private and intimate stories of their lives. Old men squatted and old women kneeled when asking for my services—gestures usually accorded to elderly people or important members of the community. Old people would ask me to write letters to their sons who were enticed to the city and were no longer prepared to come home. What I dreaded most was to read letter, telegrams, and messages informing the relatives about deaths in the family. This was not uncommon for a community where people worked on the mines. I would watch helplessly while my aunt tried to comfort the poor father, mother, wife. At the tender age of ten, I was a letter reader and a letter writer for my village.

To appreciate that the cultures, interests, beliefs, and values students carry with them inform their reading and writing, we need to turn the telescope onto ourselves as teachers. Over my time in teacher education, I have encountered many different kinds of people who are ruled by their cultures, their convictions, their passions, their belief systems, their interests, or a combination thereof. No two students have ever been the same, and each one had a different take on what it means to be a teacher. With this in mind, identity can be seen as the prevailing force in teaching and learning, as the impetus for our planning and assessment of students. That is, is it possible with all of this multiplicity, to create a framework that can assess literacy development?

In my research and writing on my own and with Kate Pahl, I am particularly interested in how we bring our own identities to bear on our teaching, how we interleave our own experiences and backgrounds with those of our students. Kate Pahl describes this fundamental part of meaning-making *sedimenting* our identities into the texts and practices we use as we engage with print and other media (2002). The theory of New Literacy Studies is built on a belief that literacy is mediated by what we bring to a literacy event and practice. A prime example is Shirley Brice Heath's (1983) influential study of literacy practices in

the Carolinas, which demonstrated how three different households carried three different versions or models of literacy premised on oral language, written language, or read alouds. Importantly, only one of the households supported literacy practices that matched the local school's teaching of literacy. This groundbreaking longitudinal study powerfully illustrated how literacy takes place in each household, but it shifts based on culture, on the people and their household practices, and on the perspective. Each one equally meaningful, however, one is honored at the local school and the others are not.

In my interviews with teachers, time and time again, they refer to how their own experience learning to read and to write informed the way they teach and understand literacy (Rowsell & Rajaratnam 2005; Rowsell, 2006). In this way, our identities are a lens through which we teach literacy skills.

Eve Gregory (1996) considers the role of social context in literacy. She notes that children learning to read may or may not identify with what is being said, depending on the underlying cultural assumptions in the text. She cites the example of a book that refers to marmalade, which makes complete sense to a child who is a native English speaker, born in the United Kingdom. Another UK-born child, whose first language is Cantonese, lacks the material reference for the word, thus making the text incomprehensible. Gregory points out that bilingual children "must lose their 'strangeness,' not only to the new language, but to a strange culture through experiencing everyday new routines and ways of life" (Gregory, 1996).

Thus, language assessments can never be simple tests of vocabulary comprehension, but are always entangled with cultural assumptions that may or may not be understood by the students (Gregory, 1996). Gregory, however, does not frame this strangeness to the new culture as a deficit. Instead, she leads us to consider the strengths that "emergent bilinguals" bring to the task of language learning.

Literacy Moment

Finding Language through Collage
by Hilary Inwood

A new student, Sarita, has recently been added to Mr. Wong's Grade 7 class; she is a recent immigrant from India and speaks little English. Unfortunately, there are no other students in the class who share her native language, so communication with her is difficult and is accomplished by hand signals. Sarita has a hard time making friends in the first few weeks, as she is too shy to accept the invitations other girls extend to join them for lunch. She smiles and nods when Mr. Wong asks her if she understands an assignment, but then sits and stares vacantly once work time begins.

But Sarita finds her place during art class. Mr. Wong shows artworks to the class as a mental set for each lesson, this week showing self-portraits of artists as inspiration. Sarita looks at the works intently, focusing on their features, and seems to listen carefully to class discussion. She looks at the sample of the project that Mr. Wong holds up to inspire the class, and she nods and smiles when he ask if she understands the assignment. And this time she gets right to work, rendering her own collaged self-portrait using a combination of drawing and cutouts from magazines. She smiles shyly as a few of her classmates compliment her on her work. It is the first school project she has completed since her arrival in class.

"We, as teachers, share our various ethnic backgrounds with each other. This helps to enrich us as a group working together. And not only that—the children also share their backgrounds with each other and with the teachers. The whole basis of the subject content matter is who we are in this school."
— Courtney Cazden

Culture and the ESL Student

In 2003–2004, Judy Blaney, Marianna Diiorio, Elaine Chan, and I conducted a series of focus groups with teachers and student teachers at an inner-city school in Toronto in which we discussed the role of culture in literacy teaching and learning. In particular, we focused on ESL teaching and learning, and how culture can be used as a tool in language teaching. The focus groups illuminated some key findings about the powerful role of culture in how we learn language skills:

- Talking About Cultural Experiences: "Having ESL students talk about their worlds is key. Like, if there's a holiday or a celebration as opposed to just finding things on it. When they talk about it, they have ownership of it" (Mark, Grade 4)
- Relating your culture or ESL experience to student experiences: "I have a lot of ESL experiences, myself, all of my life. I started English when I was 12, so it's not like I started early. I started in junior high, so I'm an ESL learner, and something interesting about an ESL learner is once you are an ESL learner, it doesn't matter how old you are, and how many years you have been speaking English, you are an ESL learner all your life." (Chi Mai, special needs teacher)
- Link with Home: "I would say link with home. No matter how hard it is, try to make contact with the parents, because I think, once they feel that there's a link, they will talk to you. If there's some kind of dialogue that can be done… a lot of people too, coming from different cultures and they aren't aware that you get to talk to teachers. And I think that's important, and then you have to have a consistent message." (Rita, Grade 1 teacher).
- Translate school documents and correspondence: "We translate newsletters in our school so that parents know what is going on in the community." (principal of elementary school)
- Cultural Sensitivity: "There is a shy ESL student in my class and we all know that giving her space is important, because in her culture women are not necessarily given as many opportunities to speak up, or expectations to speak and participate as often." (Mark, Grade 4 teacher).
- Bridging cultures through book bags: "We purchased a number of books for our Kindergarten children. Then we purchased a number of book bags. In the book bags we put a copy of the book and a series of activities (on a laminated sheet of paper) to go with them. The Ministry expectations (Ontario Ministry of Education) were also put on the sheet along with the activity, which reinforced the expectation. Then all of the sheets were translated into a variety of languages appropriate to our community. I should also mention that in the book bag were included all of the manipulatives needed to complete the activities. Teachers gave out the books on Wednesdays and they were returned the following Monday. To minimize having the manipulatives lost, we had a checklist of all of the articles that were included in the book bag, taped to the outside of the bag. When the bag was returned, an older student in the school would review the contents with the Kindergarten student to make sure it was complete for the next child borrowing it… The rationale for the program was to have parents read and spend meaningful time with their Kindergarten child." (Tanya Sterioff, principal of elementary school).

- Talk and the ESL Learner: "I think talk is very important, and our ESL students only have the six hours a day at school to practise their English. So there has to be that balance of wanting them to know that you appreciate their first language, that you support them speaking their first language, that you value them speaking their first language, having their culture, but also understand that this is their chance to practise their English. And there has to be that balance, and it is a fine line when you have students fresh from another country. As they are learning their new environment, you need to create a buffer for them." (Suzanne, Grade 3 teacher)
- Giving space and finding buddies: "So you have to give students some space until they feel more comfortable doing that or doing small group work where there is some dialogue so that they can converse." (Mark, Grade 4 teacher)

What emerged from the focus groups is the necessity for classroom teachers to be aware of their own culture as they work with students new to a culture. There was a direct tie between feelings of cultural dislocation and underachievement. We "lose strangeness" (Gregory, 1996) when we accept that entering and exiting contexts requires constant and insistent mediation. All of our students, perhaps particularly our ESL students, have a tacit awareness of language and how it shifts when we cross from one place to the next.

Literacy Moment

Culture Goes to School

Marianna Diiorio remembers a girl in her class who was so shy and quiet that she hardly ever put her hand up. During an activity called *Who are you?*, she stood up in front of the class with incredible presence. At recess, Marianna approached her and commented, "Mashid [a pseudonym], you did such a wonderful job on your oral presentation." She responded, "Well, you know, I have to get up in front of everyone at Mosque and recite the Koran every day." This young woman had been doing public speaking every day after school and Marianna had not realized it. She had public speaking mastered and much of it came from her practice at her local Mosque.

The way that we deal with language in schools plays a role in structuring inclusions and exclusions, in validating and marginalizing cultures. The findings of a study conducted on the role of culture in ESL teaching clearly demonstrate a need to bridge cultural practices in urban classrooms, both in teacher education programs and in teaching and pedagogy. The ESL experience is not only about a linguistic divide, but equally about a cultural divide. The findings of the study spoke not so much to cultural difference itself, but to how it is taken up and even constructed in the classroom environment. To overcome this divide, teachers need to build in recognition of similarities and differences:

- Discuss texts written in different languages from local store (if the school community has dominant cultures), from the Internet, or from the library. You can even ask children to bring texts in their own language from home.
- Ask students to bring in photographs of celebrations, such as Eid, to school to discuss what is happening and what it means to them.
- Find out about your students' "literacy ecosystems" (Kenner, 2004) by asking them who helps them with their literacy at home. This information

will help you to put together a fuller picture of their home literacies, and also to know who to contact to discuss a student's progress.

- Link in with the valuable role of siblings as literacy teachers. If some of the siblings are in your school, hold a workshop for them to come and discuss strategies that they use. (Kenner, 2004)

Voices from the Field

What about the English-language Learners?

by Nydia Flores-Ferrán

Our schools, curriculum, and even pedagogy were all designed to meet the needs of a prototypical public school student—a classic, a standard, a one-size-fits-all mold. No matter how diverse the student body was, the general trend was to move all to be good readers, speakers, writers, and appreciaters of only one language. Now, as a consequence of globalization, immigration, and changes in migration patterns, the United States' and Canada's local urban, and even rural, educational environments have changed. The public-school student body has become more diverse, and immigrant groups have ample ability to return home; increased contact with the native language and culture through fiestas, parades, and church-related functions; and a strong feeling of identity that was not overtly expressed by immigrants in the past.

However, the educational agenda of the students you teach probably remains largely unchanged. If you witness change, you are subject to adjustments that school planners make—such as lumping Spanish speakers into one group, Arabic speakers into one group, Chinese speakers into one, etc.—without taking into consideration the oceans of differences between Cantonese, Mandarin, or Taiwanese languages and cultures; Cuban Spanish and Mexican Spanish; etc. The educational perspectives and agendas have not yet been re-molded to accommodate or improve the learning conditions of the ELLs, which in many instances represent the majority in a classroom setting or a school. But let's ask ourselves these questions:

- Are our schools community schools?
- Do they represent the needs of the community they are located in?
- Should teaching and planning reconsider who is the majority versus the minority and then move forward?
- And finally, should you consider first the linguistic preparedness that ELLs come through your door with and plan an exit strategy within a reasonable timeframe having in mind the research that has been conducted in the fields of Second Language Acquisition and Sociolinguistics?

The responses to these questions, although affirmative, require change:

- If you know that a child is learning another language alongside English, you can ask her or him to show you how to write in that language. Then ask what is similar in English. This will help students gain insight into how writing works in different languages.
- Your school could extend its language learning curriculum by investigating opportunities for teaching languages already spoken by pupils.
- When observing children who speak two languages doing a writing task in the classroom, ask them to try to find the best way to represent sounds in English.
- Materials in a range of different languages can be used to raise language awareness. Such awareness prepares children to learn languages now or in the future.

- You can build a multilingual learning environment in your classroom by inviting parents, grandparents, or siblings to demonstrate activities such as cooking, crafts, or storytelling in different languages.
- Ask bilingual children to compare English with other languages that they know.

Bennet et al. (2002) examined the relationship between the family's social network and the children's literacy skills. That research was guided by three theoretical models: in the family-as-educator model, the family affects positively the language development of its children; the resilient family functions as an insulator against pressures while still providing time to foster language development; in the parent–child–school partnership, the parents are seen as activators in the home–school connection, working as agents to promote their children's language and literacy abilities. The study reported that the family-as- educator model was significantly related to children's book-related knowledge, and to receptive and expressive language skills.

To assess students' pathways into literacy (Kress, 1997) and their understanding of modes other than written ones, use the Observation Checklist on page 51 as a framework while observing students during their literacy activities.

Cultural Resources

Literacy Moment

Becky and Harriet
by Suzanne Kaplan

When my sister and I were little, my mother read us stories as part of our bedtime ritual. One of our favorite series of stories was called Becky and Harriet. Becky and Harriet were stories that my mother made up based on our own lives. My sister was Becky, and I was Harriet. One of my favorite Becky and Harriets was "Becky and Harriet Go on a Picnic," in which Harriet spills juice all over the picnic blanket. I didn't realize that the stories were about my sister and me until years later when my mother told me. My sister claims that she always knew the stories were about the two of us, yet she always loved it when my mother told them.

To discover how children learn outside of school, we need to observe with an open mind. The "stuff"—objects, books, artifacts, and mess—all represent prime meaning-making materials. Children can use almost anything to make meaning. We refer to these sorts of texts as "piles of ephemera" (Pahl, 2002).

As Kate Pahl expresses it, "early literacy activities rest on a complex sea of play, talk, writing, drawing, and modeling, among other things. All are forms of representation" (Pahl, 1999). As children enter and exit places, they bring cultural resources with them; sometimes they leave them behind. Our students use whatever is to hand—from religious books to Pokemon©—to make meaning, and we need to build on the skills these texts bring. All children write, draw, play, and symbolize within homes, and these activities are shaped by the contexts in which they were made. We need to pay attention not only to the text—how it is produced and with what kinds of materials and modalities—but also to the talk and movement around their play. We need to value what children bring to their making and composing activities. Play and using cultural resources in the home allow us to see a child's pathway into literacy. Uncovering the meanings behind the artifacts children make in the home allow us to see into children's preoccupations and narratives.

Literacy Moment

The Greatest Artist
by Hilary Inwood

Zachary, a Grade 2 student, is often referred to by his teacher as "quite a handful." While he is obviously bright, his reading is well below grade level. He has struggled since Kindergarten with attention deficiencies and behavioral problems. Unable to stay focused on a task for more than a few minutes; he fidgets incessantly in his seat and plays with any object he can get his hands on. He uses any excuse to leave his desk, and has to be repeatedly told to return to his seat.

One afternoon an artist visited the room for a special program. She read a story and asked the students to discuss the illustrations. Zachary, who had been fidgeting during the reading of the story, puts his hand up to offer his responses to the artist's questions. He listened intently to her instructions for the drawing activity, and was one of the first to begin work on this drawing. Much to his teacher's surprise, he focused on the project, drawing for 45 minutes without leaving his seat. When the artist asked him if she could share his work with the class, he agreed, and his classmates whispered in awe at his detailed and imaginative drawing. He beamed with pride as a few claimed that "he is the greatest artist."

What are Cultural Resources?

Cultural resources signify the cultural worlds of our students. They need to be present in some guise in our classroom spaces, and to be used, to varying degrees, in our planning. Cultural resources invite us into student worlds, and can include the following:

- Objects in the home: cushions, blankets, chairs from which children make meaning
- Arts and crafts: paper, different kinds of paint, markers, scissors, glue, clay, brushes, crayons, etc.
- Family artifacts: mementos, symbols, old jewelry, clothes tied to events (e.g., saris), heirlooms, dress-up clothes, family tokens that have become a part of family history and signify ways of being in the family.
- Popular culture: bedspreads, posters, CD covers, etc. that speak to student interests
- New media: handheld computers, smaller console games, game cards, etc.
- Toys: Lego©, puzzles, maps, action figures, Barbies, etc.
- Stuff: baskets, masks, binoculars, little soldiers, etc.

The Power of Play

Stories told—and read, watched, listened to, acted out—provide a basis for imaginative activities and valuable meaning-making. Consider the following activities for younger children to foster language development and to bridge a home–school divide:

- **Drama:** Place students into groups and have them set a story into a play. Ideally, they should know the story by heart and keep it simple. Incorporate art by having them create props for the play. For example, the story of Puss and Boots works well if some students create boots for the cats to wear, and gather material for the princess and ogre to wear. One group can serve as choral narrators of the story. Plays can be informal or they can be more elaborate, with sets, costumes, staging, etc.
- **Artwork:** Artwork is an ideal vehicle as a follow-up to a story. Artwork can take on a variety of formats, from friezes, to collages, to three-dimensional figures such as dioramas, to their own storybooks. Artwork provides a vehicle to spotlight students' ruling passions and to witness traces of home coming to school.
- **Role Play:** After reading a story, encourage role play by providing props and dress-up clothes to turn a classroom space into a different setting.
- **Music, Song, and Dance:** Stories or parts of stories can also be turned into action songs, set to music, or turned into mimes or dances.

With all of these activities, it is important to engage children based on what they know and what they are familiar with. With this in mind, try to incorporate familiar cultural resources that speak to their funds of knowledge. For example, if you live in a community in which saris or other traditional clothing is worn, try to have a parent or member of the community donate clothes to match the cultures in which you teach.

In *Transformations: Meaning Making in Nursery School*, Kate Pahl presents observational data from three years in a nursery school in North London. In her book, she details how children use cultural resources and how it offers a window into their meaning-making.

> When children receive an idea, they take it in and it becomes meaningful to them. For example, from one nursery child's interest in the story of Peter Pan came the idea to make a Captain Hook's hook out of the inside of a toilet roll. This idea spread and the children became preoccupied with making hooks. In another observation, the children made wings to become the fairy Tinkerbell. It is possible to track the process of hearing the story of Peter Pan to the making of models. Children may also be observed acting out the story of Peter Pan and adapting it to become part of further play and model making. Children take ideas on and transform them in their own unique ways. Through watching children listen to stories, make models, draw and write, we can uncover a fascinating and complex understanding of how ideas can be received and translated into completely different activities. (Pahl, 1999)

Over time, children pay attention to features of print and emulate them in their own attempts at writing. In our planning and teaching, we should regard these observations and acquisition of skills as representational resources that we can use in our classrooms.

A five-year-old drew a picture just after her soccer practice. It depicted a man on a stage with bright lights and a curtain. She drew five other versions of the same picture, and consistently described the scene, as "a soccer man on stage." Each picture was an exact replica of the others and that was exactly how she wanted them to be. One of her coaches was sitting on another stage during practice so she used a sticky note to squeeze him into the picture; the other coach would not fit at the bottom of the page, so she improvised with materials at hand.

The drawing is a use of cultural resources in the home to depict an important moment in the child's life. Questions that might arise from such artifacts are

- What can the image offer that words cannot express?
- How does this image resemble other kinds of texts that she sees on a regular basis?
- For a child who cannot yet read, what literacy skills are being exhibited?
- How can we help this child along her pathway to literacy to lead her into a written description of the scene?

As you work with younger children, these sorts of questions can frame your conferences with them. When working with older children and adolescents, invite them to use cultural resources in their written, visual, and multimodal work. Different genres have variable organizational structures and visual grammars. You should help students come to understand these features and have a meta-awareness of them. For instance, explore the notions of design and designing texts versus doing a series of written assignments.

Voices from the Field

Literacy as Cultural Practice

by Victoria Purcell-Gates

The theoretical presupposition of my research into early literacy development has two basic principles:

- The ease with which children learn from beginning literacy instruction is determined by their experiences with written language practice in their lives before they begin this instruction.
- These experiences with written language use are constrained by and constructed by cultural and social contexts within which the children, their families, and their communities live their lives.

The theory—that children use the concept knowledge gained informally from experiences with written language use by others in their environments—runs counter in many ways to the widely held theoretical assertion that reading and writing achievement in school rests on an oral language base. However, study after study, including all of mine, have found that it is

- the presence of books and magazines of an array of genres
- the presence of other reading materials
- habits of writing, such as personal letters and notes
- literacy practices that include children, such as storybook reading
- emergent writing
- answering child questions about print
- parent education levels that determine the level of readiness for literacy instruction, as well as the probabilities for satisfactory and higher achievement in school-based literacy tasks

Examining these types of written language activities reveals that the literacy practices of homes and communities reflect the social and cultural lives of those communities, i.e. reading and writing—including the types of texts, the purposes for reading and writing them, the norms for who reads or writes what, where, and when—mediate the social activities of people, weaving in and out of other semiotic activities, such as talking, listening, viewing, and visual representation. This means that the early literacy concepts and skills with which children begin school are the product of the ways that literacy is practised in their communities. This, in turn, is the product of the social and cultural lives of the community members.

The literacy practices of communities change to reflect changing sociocultural realities of people, not the other way around. This theory plays out in my research in the following ways:

- First, I conduct numerous studies of literacy practices within homes and communities to ascertain the types of literacy practices that constitute the written language environments of the children of those communities (see www.educ.ubc.ca/research/cpls for a sample of those types of studies that fall under the umbrella of my larger project.
- Second, many of my studies include tapping and measuring the types of early literacy knowledge held by young children within these contexts.
- Third, some of these studies focus on examining the relationships between this knowledge and different types of socioculturally determined literacy practices experienced by children.
- Finally, I have conducted studies examining the ways that children's emergent literacy knowledge at entrance into formal schooling transacts with different types of school-based literacy practices and instruction and how both of those are related to literacy achievement in school.

Observation Checklist

Students demonstrate the following:

☐ Knowledge of which aspects of a text emerge from a student and their funds of knowledge.

☐ Knowledge of which parts of a text have more prominence than others (e.g., interactivity on a web site).

☐ Knowledge of the facts, skills, and issues that underpin a medium.

☐ Ability to discern which material, discursive aspects have most relevance for the medium.

☐ Ability to describe the process of making a text.

☐ Knowledge of practices used to create a text.

☐ Understanding of what different aspects/modes offer texts (e.g., doing an electronic portfolio vs a print-based one).

☐ Understanding of how different aspects/modes constrain texts (e.g., creating an electronic portfolio hinders holding it and looking through it).

☐ Ability to capture material effectively in the medium and communicate it to others.

☐ Understanding of skills that emerge from using different texts.

☐ Understanding of genres of texts and what they have to offer.

☐ Ability to reflect on the process and product and to build on this knowledge into the future.

☐ Ability to move principles of a genre onto another medium and genre of text.

☐ Ability to critically frame discourses and visuals in texts.

☐ Ability to represent their identity or parts of their identity in their literacy work.

☐ Understanding, knowledge, and ability to work with design and notions of design.

CHAPTER 5

Using Multiliteracies to Teach

The following chapter traces a movement from theory to practice. As discussed in preceding chapters, children, adolescents, and teenagers are engaged in different acts and texts, and they use these forces to invite new skills. It is easy to forget these new sets of skills as we plan, teach, and assess on a daily basis. One of the great appeals of technology and media is that they are intrinsically motivating, and students can set goals and create their own rules. Equally easy is it to say that we need culture as a bridge to invite skills that remain confined to homes and to the roles we take on at home (e.g., son and father enjoying and storing flyers). In this chapter, we see how teachers, administrators, and researchers consider ways of implementing multiliteracies and multimodal pedagogy. The section provides a roadmap for building new frameworks into your school and creating community to do the building.

"There are the global matters of swift communications through Internet, e-mail, and digital imaging… and surrounding us are the daily reminders that news media, advertising—all the rhetorical devices of society—are using image plus language in increasingly complex ways … These changes impose urgent demands on educational practice in literacy."
— Eve Bearne

Throughout this chapter are activities tied to multiliteracies skills. In addition, there are assessment frames to offer ways of assessing multiliteracies and multimodal skills.

Literacy by Design

We know that reading and writing remain integral to being literate. Small children make their way into print by understanding letters, putting them together, and making phrases. However, anyone who has spent time with small children knows that they equally engage with objects, draw pictures, configure cultural resources (which can be anything), watch DVDs, use playing cards—and all the while understand print. In other words, they are designing or using available designs (ones that exist and that they can transform) to make meaning. The same can be said for older students and adults who engage in different activities to make meaning at school, at home, and out in the world.

Rather than taking reading and writing as a starting point in literacy, what about thinking about literacy around the principles of design? Print or electronic texts can be seen as ensembles of features, fonts, formats, and modes. Implicit to this philosophy would be a belief that we choose a mode—visual, oral, written, textured, one with gesture—that best suits a text. Certainly when a students works on web pages or blogs, they are using photographs to transmit a message as much as they are using written prose to express their thoughts. Multiliteracies pedagogy believes our students think as designers, who see page spreads or interface as available designs (Cope & Kalantzis, 2000) that can be changed around how they see fit—in doing so, they change the message to something else.

With Anne Burke, I explored the degree to which students actually acknowledge and transform designs, and how they redesign based on their own taste, experience, and know-how. With a group of Grade 6 students we noted, time and time again, how much students actually know about design and designing. Avril had the following to say about her favorite web site, one in which you can change and try out outfits. In Anne's discussion with Avril, she certainly knew how she would improve the web site:

> Actually, I would… On the lips here (points with finger to screen and traces the cell with different kinds of lips) there is a bunch of lips but they are really big. You can't just get little lips like if you wanted to get little tiny ones just normal. (indicates with her finger, tracing the lips and showing how she would downsize them). You see like this. Just under the nose a little bit… but these they go out to like your ears. They are so BIG. So I'd change that and the tops… I like the tops because even though there is only eight tops there (uses the mouse to circle items), they give you a choice to change the color. (Burke and Rowsell, 2006)

Clearly, Avril appreciated available designs that were written as much as they were visual, used sound as much as movement, and importantly, knew exactly how she would change these features. Avril concentrated on aspects of web space and reflected on what she might change if she were a designer.

It is worth noting that in all of the interviews with Grade 6 students, only one student said that they would change written text within a design.

Using Critical Literacy in Literacy Teaching

As literacy educators, we need to cast a wider net to include print and electronic texts that speak to our students' interests.

Our aim is to bring children on the margins of literacy development in. This population includes students

- whose first language is not English or whose literacy practices in the home are not acknowledged and scaffolded in our teaching
- who do not have the types of texts that are used and understood in classrooms, but who have their own repository of literacy experiences we can draw upon
- who are not interested in the kinds of texts we present in school and, as a result, do not feel motivated to read or to write
- who are proficient with new media and technology, and perhaps less with printed texts
- who have a different sense of how to learn language skills because they come from a culture with its own set of beliefs, habits of mind, and literacy practices

Collectively, these students represent a strong percentage of our student body and they need to be heard.

Multiliteracies Pedagogy and Family Literacy

"The computer, of course, is not unique as an extension of self. At each point in our lives, we seek to project ourselves into the world. The youngest child will eagerly pick up crayons and modeling clay. We paint, we work, we keep journals, we start companies, we build things that express the diversity of our personal and intellectual sensibilities. Yet the computer offers us new opportunities as a medium that embodies our ideas and our expressions of diversity."
—Sherry Turkle

In the late 1990s, a group of scholars gathered in the United States to create a framework that mediates between the complex worlds students engage in outside of school with the literacy and language work that they do in school. Part and parcel of their discussions was taking account of multimodality and the increased role of the visual in student's life worlds. In light of their meeting, they devised a framework of four types of literacy activities (Cope & Kalantzis, 2000). You will find activities of all four types in the second section of this book, scattered through the genre chapters.

Types of Activities

1. Situated Practice

Locate your teaching, planning, and assessment within student worlds.

- What do your students read and write?
- How do they think?
- What are their interests?
- What are the cultural backgrounds in your classroom?
- What do they do outside of school?
- With whom do your students engage in literacy practices?
- What kinds of texts do they read?
- How do they read and write them?

Situated practice activities locate teaching within student skill sets; textual practices; texts; and lifeworlds.

- Meaningful practice within a community of learners who play multiple roles and whose meaning-making shifts as they enter and exit contexts.
- Planning with situated practice in mind means concentrating on everyday interactions and locating your activities within student skills.
- The family literacy dimension is sharing texts and activities with parents or guardians so that they can do them at home with children.
- By using texts students read at school, parents who have limited English language skills can be reinforcing learning that takes place in school.
- As Kath Gilbert and Yvon Appleby express it, parents "can support their children's literacy by talking about texts in their home language, questioning, predicting, looking at ideas and attitudes" (Gilbert & Appleby, 2005).
- The parents can discuss a text with the teacher and then have the child explain the plot to them. There can be an intergenerational component to the activity whereby grandparents read dual language texts with their grandchildren.
- Locating planning and assessment within technological skills students exhibit is another form of situated practice.

Throughout the book, you will see instances where a text genre is present with ways of situating it in your practice.

2. Overt Instruction

Teach *to* your students' skills. Matching your instruction to the kinds of skills your students possess—Farid's flyers or the encyclopedias a family uses—as a literacy teacher you need to locate your teaching within your students' lifeworlds. Ask yourself the following questions as you plan your teaching:

- What are your students reading and writing practices outside of school?
- How can I build on their funds of knowledge?
- Am I accessing skills they possess from their use of console games or reading and writing in an electronic medium?
- Is there variety in the kinds of texts that I use?
- Have I diversified my instruction to include an equal account of printed as well as electronic texts?

Situated Practice Activities: Locating your teaching within student skill sets; textual practices; texts; and lifeworlds.
Overt Instruction Activities: Using new skills within lessons, openers, wrap-ups, activities, modifications, and assessment strands.
Critical Framing Activities: Peeling away the layers in texts and analyzing them in terms of multimodality; form; language or discourse; and function.
Transformed Practice Activities: Teaching literacy based on new skills and multimodal texts.

- Have I acknowledged different gender interests?
- Are there students who feel marginalized because of literacy content or activities?

Overt instruction activities use new skills within lessons, openers, wrap-ups, activities, modifications, and assessment strands.

- Teacher scaffolds learning through explicit teaching and teamwork between teacher and student.
- Planning with overt instruction in mind demands that teachers think about texts students use inside and outside of school; think about cultural resources in the home and how best to build them into teaching (e.g., family artifacts or different languages in the home); think about technology and our students' understanding of technology—their use of multiple texts at once, and texts with color, animation, and music.
- Overt instruction also means situating assessment within the students' skill set, and thinking about funds of knowledge and new technology skills that they bring with them to the classroom.

3. Critical Framing

Teach your students not only to understand and think about different discourses and ideologies in texts read and written in class, but also to appreciate how the format and layout of texts reflects underlying meanings.

- Who wrote the text?
- Who is the audience?
- Why was it written?
- What is the visual communication of the text?
- What is its overall message?
- Do I agree or disagree with the message?
- Does it remind me of other texts?
- What purpose does it serve?
- Can I create a similar text?
- When would I create it?

Critical framing activities involve peeling away the layers in texts and analyzing them in terms of multimodality; form; language or discourse; and function.

- Critical framing helps students frame their mastery of practice and their understanding of more ideological aspects of language development (e.g., how language changes from one genre to the next).
- Students can peel back several layers of texts. Planning activities that mobilize this skill will help them to understand the importance of a critical view of texts that they use.
- It is essential to assess critical framing as a form of metacognition, so that students are aware of assumptions they might carry in their reading of texts, or that texts carry particular perspective.

4. Transformed Practice

When you situate your practice within the lifeworlds of your students, you have transformed your practice. When you speak to skills students possess and use texts that interest them and elicit funds of knowledge, you are constructing your program based on student needs. The following reflection questions can guide your practice:

- Are students engaged in my program?
- Am I aware of literacy practices in the home and how to embed them in my program?
- Are the skills that I teach removed from their worlds and their skill sets?
- Am I speaking to one gender over another?
- Is there evidence of mediating with curriculum and worlds outside of the classroom?
- Am I representing the cultures of my classroom?
- Are there formative assessment measures that draw on multimodal skills?
- Do I equally account for electronic genres of texts as well as printed texts (even if I do not have access to electronic texts in my classroom, or students do not have access to them in the home)?
- What are my program goals and do they correspond with what my students know and enjoy?
- Have I spoken with parents or guardians about their children and what they do in terms of literacy in the home?
- If so, how can I build on these skills?
- Is my school fostering community ties?

Transformed practice activities are based on new skills and multimodal texts.

- Transformed practice is the ability to move new skills that students learn during literacy teaching to other contexts. Learners are thereby able to transfer meaning-making to different places.
- Family literacy is ideal for applying transformed practice because you can provide ways of using new skills in the home; for example, by sending books home to read with a parent, grandparent, or sibling.
- Highlighting the use of looking up information on the Internet within a social studies activity is an instance of transforming practice, of having students bring a skill they use frequently outside of school, into school.

Assessment Frames

Assessment Frames represent opportunities to assess what students bring with them into our classrooms. Each one evokes skills implicit to the genre (e.g., how blogs use visuals to mediate identity). Use assessment frames as a way of building a bridge to students' worlds and to provide a more holistic picture of each chapter.

Multiliteracies pedagogy is premised on the screen, so we must be sensitive to issues of access. We know that many students do not have computers at home, or even at school. We must open up literacy to look at family and culture alongside new communicational systems, for even with limited access students still think *in terms* of technology.

Assessment Frame
....

Text Inventory

At the beginning, middle, or end of the school year (or when you get an opportunity), take an inventory of text genres in your classroom. If you have not already done so, sort genres, put them in bins, and label them. Have you thought about including these genres?

- Graphic stories
- Chapter books

- Magazines
- Collector cards (e.g., Pokeman© or Digimon©)
- Large-format non-fiction books
- Comic books of all kinds
- Catalogues and flyers
- Artwork
- CD inserts
- Newspapers
- Single- and dual-language books
- Photographs.

With each genre, have activity cards that match skills implicit in each one. Write down assessment frames from chapters as ways of assessing student understanding of text genres.

Voices from the Field

Multiliteracies and Teacher Education

by Clare Kosnik (Stanford University) & Clive Beck (OISE/University of Toronto)

For many years we have taught in preservice education and done research and writing on our own practice and that of other teacher educators (e.g., Beck & Kosnik, 2006; Kosnik & Beck, 2003). We have found researching practice helps improve our practice. At present we are conducting a four-year longitudinal study on the preparation of elementary literacy teachers in a large school of education. We define multiliteracies pedagogy rather broadly to include social constructivist aspects, such as student construction of ideas, experiential learning, collaborative learning, and building classroom community. Almost all the new teachers we interviewed and observed were in schools with a highly multi-racial, multi-ethnic student population and a significant proportion of ESL students. We found the following:

- **Considerable attention given to multiliteracies pedagogy.** Constructivist pedagogy was widely advocated in the preservice programs and was apparent in the ideas and practices of the new teachers. A large proportion of the faculty and new teachers also emphasized non-fiction reading and writing, connecting to students' lives beyond the school, culturally sensitive pedagogy, and fostering classroom community. Some also stressed the importance of addressing digitally-based literacy.
- **Lack of clarity about the nature of multiliteracies pedagogy.** Although they advocated a multiliteracies and constructivist pedagogy, the faculty and new teachers often seemed unclear about its precise nature. As one new teacher put it, sometimes "catch terms" were presented in the preservice program rather than clear ideas. This even applied to terms such as "balanced literacy" and "guided reading" that were central to the literacy approach being advocated. Other areas of apparent lack of clarity were the teacher–student relationship, the school's role in relation to digitally-based communication, the relative weight to be given to the needs of the individual students and their home and community culture, and the role of the class community.
- **Limits to the implementation of multiliteracies pedagogy.** Although the faculty and new teachers gave considerable attention to multiliteracies pedagogy, in our view they did not go far enough in this direction. On the whole, an aesthetic or "literary" emphasis was still dominant in the approach to literacy teaching; formal reading and writing were still the main focus, rather than less formal out-of-school

literacies; the approach to literacy teaching was not as "critical" as multiliteracies theorists advocate; and multiliteracies pedagogy was not always modeled in the preservice programs themselves.

Writing and Technology

In addition to reading, the nature of writing has changed with increasing use of the computer. Editing, in particular, is a skill that our students have honed as they come to grips with researching online, formatting text, adding tables and figures, using film clips to accompany assignments. Words on the page are one feature of writing, but behind the scenes, there are so many other kinds of literacy practices involving technology:

- Brainstorming: research and invention of material (i.e., what kinds of texts—electronic and printed—will I refer to?)
- The writing process: creating and saving multiple drafts.
- Thinking through audience, impact, and purpose by referring to texts online.
- Spelling, grammar, punctuation: relying on more than technology to check all of these elements.
- Formatting and production: What font to choose? Will I incorporate illustrations or tables or figures? What sorts of distributions of meaning (i.e., how should I present the material and in what medium)?

Our students think about writing in this way because they are used to the trappings of technology, which offer not only words, but also all of the affordances of multimodality —animation/movement, sound, color, principles of design, and sundry production options. Although composing is still key, editing on screen is integral to the process.

The Writing Process On and Off Screen

1. **Writing needs to be taught as a process.** Looking at texts provides a good segue into the process of writing, by spotlighting how texts go through a process from development to production and formatting. Using different genres of texts, such as comics, as a springboard for a discussion about the writing process is a good way to illustrate that writing follows stages.
2. **Reading and writing are inextricable linked.** If you are an avid reader, chances are you have a strong awareness of voice—articulating what you want to say when you want to say it—and you understand audience. Viewing reading and writing as a continuum fosters an awareness and excitement about the reading process. This kind of thought provides even more reasons to build on the interests of your students as a hook to teaching writing.
3. **Writing evokes our passions and beliefs.** There is nothing more compelling than reading a piece of writing that strongly articulates an idea or an opinion or a belief. We may not necessarily agree, but we take the time to think through the ideas when we face good writing. We need to imbue this sense for our passions and feelings in our students. Once again, an ideal vehicle is their own experience, interests, and funds of knowledge.

Biography of Someone You Know

For intermediate students, ask them to write a biography about someone who has moved from one culture to another. Have students interview someone in their family about their migration and use photographs that they can scan in and add photos to fill out written text. They should frame their interview with such questions as:

1. At what age did you move?
2. For what reason did you move?
3. How did you find the new culture and traditions?
4. Did you have to learn a new language?
5. How did you feel as you adjusted to a new place, new language, new culture?

There should be a reflection piece within the biography about how students felt about interviewing someone they know about moving and migration.

Incorporating Family Literacy into Your School

Out-of-School Literacies in the Classroom

Jo designs her classroom with illustrations and photographs from different cultures. She has a separate reading area with soft cushions and an extensive library filled with dual-language texts, wordless picturebooks, non-fiction texts, comic books, Pokemon© cards, and stories of all sorts from fables to *Harry Potter*. It is a room that celebrates different cultures and appeals strongly to the interests of students in the class. Jo has a publishing centre in the middle of her classroom where children laminate, collate, and bind books of their poetry, drawings, and stories in English and, at times in their own languages. These books are on display around the room and in a central area of the school.

Jo has a specific philosophy of literacy that envelopes all forms of literacy and, in particular, invites linguistic diversity. Jo does not insist that students adopt one culture and one language, but instead allows and encourages them to adapt their own culture and language to their host language and culture. In this way, one language begets another.

Jo's classroom illustrates how we can harness our language teaching to culture and cultural practices by incorporating and building on student-lived experience in our teaching. When we scaffold our student's home culture and social practices within their schooling contexts, students are able to situate themselves in the process. They can find themselves in the local and in the global, and embed their identities in artifacts; for example, by placing a poem onto a digital image. After all, children are masters of our new communication systems and, by combining them with more traditional methods, we are speaking to their needs and to their interests.

Family literacy takes on different shades of meaning when we compare what small children do at home, how they make meaning in the home and with parents, and compare that with what adolescents and teenagers do. For example, surveying the field of adolescent literacy, the following findings have been made:

- In a study on adolescent reading, Mary Curtis found that Grade 6 is an ideal time to look at sentence and discourse processing for comprehension rather than word-level work. (Curtis, 2002)
- "The link between knowledge and comprehension in older readers is not straightforward…. Reading skill can compensate for knowledge deficiencies, and knowledge can compensate for deficiencies in reading skill." (Curtis, 2002).
- Studies show that the presence of reading material in the home and family discussions about school experiences and educational plans are related to reading comprehension skills. The home conditions that predict adolescents' reading achievement may be less modifiable than those that are important for younger children's reading development.
- Motivation and engagement are critical determiners of adolescent literacy development. Students often engage in sophisticated reading *away* from the classroom. (Kamil, 2003)
- Both direct, explicit instruction in vocabulary and deriving word meanings from context are important.
- Providing appropriate reading materials for ESL students may require consideration of more than text readability. Cultural knowledge and appeal of subject matter may also be important.
- Computer-based communication involves use of literacy skills in social settings and often collaborative work with peers. These activities may improve reading and writing abilities.

Barbara Comber has conducted important research in the area of critical literacy. In her work, she argues that the following factors at school make a difference to what children learn:

1. The Recognition Factor: the extent to which what children can do counts and they can see it counts.
2. The Resource Factor: the extent to which schools have human and material resources they need.
3. The Curriculum Factor: the quality, scope and depth of what is made available.
4. The Pedagogical Factor: the quality of teacher instructional talk, teacher-student relationships and assessment practices.
5. The Take-up Factor: the extent to which children appropriate literate practices and school-authorized discourses.
6. The Translation Factor: the extent to which children can make use of and assemble repertoires of practice that they can use in new situations.

In her most recent work, Comber considers how the principles of design can be used to develop literacy skills. To explore the notion of design and literacy, Comber invites architects and architecture students into junior-age classrooms to create and design spaces based on principles of design and the creation of space. Comber speaks of how deficit discourses (i.e., approaches to literacy that regard a lack of written language as a lack of literacy skills) produce pedagogies of poverty. Comber believes that we need to make a notion of place and space central in children's learning (Comber, 2006).

Assessment Frame

What Is Happening Where?

To assess your students' awareness of their home space and its funds of knowledge, have them create a floor plan of their house. Analyze what you do in each area and why they are important. Write the activities that take place on sticky notes and stick them in appropriate rooms. For example:

- The kitchen is where Dad makes chili.
- The study is where I play most of my video games.
- I like to lie in bed and read books before going to sleep.

Now ask them to list the kind of learning they do at home. They will have to walk through the house and perhaps observe family practices for a week in order to really think it through.

Defining Parental Involvement

Home involvement is never cut and dried because there are so many different family compositions. Many researchers have concerned themselves with what are known as home-environment variables, the resources that families have to support literacy, by looking at socio-economic status; parents' education; parents' literacy competence; values about literacy in the home; and environmental elements. As teachers, not only do we need to open up literacy but also to embrace all kinds of resources in the home, from cultural texts to family artifacts to televisions to video games.

As well, ties to schooling include the degree to which parents become involved in their child's literacy development by attending parent–teacher meetings or conferences with teachers, by attending student performances and athletic events, even by participating in decision-making around school reform.

Some of these factors can be changed by implementing school initiatives to involve parents more in their child's schooling and the school community. There are standard initiatives in place and school-initiated efforts that you can implement to increase or to improve parent involvement.

Joyce Epstein developed a framework to assist educators in developing school and family partnership programs. There are six dimensions to her framework. These six dimensions can help principals and teachers infuse family literacy into their school and create professional development sessions around each type of intervention.

1. Parenting: Assist families with parenting and child-rearing skills; help parents understand child and adolescent development; set home conditions for optimum literacy development. Schools should identify funds of knowledge within communities and families.

2. Communicating: Communicate with families about school programs and student progress that will affect school-to-home and home-to-school communications.
3. Volunteering: Improve recruitment, training, and work aimed at involving families as volunteers and audiences at the school to support students and school programs.
4. Learning at Home: Involve families with their children in learning activities at home, including homework and other curriculum-linked activities. You will need to provide support for this, including translating materials into primary language groups.
5. Decision Making: Include families as participants in school decisions, governance, and advocacy through parent–teacher organizations, school councils, and committees.
6. Collaborating with Community: Coordinate resources and services for families, particularly families in the community, and provide services to the community. (Epstein et al, 1995)

Family literacy initiatives that are well-organized, that are long-lasting, and that involve community partnerships as part of a comprehensive plan can improve student achievement (Desforges & Abouchaar, 2003). Programs need to provide parents with strategies for helping with homework, encouraging learning, creating a home environment that fosters learning, communicating with children, and monitoring their learning (Boethel, 2003).

Situated Practice

Documenting Literacy Events

Ask students to take pictures of literacy in the home. They will then write descriptions of what is taking place, when it takes place, and with whom. Present the literacy event to the class as a collage with pictures to enhance awareness of literacy in the home and to offer more knowledge about students and how they make meaning outside of school.

Voices from the Field

Forging Community by Setting Up a Tutoring Program
by Kathryn Broad and Mary Lynn Tessaro

Drawing on the resources of the local community can be a powerful strategy for helping students with their literacy learning. When students are struggling with literacy, individual or small group tutoring is beneficial. Students are given time and attention to develop necessary skills as they are tutored. Parents and other willing adult volunteers can be brought into the school, and with some training, can work with administrators and teachers to tutor identified students.

• Tutors and students are engaged in constant communication through talk. As tutors model talk, students can learn a great deal about language by hearing new words and new ways of expression. Having a strong foundation in oral language helps students with reading and writing.
• Reading to children is very important and tutors should be reading to their tutees. Favorite materials can be read and reread during sessions along with the new material being introduced.

- It is well known that when children are learning to read they need a great deal of practice. By listening to students read and offering guidance, tutors provide invaluable support to struggling literacy learners.

1. A thorough orientation to the program will assist tutors to work more independently and with less direction.

- Welcome and orient new tutors by providing contextual information as well as training and guidelines for the tutoring process.
- Tour the school to familiarize the tutor with key personnel and locations, including restrooms, the school office, the library, and the quiet, yet public space designated for tutoring sessions.
- Provide information regarding school hours, fire exits and emergency protocols.
- Offer a space for storing materials and begin with a good supply of pencils, paper, scissors, etc. Outline the procedure for obtaining additional materials.

2. Explain classroom/school guidelines for behavior to the tutor.

3. Provide information about the strengths and areas for growth of the student to assist the tutor to develop an effective tutoring plan.

4. Determine the work schedule for the tutoring sessions in alignment with the school calendar of events. Ensure that the student and classroom teacher have copies of this plan.

5. Describe the format for communicating with the classroom teacher. A tracking sheet that lists the activities accomplished during the tutoring session may assist the classroom teacher to plan more effectively for the student in the classroom setting.

Literacy Moment
....

Multimodality for a Day

Every year, Susan Elliott and Tina Jagdeo organize a technology day at their school. At the beginning of the day, students are introduced to an assignment, *Who am I?* After completing the writing process in class, the next step is to create a multimodal version in the computer lab during the scheduled Tech Day. Students use their essays on *Who am I?* as springboards to learn, experiment, and create with computer technology. Open-ended software programs—including Inspiration©, Key Note©, iPhoto©, Garage Band©, and PowerPoint©—are used in their designs. Embedded in the creations were photos from home, school, and the Internet; even their own musical compositions were represented.

At the beginning of the day, the teacher reviews the assignment and the assessment criteria. Then, a series of mini-lessons and experiments begin. Students zip from one digital tool to another; for some, the day gives time to go deep into the detail of what one program can do. One of the best parts of the day is that students teach each other (and at times the teacher) using new digital skills and software.
....

Promoting Family Literacy in Your School

To promote family literacy in your school, there are certain measures and supports that you can put in place.

1. Adopt policies that promote family literacy.
2. Develop the capacity of school staff to understand and work with diverse families.

3. In school with large enrollments of students whose first language is other than English, staff who speak the other dominant language can be invaluable.
4. A parent coordinator or home–school liaison can simplify communication. The coordinator should come from the predominant group in your school community.
5. Welcome parents into the community. Create a welcome room for parents new to the community and to the culture.
6. Maintain regular communication with families.
7. Help low-income families gain access to community services.

At the beginning of the school year, consider using these strategies to start building community:

- interviews and questionnaires with community members
- introduce some community members
- create a bulletin board with community information, such as maps, local stories, profiles of people in the community, key resources in the area
- share stories of the lives of community members
- share student stories about the community

Voices from the Field

Case Study of Family Literacy in a School

by Sandy Arbuck, Principal of Discovery Public School

Our School Plan for Continuous Improvement (SPCI) clearly identifies Literacy Development in our students as our number-one goal. Discovery Public School is a large elementary school, with 745 students from Junior Kindergarten to Grade 8. The school is very multicultural—English is the first language for only 45% of our students.

Over the last three years, we have seen a steady improvement in our students' literacy levels based on a variety of standardized reading tests and report card data. This steady improvement is a result of our focus on establishing our school as the hub of our community. As a staff we looked at our community—participation of parents, English fluency of parents, reading materials in the home, and frequency of English usage beyond school hours. We made the decision not to lay blame on families for sending us students who did not speak English well, write well, or care to read, but instead to find a way to fill the gaps our students demonstrated. We set out to establish a school that would provide the literacy enrichment that so many of our students required. Our outstanding literacy teacher has been working very hard with all staff to ensure that the programs in classes are of the highest calibre; however, this is not enough. We had to look beyond the traditional school day, traditional school responsibilities, and traditional homework.

At the very foundation of literacy development is speaking. We had to find a way to get our students speaking more English. We knew if we could enrich and reinforce student's spoken language beyond the school day, it would transfer to their reading and writing skills. Extracurricular activities in the areas of sports and the arts were a great beginning; however, we went further. We brought in low-cost community-based programs, which were fun for our students and gave them opportunities to practise English. As well, parents had to pick their children up from these programs, so we could use these times to meet parents in a non-threatening environment.

It is easy to say, "We must get parents more involved with their children's learning, they must come to curriculum night, they must come to parent interviews"; however, the current reality is that parents do not. We must find creative ways to get our messages out to parents: training students to give "oral newsletters" describing learning that goes on at school; classroom newsletters, which are short, easy to read, and always contain clear activities parents can do with their children; and literacy messages on the school sign that parents drive by daily.

We must provide multiple opportunities for parents to come to our schools for events that do not necessarily require them to interact with the teachers or administration. We all know that significantly more parents attend school concerts than curriculum nights. We can provide non-threatening connections to learning at every one of these events. Family fun fairs, barbecues, and carnivals are ways to get parents into school with their children, so they can see the work on the halls and walls and feel comfortable in the school environment. At each of these events it is crucial to reinforce your school's message about literacy. We always have "small talk" about reading and writing, and give a couple of strategies that parents can use to support their children.

All teachers are expected to make at least one "good news" phone call per student per term. Calling parents to tell them that their child has moved to the next level in reading or has mastered a difficult concept in writing, or just to thank them for making sure homework has been completed, establishes a positive relationship. Such a relationship is necessary when you have to move on to the more difficult areas of making recommendations to parents, or dealing with discipline problems. Teachers often report that they use these phone calls to ask for old books (particularly in students' own languages) and games to be donated to the class. Parents report that they feel a greater connection to the school because they have contributed.

Student-led conferences are another great strategy for getting parents into the school for interviews in a non-threatening way. Students are trained to talk about their strengths and needs, and strategies they are working on to improve their performance in school. This requires a lot of practise with peers and teachers, and it is an authentic opportunity for students to demonstrate their oral language skills. We always encourage students to do these conferences in English first and then translate into their first language for parents who do not understand English.

Our school currently runs a preschool program. Two mornings a week parents, grandparents, and caregivers can come into the school with their toddlers and make crafts, play games, sing songs, hear stories, and get to know other people in the community. Often it is grandparents or babysitters who bring children to this program. Great benefits are achieved, regardless of which adult attends the program, because toddlers are being exposed to "school" experiences in the school environment. Transition to our Kindergarten programs is much smoother for the students who have already had opportunities to be in the school environment, to learn some English, and to spend time away from their home.

Most students in our community do not attend summer camps or engage in any type of learning activities over the summer. We have worked with our school board and the local Parks and Recreation department to establish a low-cost summer camp in our school. For our at-risk students, those who read and write below level, we have built a reading camp into this summer program. Teachers, volunteers, and community workers provide reading instruction to students so that they can maintain their skill levels over the summer. In conjunction with this program, we have opened up our school library during the summer.

Family Literacy Night is always a hit with young students. Often we have parents attend a short information session with the staff while the principal reads to all the children. Teachers talk to the parents about strategies that parents can use when reading with children at home. They model for the parents how to read to children, what types of questions to ask, how and when to sound out words; they often just encourage parents to read to their children. Following the parent session, the families reunite on pillows with stuffed animals and read together. Teachers circulate through the room, supporting parents with the reading strategies and reinforcing the good practices we encourage parents to use.

Each year we run a major fundraiser. The money raised from this event goes to purchasing materials that support our literacy initiatives. For the last three years, the major fundraiser has been a school-wide Readathon. Students raise money and spend a portion of a day reading. The highlight of the Readathon is often the guest readers who attend, bringing their favorite books. We have had police, firefighters, the Director of the Board of Education, parents, grandparents, siblings who have graduated, crossing guards, buss drivers, and local storekeepers. We encourage our students to seek guest readers from their family circles.

Part 2

New Texts, New Skills

> "In sum, I have argued for a pedagogical approach in which teachers—and administrators, parents, and the public—are sensitive to the ideological as well as social dimension of literacy and, moreover, one in which teachers respond to and build on what the children know and can do but, also, help the children respond to and build on what each other knows and can do."
> — Anne Haas Dyson

This section of the book looks at text genres and the skills that they bring with them. Some are relatively new, while others have been around for a while. Whether texts are web-based, are in print, or have multiple dimensions, they capture the minds and interests of our students, and they need a place in literacy teaching, planning, and assessing. Some text genres remain a mystery to us as adults, but for our students they are part of their life worlds.

Some of the chapters are by me, while others are by teachers, researchers, and scholars who are passionate about issues relating to literacy, multimodality, and student meaning-making. With an equal measure of my voice and other voices, chapters vary a bit, and some have brief biographies with featured skills. Chapters include

- moments or memories of using the featured genres
- presentation of the focus genres
- multiliteracies activities (Situated Practice, Overt Instruction, Critical Framing, and Transformed Practice)
- media connections that compare and contrast other genres featured in this book
- assessment frames

Concepts and beliefs presented in the first section of the book lie beneath the surface of this section:

1. *Each text has different modes:* modalities are identified alongside how they make students think differently and how they use them in certain ways for certain reasons. As a result, each text has movement, visuals, sound, textures, words, etc.
2. *Design and available designs* are prevalent, and are the basis of activities and assessments.
3. *Funds of knowledge*, as currency that our students bring to the classroom, are spotlighted, as are ways of building on skills and cultural practices in planning, teaching, learning, and assessing.
4. *Context* and how it shapes literacy is taken into account.
5. *Text form and function* both play a key role in understanding texts.
6. *Student interest* and motivation are a vital part of each chapter, and remind us why we need to think about these texts to begin with.

7. *Negotiating* what we know to work and coming to terms with new texts and new skills is part of the process.

Media Connection: Students will often use media and popular culture as cultural resources (see pages 46–50) in their work. Try to use their funds of knowledge of movies and popular trends in your teaching. For example, in Marika Autrand's chapter she discusses how rap and hip-hop are contemporized forms of poetry.

The Internet

by Isabel Pedersen

Isabel Pedersen is an Assistant Professor of Professional Communication; she studies our relationship to computer interfaces, including how they persuade us, how we interact with them, and what makes them unique forms of communication. In her chapter, she shares her expertise about web spaces by spotlighting the following key skills:

• Using metaphorical activities in online spaces
• Understanding how other media practices relate to Internet use
• Practicing web design and understanding design principles

Literacy Moment

Drop-down Menus

by Tony Balazs

Simon Balazs is six years old and has autism. Two of his favorite activities are reading word-and-picture books and using his laptop. He loves pointing to words he recognizes in the books and telling us what they are. Sometimes he asks us to read to him, indicating that we should point to the words as we go. He seems fascinated by letter shapes he sees in the world around him. Simon first became fluent at recognizing features of words by figuring out how to use the browser's drop-down menu to find the BBC children's website. He can now navigate to several sites he enjoys. The laptop taught him how useful it can be to recognise words and long strings of letters.

The Internet and Metaphor

Many consider "As We May Think," Vannevar Bush's 1945 article in the Atlantic Monthly, the first early conceptualization of the World Wide Web on the Internet. In it, Bush imagines a "memex," an electronic collection or library holding mass amounts of knowledge. The memex would support the mind, that "snaps" from thought to thought "in accordance with some intricate web of trails" (Bush, 1945). Bush conveys his ideas with metaphors that use familiar concepts to help us understand the unfamiliar. He projects *known* concepts onto the *unknown*: the mind does not really "snap," but the metaphor of *snapping thoughts* makes the idea more familiar and, consequently, his memex invention seems more plausible.

Mark Johnson, a cognitive metaphorist, explains that metaphor in language emerges from our physical experience of the world (1987). He means that we draw on our physical lives. Currently, metaphors in language help us understand Internet technology; the web is chockfull of activity-based metaphors (Randall & Pedersen, 2000). For example:

- **Hyperlinking** feels like a leap to another location. The metaphor of the web as a set of travel destinations is dominant. To surf is to *go somewhere*. You *follow* a link *destination* when you *go* to a web *site*. In one sense, links imply linear trips from point A to point B. At the same time, the web constitutes a mass network of hypertext, which is "text composed of blocks of words (or images) linked electronically by multiple paths, chains, or trails in an open-ended, perpetually unfinished textuality" (Landow, 1997). In a sense, hypertext implies ubiquity, meaning that you can go anywhere you want from any one place (i.e., You are everywhere at once). As web users become savvier, they learn how to navigate hypertext with purpose rather than randomly wandering through texts. Hyperlinking through hypertext develops critical skills in deciding what is a relevant and what is not.
- **Searching** draws on travel metaphor as well. The word "search" comes from the Latin *circare* —"to go about"—pointing to a physical conception of *looking for something*. On the Internet, search engine sites like Google.com broker most web searching; Google's mission is "to organize the world's information and make it universally accessible and useful." Yahoo's *Yahooligans* site offers seven- to twelve-year-olds a massive hypertext for searching and browsing.
- **Browsing** is more like *picking* things at a fruit stand; each link presents itself like a waiting apple or banana.
- **Hovering**, or moving over hidden spots on web pages, draws on other physical metaphors. Hovering implies that you are two places at once. Hummingbirds, helicopters, and flying saucers hover: they suspend themselves in the air, but interact with land. Pollypocket.com's Kooky Kitchen game relies on hovering as the main interface activity: players hover over cupboards and appliances to find misplaced items, like elephants under the kitchen sink.
- **Clicking** is probably the first interface activity we learn in a desktop context. The interrelationship of the hand–mouse–cursor makes *clicking* feel like we are tapping on the screen to indicate choices. Some Teletubbies games at PBSkids.org focus on clicking as the sole interface activity, because the target age of user might only be two. Generally, children can master a mouse before they learn an alphabetic code.
- **Dragging** works in concert with *clicking*. Dragging feels very much like grabbing hold of something and pulling it across the screen ("There, I've got you!"). *Charlie and Lola*, a British children's TV show, features a web site where visitors can drag dress-up clothes from the "jumble box" and drop them onto Lola.

Of course, there are many more metaphor-based interface activities that go on in a web context. By identifying a few of them, you develop both a common vocabulary for classroom discussion, and an awareness of how we generate language out of bodily experiences.

Find the Metaphor

To develop watching skills, listening skills, and web-based vocabularies, ask students as a class to identify activity metaphors at web sites.

- For older students, pick a complex web interface like *Google Earth* (www.earth.google.com), which allows you to use a satellite to explore fantastic images of the earth. As you zoom in on your own school or a famous landmark, make a blackboard list of all instances of hyperlinking, searching, hovering, clicking, and dragging to demonstrate interactivity in a whole text. Ask students to brainstorm other interface activities they recognize (e.g., How is *zooming* metaphoric?).
- Show younger students PBS Kids (www.pbskids.org) and get them to explore and discuss interface activities through web games suited to them.

Media Connection: No media is remote from other media. Internet media, in particular, spring from their relationships with more traditional media. E-mail fashions itself out of postal mail. Flash animation borrows from the medium of movie trailers. Web pages adopt the visual conventions of print (e.g., navigation links look like tables of contents). All of these connections are instances of "remediation" (Bolter & Grusin, 1999). Remediation is the way that "new media refashion prior media forms" (Bolter &Grusin, 1999). Our kids constantly sift through complex layers of remediation on the Internet every day. In a sense they are themselves remediators in this process of transformation and hybridization.

Remediation

Dora the Explorer is both a popular television show and an extensive web site. Each medium remediates the other. The Dora TV show remediates computer media in several ways:

- Dora "exists" inside a computer game. The opening sequence pans into a room and zooms over to a computer screen to start the show.
- A large animated cursor highlights key ideas on the television screen, as the seven-year-old adventurer travels to three points on her map (e.g., crossing a bridge, passing through a maze, and climbing a mountain).
- The show remediates computer sounds (e.g., beeps) to demonstrate how Dora progresses through her narrative quest.

Likewise, the Dora web site remediates the television show:

- The TV jingle plays at the start of Dora web site games, mimicking the start of the show. Jingles are not generally a convention on the web.
- The design features camera angles mimicking television rather than the print-page style of most web pages. For example, in the La Casa de Dora game, the web designers have the viewer follow Dora as she enters her house, rather than situating the viewer directly inside the house from the start.

When the Dora creators remediate computer conventions, they enable young viewers to combine a whole set of meaning-making resources from both television and the web.

Becoming Remediators

To develop critical skills, ask students to find instances of remediation in two different media. Circulate through the class a popular children's magazine (e.g., *OWL* magazine in Canada) and ask students to compare it with the web site counterpart (e.g., www.owlkids.com). Discuss ways that each medium borrows from the other in terms of

- layout
- graphical style
- typography

- wording
- tone of voice
- interactive features

Try to draw out the benefits of two media acting as counterparts.

The Internet and Design

Benjamin and Peter Selfridge's *A Kid's Guide to Creating Web Pages* is a great resource for learning how to make a web page with HTML (Hypertext Markup Language), the basic software code of the World Wide Web. Benjamin Selfridge identifies himself as a thirteen-year-old who has "been messing around with computers for a long time" (2004). Even young children can *author* web pages by entering their names at certain sites and altering the content. Internet technology liberates the subject who wants to self-publish; creating a web page has become common practice.

The web, however, also invites the chance to *design*. Gunther Kress writes that "designing is the action of setting an agenda of future aims, and of finding means and resources for carrying it out" (1998). Designing a web page invites skills like imagining, brainstorming, planning, collaborating, compromising, and organizing.

"Paper-prototyping" is a method for designing user interfaces implemented by usability experts in the field. A prototype is a model that demonstrates a design before it is actually made into an artifact (Preece et al., 2002). Using paper, or some other low-fidelity medium, lets you plan your design and test it out before a web page is actually coded in HTML. It is basically a rough plan of what your web page will look like and what it will do. Students can learn about web pages and make paper-prototypes to demonstrate design ideas.

Here are the steps for creating a simple paper prototype:

1. Form a small group of "designers" (i.e., three or four students).
2. Decide a high-level goal for your web page (e.g., Teach people about the importance of road safety).
3. Consider the audience for a web page. Who will be visiting the site? (e.g., adults, children, teachers, etc.)
4. Consider the interactions visitors will be doing at the site (e.g., reading information, searching for answers, playing educational games).
5. Think about metaphor and remediation, and how they can aid in the process of designing the page.
6. On paper, sketch the web page. Draw in areas for each interaction, including hyperlinks, search areas, and other activities.
7. Rough in graphics and places for written text.

Paper Prototype for New WEbsite

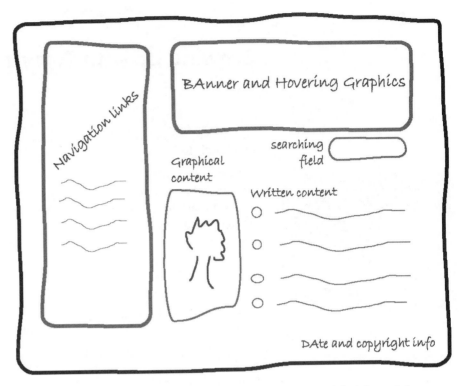

8. Test the paper prototype by sitting down with a potential visitor. Ask your visitor to imagine that he or she is visiting the site and doing some of the interactions. Watch for difficulties or confusion. Ask for feedback in the form of criticisms, comments, and new ideas.
9. Sketch out new ideas right on the paper-prototype.

After you complete the paper-prototype, you can make it into a real web page. At the same time, a prototype serves as a complete design text, demonstrating extensive planning and creative thought. Done as a group project, it also imitates a real usability job that takes place in the field of interaction design.

The Internet infiltrates our lives in multi-faceted ways. It orients, informs, teaches, and amuses us. It invites very practical skills (e.g., we use it to find jobs and prove ourselves worthy of jobs). However, it also invites us to metaphorize, remediate, design, and create in ways that are wholly liberating.

Assessment Frame
....
Using an Internet Journal

Ask students to visit a different web site every week under a theme such as dinosaurs, astronomy, cooking, or art history. Get them to compare and contrast the sites in an ongoing journal. At the end, ask students to give a short presentation of the best site of the set. Encourage them to use the vocabulary that they learned in classroom lessons and discussions.
....

Growing Up with Television

Literacy Moment

Too Much TV!

Our five-year-old daughter, Madeleine, watches too much TV. I appreciated this as I sat with her and we scanned through channels while she gave me a detailed profile of shows and their characters, such as Sponge Bob whose best friend is Patrick, and overly energetic Sandy who likes Mr. Crabbs but who finds him dogmatic and bossy. Whether it is *Timothy Goes to School* or *The Xes*, Madeleine loves the medium and cannot get enough of it. She is not alone in her obsession with television, as I have witnessed first-hand the mesmerizing stare of children as they gaze at the box with moving pictures. Given Madeleine's fixation with TV, we had to find ways of limiting her overzealous viewing time, and of somehow harnessing her learning to the Box. The moment came when she began phonics activities at her school. Her teacher made little books—the size of an index finger—containing similar sound patterns. One day Madeleine and I decided to make a series of these books, but instead of using words taken from her lifeworld, we chose words within her TV world— "Scooby," Scrappy," "Shaggy," etc. We chose words that followed a pattern, but one she could relate to. Wouldn't you know it, she became engaged; she started to make them herself and sound out letters.

As an older technology (i.e., it has been around since the 1930s) compared to the Internet or text messaging, television still very much occupies the attention of our students. Television operates as a monologic technology, in that we cannot interact with it or inject our own thoughts, the way we can with the Internet through e-mail and instant messaging. Television is not personalized in that it is not directed to one person or a group of people, but instead to limitless numbers of people all of the time. The part of television we actually watch and consume is the text. Media studies uses the term "text" to refer to the material that television produces such as reality shows or cartoons or soap operas. Like all texts, TV shows grow out cultural interpretations of the world.

Research has shown that, "we spend more time viewing television programmes than on any other leisure pursuit, including going to the cinema, listening to CDs or even playing computer games" (Marshall & Werndly, 2002). Television that children watch should not be regarded as a time-wasting enterprise (although it is obvious that moderation should be the ideal). Like video games, genres of music, comics, and magazines, television is a part of our students' lifeworlds, and it is important that we recognize skills that emerge from the medium.

Critical TV Skills

To develop critical listening and watching skills, ask students to compare and contrast the following elements of TV shows across genres, including a cartoon, a reality show, a sitcom, and a news program. In pairs, compare and contrast these features:

- language used in the show
- characters' clothes
- relationships between characters
- objects characters use
- settings in the show
- introduction and conclusion

Discuss your findings with your partner and present them to the class.

TV as Narrative

Television, like film, is a moving medium combined with spoken language. "Reading" television texts involve a process that involves selecting images and combing them according to rules and conventions (Marshall & Werndly, 2002).

Obviously settings and people play a key role. Take, for example, shows like *Seinfeld* or *Friends,* in which settings are less important than characterization. In contrast, in shows like *CSI Miami* or *Lost* settings are key to the story, and there are strong visual narratives. A narrative represents the organizational structure of a story and cuts across most genres of texts. Familiar narratives would be the beginning–middle–end construct; however, there are variations. Typically in sitcoms and dramas, the narrative relies on a beginning, a disruption or conflict or event, and a resolution. Students implicitly understand these constructs and impose them on their interpretation of moving-image narratives, as well as on fictional work. We can use television as a powerful model by developing this skill of mixing genres and building on their innate ability to make inferences based on narratives.

Television Critics

Talk to students about what they watch, when they watch certain television programs, with whom they watch television programs, etc. Note their responses on a large sheet of paper. Then ask students to feature their favorite show with visuals and answers to questions about the conditions of viewing. Be sure to have students critique all aspects of the show: visuals, gesture, movement, dialogue, premise, etc. As their teacher, present your own favorite television show to the class to model the activity.

TV Timeline

1947: *Howdy Doody* — 1949: *Bozo the Clown* — 1955: *Captain Kangaroo* — 1955: *Mickey Mouse Club* — 1963: *Mister Rogers' Neighborhood* — 1969: *Sesame Street* —

1971: *The Electric Company* — 1979: Nickelodeon (network) — 1981: *The Smurfs* — 1984: *Transformers* — 1987: *Teenage Mutant Ninja Turtles* — 1992: *Barney* — 1993: *Mighty Morphin' Power Rangers* — 1996: *Blues Clues* — 2002: *Rolie Polie Olie* – 2004: *Jimmy Neutron* — 2005: *The Grim Adventures of Billy and Mandy* ...

Have a class discussion about how television has changed over the years.

Television Genres in Student Worlds

There are many different types of shows on television, and the number is ever increasing. There are a number of television genres students particularly enjoy, and skills related to these types of shows.

Cartoons

There are new cartoons introduced all the time, so that there are different genres of cartoons within the cartoon television genre. There are funny cartoons, such as *Sponge Bob* and *The Simpsons*; action-driven cartoons such as *The Xes*; supernatural, spooky cartoons such as *Foster's Home for Imaginary Friends*; instructional cartoons such as *Dora the Explorer* or *Blue's Clues*; and, of course, space adventure cartoons such as *Atomic Betty* or *Kim Possible*. Each one offers an array of new literacy skills. In watching these shows in moderation, children and adolescents develop a sense of character, of settings, of what is believable and not believable, of new language (e.g., Jimmy Neutron introduces new science words each episode), of acute visual awareness, of notions of good and evil and morals of stories, and of emotional language such as sarcasm. There are some good and some not-so-good cartoons on television, just as there are some good and some not-so-good dramas on television.

Skill Check-in: visual awareness; characterization; inference

Reality Shows

The voyeur factor of reality shows makes them appealing. Watching authentic dialogues between real people gives us an enhanced picture of the human condition, complete with foibles, insecurities, and ambivalent natures. Once again, there are some interesting, and at times valuable, reality shows, and some that offer limited substance and depth about the human psyche.

Skill Check-in: body cues; conversation analysis; our sense of right and wrong in life and relationships

Dramas and Soap Operas

Dramas and soap operas are primarily concerned with interpersonal relationships. Much of the content is not appropriate for children, but teenagers watch and enjoy them. Often dramas and soap operas focus on particular communities and the goings-on in their worlds. Characterization plays a key role.

Skill Check-in: developing a sense of character and trajectories of stories; deeper understanding of human nature; understanding of formal and colloquial language, with code switching between familiar characters and more distant relationships.

Sports Shows

Whether it is football, baseball, basketball, soccer, or hockey, adolescents and teenagers enjoy watching sports on TV. Sports on TV give them a sense of the game, but also commentaries on the game and facts to support commentaries. They are a rich source of information for our students, honing their knowledge of numbers and facts, and feeding into their keen interest in spectator sports.

Skill Check-in: analyzing athletic activity; understanding commentaries on moves by athletes; reading sports text during game time; digesting facts to support teams and players.

Sitcoms

Adolescents, teenagers, and adults alike enjoy sitcoms and become ensconced in sitcom worlds. Characters tend to fall into types, from the quirky Kramer on *Seinfeld* to the neurotic Chandler on *Friends*. Our students know and appreciate these nuances, which make them an excellent springboard for literacy work that looks in detail at characterization.

Skill Check-in: understanding of nuances of characters; understanding of narrative —opening, middle, and resolution

Media Connection: There is a special relationship between zines (see Zines chapter) and television. The first zines were paper publications (sort of like newsletters) that made available fan writing—mostly fiction—based on the original *Star Trek* series. These fanzines quickly spread to other series and then other subjects.

Media Connection: TV is not the only genre with hybrids. Clearly, genres of cartoons and newspapers can be considered hybrids; for example, a graphic novel is as much a cartoon as it is a novel.

There are also genres that tend to be more adult-oriented, such as detective and police dramas, quiz and game shows, news and entertainment shows, and documentaries. Each genre has its own narrative structure, use of visuals, characterization, sense of context, etc. There are also hybrid television shows, such as *The X-Files* which combine detective and science fiction genres.

Overt Instruction Activity

Analyzing TV Genres

Find two or three shows you think may be hybrids of television genres. Discuss how they are hybrids by looking at plot, characters, themes, situations, visuals, and setting.

Transformed Practice Activity

TV Storyboards

Once students have written the opener, conflict/event/denouement, and resolution in groups, ask each group to storyboard each scene in their show and write descriptions of the visual narrative. Then analyze the storyboard to ensure that all scenes make sense. Have a group discussion about coherence in stories within all genres: Does a character work in the plot? Do his or her actions match the characterization? Does the story make sense (watch out for holes in the plot, especially with detective shows)? Is there a sense of setting? Does the dialogue get at characterization? Have you thought about the title sequence, the opening scenes with the program title, credits, music, etc.?

Inventory of multimodal skills that TV draws on:
- **Visual:** camera shots, camera angles, character positions, settings, clothes, title, credits, makeup, costumes, objects or artifacts used
- **Oral:** music, dialogue, sounds, voices
- **Written:** text scrolling on screen during news programs, close captions, sports text, subtitles
- **Movement:** character positioning and actions, icons moving on screen
- **Tactile:** identifying elements of shows; e.g., *Dora the Explorer* or even blooper shows
- **Dimensions:** animation, using camera shots and technology

The Language of TV

Television shows are dependent on a combination of spoken language—sometimes written language—with visual images. In analyzing the language used in TV shows, we need to take account of visual components. Visuals and language work together in the grammar of visual design (Kress & Van Leeuwen, 1996) of shows. Television is particularly complicated because visuals and language/dialogue are combined with sound—they are multimodal texts that feed into students' innate *synaesthetic* understanding. Television scripts therefore need to take equal account of words, pictures, and sounds.

Grammar

There is a hidden grammar to television production, which is a bit like a grammar in language, based on camera angles that are used to create mood (Marshall & Werndly, 2002):

- **Close-ups** are frequently used in soap opera scenes, because they communicate relationships between people and are a cue to concentrate on emotions and feelings of characters. Dramas also use close-up shots to show intimacy or feelings.
- **Long shots** are used in action films and action-packed cartoons, where spectacles and visual effects are emphasized.
- A shot taken at **eye level** emphasizes a character's power, because our perspective is as if we are looking up at them.

Situated Practice Activity

Scooby and the Gang

Scooby Doo has withstood the test of time.

- Ask students who love Scooby and are struggling with literacy to think about characterization in a Scooby storyline.
- To illustrate what it means to analyze characters and their dispositions in texts, ask students to study in-depth character traits in a *Scooby Doo* episode for homework.
- Use multiple types of texts by having students read one of the many Scooby Doo books and watch an episode of Scooby Doo.
- Ask students to write a character profile of each character: Velma, Fred, Scooby, Shaggy, and Daphne. Then ask them to take on one of the Scooby Doo personas. Have students pair up: one student is an interviewer and the other is a character of their choice. Interviewers need to develop questions and then conduct an interview with the character about why they made certain decisions or actions in an episode or book.

Televisual Conventions

Connotation is about how words or images or sounds have specific meanings and associations within our culture (Marshall & Werndly, 2003, p.30). Connotation grows out of our cultural beliefs, attitudes, and values, and it informs the way in which we understand moving images. Connotation can carry positive and negative signs that aid us and our students in interpreting television. Television shows play on connotations to guide our interpretations of the plot—they play on our ideals and our feelings and our values as watchers.

Just as fictional works use symbolism and metaphors, so too does television carry ideologies to transmit messages. The image of darkness falling upon a room can foreshadow something ominous in a mystery or detective story. The symbol of a rose in a drama can betoken love. Metaphorical language is as pervasive in TV as it is in printed literature, and our students' capacity to spot symbolism and metaphors is a skill we want to evoke in their language work. One frequently sees symbols and metaphors used in documentaries to unite the narrative. For example, in a documentary about women and the Taliban, a *hijab* can serve as a symbol transmitting a message. Many shots, speeches, scenes, and narratives in TV shows are metaphorical, in that they represent one thing in detail or a multiplicity of things. We see this particularly in advertising, where an object is the key feature of a narrative. Music and sounds can evoke emotions and set the tone for a scene. Television advertising often uses visual images and music to send a specific message.

Storyboards are often used by producers to lay out stories and to analyze openers, music, dialogues, character positions. Storyboards give directors thumbnail sketches of what will happen in each sequence and if the story works together.

Overt Instruction Practice

Spot the TV Genre

Create a series of openers for different genres of TV shows:

- Sitcom begins with a conflict between characters over a broken object
- Soap opera starts with a private conversation about someone who suddenly walks in
- Reality show revisits a scene from the following week and characters discuss the outcome
- Detective show begins with a murder in someone's home with the door open at midday
- Drama begins with feuding housewives
- Cartoon about a sponge who decides to help his boss meet a partner in life
- Quiz show begins with the introduction of contestants

Once you have given different groups their TV opener, they need to develop a conflict and a resolution to fulfill the narrative. To reflect on the process, ask them how the narratives might be different if they were in another genre, such as fiction or a video game.

Teaching Strategy

Smart TV Viewing

1. Develop assignments that review critical TV viewing of shows of your choice (i.e., shows that you feel will teach students something).
2. Ask students to relate their readings to a character on television.

3. Encourage parents to watch TV with their children and discuss what happened.

4. To develop more discerning TV viewers, discuss different shows and why some are better than others (the way you would suggest certain books over others).

Assessment Frame

TV Portfolio

Have your students create a portfolio of their TV watching. They can organize their portfolio however they like, for example:

- **Favorite Genre:** TV show with a description.
- **Favorite Character:** Why they like them.
- **Favorite Theme of Show:** Talk about a particular episode
- **Favorite Setting:** Talk about the context of a show and why you like it.

Once they have compiled their categories and support materials, they can present them to the class.

Music between Generations

by Anne Burke

Anne Burke has been a secondary school teacher for twelve years in Ontario and Newfoundland. She is currently an Assistant Professor at Memorial University with expertise in the area of students' use and understanding of web-based texts and popular culture. Her chapter on music highlights the following skills:
- Identity and image creation through music
- Word play and the complexity of language in musical lyrics
- Capturing words visuals and through movement in music videos
- Reader response to music videos
- Analyzing music videos

Literacy Moment

Rekindling the Music of Our Youth

Gavin loves music and, like many thirteen-year-old musicians, would love to hear his songs played on the radio, to become a rock star, to fly around on a private jet and live the life of the rich and famous. His desire and interest in becoming a famous musician consume much of his home literacy practices: reading guitar magazines, writing his own lyrics, learning new songs with guitar in hand, surfing the Internet for sites that provide song tabs (a listing of the essential chords and lyrics) of the artists that he admires and listens to on his computer and Ipod. For Gavin, the practice of visiting and revisiting music sites on heavy metal bands, such as Metallica and Guns and Roses, stems from a shared music interest with his mom and dad.

On a rainy day in May, Gavin shared with me Internet sites he and his parents visit: to return to their youthful love of heavy metal; to increase his knowledge and interest in the history of heavy metal bands. As he spoke, he reminded me that music speaks to each of us in a way, identifying with who we are through lyrics that express universal experiences in life. One day during class, I asked Gavin what music site he was looking at and he replied, "Metallica. This band rocks, they were what my mom and dad listened to a long time ago… I found a box of old tapes that Dad had and I listened to one and I decided to look them up on the Internet."

As I glanced at the interface of the web site, I saw a number of links that would capture the interest of any avid music fan: discography, band news, history, videos, and tour schedules. The opening interface invites site visitors to download wallpaper of the band for their computer screens and Metallica music ring tones for their phones. This speaks to changing technology and music consumption of today's listeners; it lets us compare Gavin's experience with his Dad's love of music in the form tapes for his car radio. I asked Gavin what he likes about the web site and he replied, "Well it's really cool and it gives you information about the band, and it has media—look, you can watch some video clips and it has a history of the band." Curious about whether sharing his family's music interest included visiting Internet sites, he exuberantly replied "Yeah! Dad couldn't believe how much more you could find out about the band, like you can get their complete discography, touring schedule, and cool pictures!"

When looking at learners such as Gavin and his home literacy practices of engaging with music through listening, playing, and surfing the Net, as educators we may see a way to connect with Gavin's interests as a budding musician. Using his love of music, looking more closely at web sites, and seeking information to satisfy his curiosity about older music genres is one way we can harness the tacit skills that Gavin carries with him into school.

Writing a Hit Song

What makes a hit song? Everybody knows what a good song is, but ask five people what their favorite songs are, and you will be surprised at how the answers vary. Teenagers on *American Bandstand* always had the same answer when asked to rate the latest singles—the best "had a good beat and you could dance to it." Add in a catchy tune and some good lyrics, and everyone could write a hit. It seems as simple as that. Or is it?

Many of the songs we hear on the radio today appeal to our identity, our senses, and our experiences in different ways. For Gavin's interest, his parent's connection to the music of their youth was what propelled Gavin to discover more about Metallica. His sharing of the web site with his dad showed how he connected with his father's past interest. Using technology as medium for further knowledge, he bridged his father's interest into his own learning. Bands like Metallica often have second-generation fans, but what sets them apart from the "one-hit wonder" bands is their ability to produce lyrics that speak to many people at once. The best songs have a universality about them that invites us to want to hear them over and over again. Writing one would seem like an easy feat, but the blend of melody and lyrics is a delicate one, and even the most successful musicians do not get the recipe right the first—or the second, or even the hundredth—time around.

Situated Practice Activity

Student Spaces of Music

Ask students to create their own personal chart of their favorite top ten songs. In the chart ask students to include the following:

- name of artist
- song title and album name
- favorite lyric from the song
- explanation of why the lyric image appeals to everyday experience

The Radio Formula

Most songs aimed for radio play use a familiar formula. Musicians who are concerned about performance or album sales rather than radio play have an easier time of producing songs. But for those who want to hear their songs on the radio, they almost always have to start with a deeper understanding of their audience.

Writers who have learned to write lyrics that send a message to the listener, a theme that relates to their own experience, have had great success with radio play. Love lyrics are by far the most popular, but songwriters tell stories, talk about political problems, or address any other issue that appeals to them. Musicians try to make the chorus the most dramatic part of the song, with powerful melody underlying the key message of the song. Each song consists of the following parts:

- verses that relate the theme or narrative of the song
- a chorus that underlines the main theme of the song
- a bridge, or melodic piece that allows us to remember a song.

All of these aspects are a part of the pop songs that we hear and hum along to on the radio on our morning drive to work.

All these elements, however, may still not be enough to make a song popular. When musicians write poetry or song lyrics, they often hope it represents true feelings that will be felt and appreciated by their readers and listeners. The reality is to achieve radio play (and hopefully large CD sales); a song's lyrics need a universal appeal, experiences so vivid that the lyrics can relate to the experiences and emotions of many listeners. This has to be combined with melody that can appeal to just as many people. Simply put: if one was to listen to the songs played on the radio, there would be four common denominators present in all songs, no matter what kind of music you were listening to.

Critical Framing Practice

Four Denominators in Hit Singles

Ask students to bring a song they like that is being played on top-40 radio. Ask them

- to share the melody
- to explain what part they like
- Are the lyrics personal and poetic? Why do they appeal to you?
- Is the rhythm catchy and infectious? What part stays in your head?
- Why do you want to hear it again?

Media Connection: Today, the medium of music cannot be isolated from the video medium. The making of videos expands the mind's eye and captures the visual representation of the lyrics. In multiple modes of representation, the video entices the listener and viewer to capture the essence of the song, which the video producer and band feels portrays the video in a narrative form.

Music Videos

Like most adolescents, the appeal of being a famous musician is to have your band's video in heavy rotation on a music television channel. As a narrative form, videos became popular in the early 1980s. Now a band's videos are almost as important to a musical career as songwriting and performing. Almost all videos are produced by record companies on behalf of artists. While they may be dramatic, funny, or very elaborate, they are essentially commercials for the songs and musicians.

Critical Framing Activity

Body Image and the Music Industry

In Michelle Brazil's class, she addresses students' perception of body image and as a part of a lesson to inspire her students to write poetically about the mass media's portrayal of females.

- After small group discussions of the lyrics in the video, she invites students to watch a music video entitled "Beautiful" by Christina Aguilera.
- She asks students to read the lyrics and to try to match images the video director and artist portray in the video to the song lyrics.
- As a closing activity, students gather in small groups and discuss how the power of the lyrics is enhanced by the moving images and camera shots used in the video.

Creating a Video

When a record company, artist, and manager decide which song from a record will be released as a single for radio play, they decide on a budget and set the task of finding a video director. The video director submits a brief script of about two pages. As most music videos do not have dialogue, the script will describe the main scenes, characters (apart from the band or artist), location, and—if there is a storyline— an outline of the plot. Accompanying this will be a rough list of shots the director intends to use. Even though there may only be two or three scenes for a video, they may be filmed at many different angles, using different lighting, moving the musicians around. All of these decisions present a very different representation from the lyrics alone. Many bands have soared to great fame after video releases; some have seen their popularity plummet. What is interesting is how each of us perceives the representation of lyrics in our own contexts.

Assessment Frame

Critiquing Music Videos

- Ask each student to choose a video from a top-40 song list.
- Situate the students' practice and association with the video by asking them to write a short narrative of their chosen video.
- Ask students if the video director's portrayal holds the same narrative as the lyrics or differs from their understanding of the lyrics?
- In critically framing their learning, ask them to deconstruct the video according to the camera shots, camera angles, and camera movement used in the video.

• As a transformed practice, ask them as a video director to create a two-page summary of the video they felt would portray the lyrics.

Camera Shots

Wide Shot: Holds the whole scene and sets the stage for the video.

Medium Shot: Camera is closer to the subject. Used also for transition from wide shot to close-up shot.

Close-up Shot: Used for showing personal details, emotions, or details of the set that hold symbolic significance to the narrative of the video

Sequence Shot: Series of shots that show movement of time, place, or character's narrative actions.

Camera Angles

Eye Level: Common shot used at eye level of subject.

Low Angle: A shot that looks up at the subject, making the subject seem important, powerful, and larger to the viewer

High Angle: This shot looks down on the subject and minimizes the subject's importance. It can give the viewer a sense of power and show the helplessness of the subject.

Shot Movement

Pan: Movement that is horizontal

Tilt: Movement that is vertical

Zoom: Movement that closes in on the subject

Reverse Zoom: Movement away from the subject.

Comic Books: Heroes and Villains

Literacy Moment

Profile of a Comic Illustrator

Since Dave was four years old, he wanted to be a superhero. In fact, Dave and his brothers thought they *were* superheroes. As his neighbor of many years, I remember watching Dave, Andy, and Ian wearing Batman, Superman, and Spiderman costumes, doing acrobatics and simulating action scenes, pretending they were facing their foes. Action heroes like Spiderman or Batman absorbed much of their time, whether they were pretending to be them or reading about them from their archive of comic books.

I was not surprised in the least when I learned that Dave became a comic book illustrator… and married one. What is more, he drew superheroes in the fashion of Stan Lee's classic Spiderman, while his older brother, Andrew, wrote text to accompany his illustrations. When I asked Dave if he and Andrew got along when they worked, Dave said that they argue a bit over what comes first—pictures or words—but that this conflict is essential to the process: "The most important work is the work between the writer and artist… to work well together you have to play off each other's ideas."

Dave can appreciate the newest rage in comic books, like Japanese *anime*, but his heart will always be with good ol' Spidey.

Comics are a part of home life for many families—whether in print or on TV. My husband Fred, who had difficulty learning to read, found that comic books were the only books that really got him excited. He learned how to read by spending many hours reading *Asterix* by himself.

The comic book world has become quite complex over the turn of the 21st century. Comics are differentiated from cartoons by range of expressions: cartoons are solely humorous; comics come in many forms—at times funny but primarily with plots and characterization we come to know and admire. An important characteristic of comics is the way pictures depict actions, emotions, and characters.

Situated Practice Activity

Analyzing Comics

Invite students to bring in any kind of comics or cartoons they can find at home. In a group discussion, ask them the following questions:

- What different ways can these comics be classified?
- What style of illustration does the artist use?
- How might these comics be organized in a classroom for other students to read?

Extra Practice: Ask students to go on the Internet to find other genres of comics and cartoons to discuss.

Elements of the Comic Book

- Style of illustration is particularly important and can create an image and ethos for a comic; for example, the infusion of Japanese *anime* into popular TV shows such as *Inuyasha* or *Pokémon* has defined a new genre of TV program.
- Comics are organized into sequential units that are graphically separated from each other; they are composed of sequences of panels, while cartoons comprise only one panel.
- Comics are multimodal in that they stimulate different senses by imitating or simulating unspoken gestures, using musical notes to express singing or facial expressions to show happiness or fear.
- There is much use of onomatopoeia: words take on sounds to resemble actions, such as *click, bong, gulp*, etc.
- In comics, words and pictures exist side by side. Words appear handwritten, giving them different latitude for expression than type.

Comics can help us explore characterization, plot, settings, the nature of good and evil, visual communication, language features (e.g., onomatopoeia), and even critical awareness of genre shifts within the comic world (e.g., graphic stories vs more traditional comics such as *The Phantom* or *Spiderman*).

Mixing Genres

by Lauren Amato

Lauren Amato's Imagery Comic Strip activity is a creative way for high-school students to show their ability to understand images in a poem.

- After reading Sir Thomas Wyatt's "Whoso List to Hunt," a sonnet full of imagery, students get into groups of three or four. In these groups, students discuss the various images that come to mind with each line. They ask one another questions about how they arrived at certain images, as well as to debate them. This is a chance for struggling students to understand how their peers arrive at images. The group work serves as a brainstorming session that is not intended to be assessed. The lesson takes 10 to 15 minutes.

- Upon completing group work, students work independently on an assignment that asks them to create a comic strip of at least five images from Wyatt's sonnet. These images should be in chronological order, matching the order of images in the poem. Below each panel, students write a summary of what the images represent, and write the line of poetry that evokes this image. Students decide whether or not to use dialogue in their comic strips. Either way, there should be a summary below each individual image in the strip. Teachers can assess these comic strips for understanding imagery in the sonnet.

The Visual Landscape of Comic Books

- Each page of a comic book is separated into about nine rectangular frames called panels. Each panel depicts still instances of action, and may contain dialogue that represents a portion of the narrative.

- Each panel is separated from the others by the gutter, a blank space between each still instance of action. Like a period and space between sentences, a gutter separates moments in the overall narrative.

- Speech balloons are the spaces in which thoughts are expressed as dialogue or a monologue of thoughts in a character's head. The tail of a balloon points to the speaker.

- Captions make up another written part of a comic. Typically, captions appear at the top of a panel. Captions add information to the narrative in addition to character thoughts.

Media Connection: With cartoons, like *The Simpsons,* there is a merging of sit-coms with cartoons; as in a sitcom like *Leave it to Beaver* or *My Three Sons,* we follow the adventures of a family we have come to know and love.

Manga Cartooning

A few years ago, *manga* took the comic book world by storm; "*manga*" is the Japanese word for comic. *Manga* characters wear bright, colorful clothing and have wild, pointy hair. The stories are usually about romance, sports, or science fiction, and are published as magazines or paperback books. *Manga* books are bound in the traditional Japanese way: the spine of the book is on the right side, and pages are flipped from the left, as if you had turned a regular book over and read it back to front. The *manga* art tradition and its associated philosophy— strategy and gamesmanship, heavily reliant on problem-solving and mathemetics—add a decidedly more global feel to comics.

Critical Framing Activity

A Comic Book Collection

Collect various types of comics—adult comics, graphic stories, older or "vintage" comics, and even cartoons—and analyze similarities and differences among them in the following ways:

- Do they use comic-book conventions differently (e.g., balloons, visual–verbal cues, gutters, etc.)?
- Are captions used; if so, how does the use differ?
- What style of illustration do they use? Do you like the style? If not, why?
- What is on the cover?
- Are there villains? If so, what are they like? How are they different from action heroes and heroines?
- How do the visual and verbal characteristics interact?
- Does gender play a role?

Have students elaborate on these questions in groups and critically frame such issues as stereotypes or gender issues in comics.

Point of View in Comics

1. **Conceptual Point of View:** Involves someone's opinions; e.g., Batman's views on Penguin and his plots to avenge him for thwarting his evil plans.
2. **Visual Point of View:** Involves an illustrator's depiction of characters, costumes, settings, action scenes, emotions, and mood.
3. **Interest Point of View:** Involves the impact actions might have on characters; e.g., in response to Green Goblin's attempts to torment Spiderman, it is in the best interest of society for Spiderman to sabotage Goblin's evil doings.

Point of view can function on different levels, and be manifested in visuals through distance and closeness; it can work through subjectivity with the thoughts of characters, or objectivity in a caption; it identifies the relationship of the reader with the characters; it helps the reader gain access to characters' emotions (Saraceni, 2001).

Overt Instruction Activity

Being a Superhero or Villain

Find pictures of a series of superheroes—Batman, Spiderman, Wonder Woman, etc.—and ask students to name their archrivals/enemies. As a group, develop descriptions of each superhero. Tell students to imagine that they could become any of these characters. Students write an explanation why these chose this particular character. Students should consider the following:

- Why might people admire you?
- What adventures might you expect to have?
- What challenge would you want to have?

Extra Practice: Create an event that gives you superpowers; e.g., being bitten by a radioactive spider turned Peter Parker into Spiderman.

Create Your Own Comic

To complete a story, Dave has to follow these steps:

1. Create thumbnail sketches (miniature pictures of each scene) of the story and go over it with his brother Andrew, who writes the text.
2. Sketch out the story with stick figures.
3. Add flesh onto arms, torso, and legs, working his way from larger areas to smaller ones.
4. Define the body, muscles, and clothing.
5. Send images out to be inked (someone else does that).
6. Scan images and use his computer to add color.

At some point between steps 3 and 4, Dave creates speech bubbles and meets with Andrew to discuss dialogue. Once he puts color into images, the agreed-upon text goes into speech bubbles.

- Ask your students to assemble three different panels, each expressing a different point of view. They can find images at home or draw them themselves. Students explain their choices.
- An extension of the activity might be to choose a panel from each of four different comics and cut the panel out. With a partner the students describe what is happening in the scene and how it might fit into the overall narrative of the comic.

Extra Practice: Review the process of creating a comic (in the margin at left). Ask your students the following reflection questions:

- Following Dave's steps, add your own spin onto them to create a superhero story. What will your hero or heroine look like? Who is her or his foe? What will take place?
- How will you structure your story? What style of illustration will you have?
- Will you write your own dialogue or will a friend write it?
- Will your action figure have superhuman mental powers, superhuman physical powers, or both?
- Reflect on the process of creating an action figure comic. How is it different from writing a poem or an essay?

Create Your Own Comic

To test student comprehension of a book they are studying, draw eight empty panels and ask students to make a comic of the story using visuals and dialogue. Then ask them to cut out each panel and change the plot of the story by moving putting the panels in a different order.

Online Chatting and Texting

by Louis Chen

Louis Chen has been a teacher for some time and has completed his Ph.D. on using texting and online forums as vehicles for teaching and learning. In the following chapter, he highlights the following skills:

• Abbreviating and abridging text related to summarizing and condensing
• Using creative and figurative language in web-based genre
• Exploring cross-curricular subjects online

Microsoft Network Messenger© (MSN) is a free instant message software designed to connect people online by allowing anyone to carry on a live conversation through texts, images, and sound. It is a popular technology that the current "wired" generation depends on to mediate their social pathways. A Canadian survey reported that 80% of adolescents between 16 and 19 use instant messaging (Randall, 2002), a slightly higher percentage compared to their U.S. counterparts at 74% (Lenhart, Rainie & Lewis, 2001). The study presented in this section focuses on aligning adolescents' literacy and technological skills with their school learning. Mike (the participating teacher) and I incorporated MSN into an integrated curriculum unit (math and geography) in a Grade 9 academic math class that was selected based on the number of students with access to computers and the Internet at home (100 percent). The chapter focuses on how Pavan, Will, Suk, and J.B. utilized the literacy skills associated with recreational use of MSN use to collaboratively carry out academic discussions and complete a group project.

Situated Practice

Creating Communities of Learners

As a homework assignment or extension activity, have students form into "communities of learners" by distributing topics and questions on areas you are covering in social studies, science, or language arts/English. Have a lead person who begins a discussion, using questions and topics to elicit comments from three other classmates, by means of texting. Ask students to text about a key topic and report back the conversation. Since MSN automatically saves conversations, have students print them out and share them with the class.

Doing Schoolwork on MSN

Students participate in a particular community-forming "netspeak" (Lotherington, 2004) consisting of explicit instructions interwoven with use of abbreviations (lol), homophones (u), creative capitalization and spelling (WUT) as a part of speech conventions. Their linguistic creativity and awareness combine to form a superbly efficient online discourse for organizational work and data search, such as file sharing, web site exchange, and instructing one another how to assemble the information. Students can extend and project the function of oral literacy in written form to conduct different levels of discussions on MSN. Their online discussions result in a hybridized "written talk" that enables them to efficiently access information and navigate through web sites. Take the following example from my own research study:

PAVAN: yo wht u sent me aint quota limits
   (what you sent me ain't quota limits)
SUK: i noe buh tht needs _2 b_ reprinted
   (I know but that needs to be reprinted)
PAVAN: kk (ok)
J.B.: WAT (what) NEEDS TO BE REPRINTED(?)
SUK: http://www.statcan.ca/english/Pgdb/econ125a.htm
SUK: THT (that)
PAVAN: i already printed it
WILL: cuz just send it so i no like how to write it up
   (because just send it [quota limits information and website links] so I know like
   how to write it [the final report] up)

This short exchange of sentence fragments is subsequent to the instant nature of MSN and the space limitation of the text box. For example, a commonly used phrase, "laughing out loud," requires 14 key strokes to correctly input the phrase; however, the same phrase is generally input with only three key strokes as "lol" in order to maintain the flow of a conversation. The very limitations of the technology elicits creative expressions, from recreational chat to organizational language for academic purposes. Text interactions are deliberate and concise, and provide social groups with clear instructions for the task at hand.

Overt Instruction Activity

Comparing Texting with Other Genres

Take a dialogue that comes from a text or resembles texting, like the one below, and ask students to compare it to another genre, such as an expository essay on Canada's agriculture industry. Ask the following questions:

- Which did they prefer? Why?
- What is the difference between the genres?
- When is one more appropriate than another?

   This activity will illustrate the notion of register—the capacity to find the most appropriate writing style.

J.B.: yo will v need comparsions b2ween other countries
   (yo, Will, you need comparison between other countries)
J.B.: lke canada and da us
   (like Canada and the U.S.)
Pavan: ya like mainly united states
J.B.: and the europe (European) countries
J.B.: so whos gonna do dat
   (so who's going to do that?)
Will: or..
J.B.: da comparsions
   (the comparisons)
Will: comparisons of...imports exports? production totals?
J.B.: Canada Vs US
J.B.: how v r diff from dem
   (how you [Canada] are different from them [U.S.])
Will: if we can find the good stuff

Will says: cause (because) member (remember), we're arguing saying we're good
in agriculture, just info that supports that, remember.
J.B.: yeah

Assessment Frame

Texting as a Form of Observation

As MSN allows users to automatically save their conversations, students' online
transcripts can be made available to monitor student progress and assess the level of
participation. One of the important advantages of this technology lies in its flexibility.
online texting can be adopted to extend classroom activities (e.g., group work) beyond
class time to address specific concerns. Students can be asked to use the saved
conversation logs as references to reflect and identify instances whereby their
discussions translate into oral presentations. Peer and self-critique assessments can
ensue to track students' progress and gain additional insight into how to critique
information they find, and how they organize and delegate their work (see Group
Work: Self- and Peer Critique on page 96). Assessment measures can be modified into a
rubric that matches the Ontario curriculum and self and peer evaluation (see Sample
Testing Rubric on pages 94–95, based on those produced by the Ontario Education
Quality and Accountability Office).

Sample Testing Rubric

Category	Level 4 80–100%	Level 3 70–79%	Level 2 60–69%	Level 1 50–59%
Final Report	• Final report is neatly presented and includes all required information.	• Report includes all required information and is legible.	• Report includes most required information and is legible.	• Report is missing required information and is difficult to read.
Data: Quantity and Quality	• A wide variety of data is provided. • Data clearly relates to the main argument. • There is enough data to create 6 or more arguments	• A variety of data is provided. • Data relates to the main argument. • There is enough data to create 5 arguments	• Data is provided with some variety. • Some data relates to the main argument. • There is enough data to create 3 or 4 arguments	• Data is provided with little variety. • Little data relates to the main argument. • There is enough data to create 1 or 2 arguments.
Analysis/ Conclusions	• Demonstrates analysis that is almost always correct and appropriate. • Displays insight in ability to make conclusions and reflections.	• Demonstrates analysis that is generally correct and appropriate. • Displays competence in ability to make conclusions and reflections.	• Demonstrates analysis that is frequently correct and appropriate. • Displays some competence in ability to make conclusions and reflections.	• Demonstrates analysis that is rarely correct and appropriate. • Displays limited competence in ability to make conclusions and reflections.
Diagrams/ Graphs & Illustrations	• Diagrams/graphs and illustrations are neat and accurate, and add to the reader's understanding of the topic.	• Diagrams/graphs and illustrations are accurate, and add to the reader's understanding of the topic.	• Diagrams/graphs and illustrations are neat and accurate, and sometimes add to the reader's understanding of the topic.	• Diagrams/graphs and illustrations are not accurate OR do not add to the reader's understanding of the topic.
Organization/ Mechanics	• Information is very organized with well- constructed paragraphs and subheadings. • No grammatical, spelling or punctuation errors.	• Information is organized with well-constructed paragraphs. • Almost no grammatical, spelling or punctuation errors	• Information is organized, but paragraphs are not well-constructed. • A few grammatical, spelling, or punctuation errors.	• The information appears to be disorganized. • Many grammatical, spelling, or punctuation errors.

(created by Louis Chen and Mike Morin)

Sample Testing Rubric (continued)

Category	Level 4 80–100%	Level 3 70–79%	Level 2 60–69%	Level 1 50–59%
Presentation	• Demonstrates depth in understanding of topic and/or data analysis. • Presentation and use of technology convey ideas and findings to a great degree.	• Demonstrates understanding of topic and/or data analysis. • Presentation and use of technology convey ideas and findings.	• Demonstrates some understanding of topic and/or data analysis. • Presentation and use of technology convey ideas and findings to some degree.	• Demonstrates limited understanding of topic and/or data analysis. • Presentation and use of technology convey ideas and findings to a limited degree.
Sources	• All sources (information and graphics) are accurately documented.	• Most sources (information and graphics) are accurately documented.	• Some sources (information and graphics) are accurately documented.	• Few or no sources are accurately documented.

(created by Louis Chen and Mike Morin)

Group Work: Self- and Peer Critique

Self-Critique

Name: _____

1. What parts of the project did you complete?

2. Of the tasks that you did, what do you feel that you did well?

3. What could you have done to improve?

4. Use the scale below to indicate your participation level in the project.

____ I did almost nothing.

____ I did less than my fair share.

____ I had to do more than my fair share.

____ I did my fair share.

Peer Critique

Name of Partner: _____

1. What parts of the project did s/he complete?

2. Of the tasks that s/he did, what do you feel that s/he did well?

3. What could s/he have done to improve?

4. Use the scale below to indicate his/her participation level in the project.

____ S/he did almost nothing.

____ S/he did less than his/her fair share.

____ (S)he had to do more than his/her fair share.

____ S/he did his/her fair share.

(adapted from Louis Chen)

Newspapers: Artifacts of a Bigger World

Literacy Moment

Newspapers as a Legacy

by Isabel Pedersen

I am the daughter of a newspaper journalist and a newspaper librarian, so the topic of writing was as everyday a thing as preparing supper or mowing the lawn. My father clacked away on his manual typewriter on most days, drank coffee, and raved to himself about editors, interviews, and wording. He traveled constantly, meeting with politicians, criminals, cultural icons, or sports figures in order to get the story. And the story gnawed at him until he wrote it down.

My mother hated to write anything beyond a shopping list. As a librarian, I think she considered herself a custodian of writing. An unknown word prompted a serendipitous dive into her big dictionary. Ask her anything and she could find the answer, but she expected someone else, "a writer," to author it.

Going on in the background, I learned to read and write like any other kid. I was not great at either. Most of the time I think I was more interested in movies and TV. I remember feeling quite sorrowful when I was supposed to move from picturebooks to chapter books that had no images except for the cover graphics. I felt cheated by authors who were not going to provide pictures to embody their wonderful tales.

When I hit grad school, I remember feeling that I could finally get back to my pictures. And now I study meaning-making in combinations of writing, visual image, and sound that appear everywhere, be it in TV advertisements or on computer screens. From my father I inherited that gnawing feeling that makes me want to write the story. My mother gave me a sense of that vast, vast context of other people's writings that shapes us always.

Isabel's experience growing up with parents who were in the business of newspapers informed her early memories with print. It was second nature for her to think about voice, being edited, and how visuals mediate texts; in the end, it informs her theorizing of texts and electronic texts and how they preside over our meaning-making.

Like television, magazines, and comics, newspapers cannot be seen as equal with each other in that they fall into genres: broadsheet newspapers such as *The New York Times* or *The Globe and Mail*; middle-range tabloids such as *The Toronto Star*; and tabloids such as *The Sun* (Reah, 1998). Equally, newspaper content cannot be created equal—content is not exclusively news items, but includes a variety of items: editorials about a world issue; articles on sports, careers, cars, the arts; and so on. In this way, newspapers give a picture of the spectrum of experiences in our worlds that allow us to reflect on these events and practices. Newspapers are artifacts of the commercial and political world (Reah, 1998, page 3). Much newspaper content is devoted to advertisements.

Navigating Newspapers

Bring different kinds of newspapers to school—local ones and more international ones. Give a newspaper to each pair of students. Ask students to find particular sections in the newspaper:

- On what page is the index?
- On what page is the sports section?

Then ask very specific questions such as,

- What is the weather in White Horse today?
- What is the weather in Memphis?

Ask for current news of the day. Then give them vocabulary associated with newspapers:

- What is a headline?
- What is a byline?
- What is a subtitle?

Newspapers as Communication

Newspaper content is about choices that writers and editors make about what to include and what to exclude. What separates one newspaper from another is how they present events and the types of details they choose to privilege. For example, a broadsheet might focus on the political ramifications of a president's indiscretions, whereas a tabloid might focus on personal elements of those same indiscretions. A story about the same event can have a different kind of lens imposed on it: one that turns the telescope onto the person or societal consequences; a moral take or a financial take. Whatever lens a newspaper chooses speaks to a particular kind of reader, often of a particular kind of socio-economic situation with particular political views.

Typically, newspapers have a narrative style, for example, newspapers in more of a tabloid genre tend to begin with openers that state incredible facts and then the story. Broadsheet genre papers, on the other hand, tend to begin with more metaphorical openers.

Visual Communication of Newspapers

For a lesson on perspective in writing in the junior grades, take four local and international papers and lay them side by side on a table in your classroom space.

- For the whole-class component of the lesson, have students gather and discuss as a group differences among the four papers.
- Divide the class into four groups with one of the four newspapers assigned to each group. Then ask each group to analyze the role of voice; the visual design and layout of the newspaper; the types of headlines and what they say; the selection of photographs; the sections (what they feature and how they feature them); and finally, importantly, the target audience.
- Have students separate these topics for display on chart paper. After about 30 minutes, have students present findings of their discussions to the class. As a class,

discuss how newspapers are geared for specific populations and how perspective speaks directly to this audience.

Extra Practice: Highlight how the visual communication of newspapers signals particular audiences; i.e., less text and more visuals speak to a population who wants to read a newspaper quickly to get key items or who may not find broadsheets too "high brow."

Headlines

Headlines grab your attention. They give you a picture of a story in just a few words: "headlines have the capacity to encapsulate a story" (Reah, 1998). With headlines, writers have to use words that are short, attention-getting, and able to encapsulate a story. Journalists often play on sound in headlines, playing on phonological similarities of words in headlines to grab your attention.; e.g., *Tripping Up On Trips*. Many headline writers use homophones because they sound the same but mean a different thing (e.g., Holmes on Homes). Clearly, connotations feature prominently in headlines such as *Stern's Justice: It is Swift, But Is It Fair?* signaling a particular view of a writer on a sports matter.

Another device journalists draw on is intertextuality. Familiar turns of phrase or ideas can be aligned with events and topics; for example, *A Curiosity Shop With Stock to Covet From Around the World*, alludes to a Dicken's novel, as does *Old Curiosity Shop*, the headline for a *New York Times* article about the 52nd Annual Winter Antiques Show on Park Avenue. Such clever turns of phrase foster a meta-awareness in students about how phrases, idioms, and literary allusions are interwoven into journalistic texts.

Headlines can have a persuasive effect on readers. Take a headline such as, *Why TV is Good For Kids*, and you know at first glance it will be in support of TV watching, an endorsement of new media and child development.

Critical Framing Activity

Story for a Headline

The following headlines come from one edition of the *New York Times*.

> *Google Resists U.S. Subpoena of Search Data*
> *Tomorrowland: Apple Chief Set for Disney Role*
> *Crying Much Worse Than Wolf*
> *Fish Out of Water, In India This Time*
> *Après-Ski, It's Bottoms UP*
> *Super Bowl Dream Passes From the Father to the Son*
> *How Should a Book Sound: And What About Footnotes?*

Write each headline on chart paper, making multiple copies in case you run out. Read them to the class. Have students get into pairs; each pair gets a headline. Ask pair groups to invent a story around the headline and a visual to accompany the story. To complete the assignment, students will have to

- decide on a newspaper genre
- choose a voice
- establish a take on the story

- decide where the article will sit in a section
- and figure out a visual and the layout.

Visuals

Visuals and headlines frequently work symbiotically or at odds with written text. A photo or image can either support a headline or spoof it. It is important, when using newspapers as a teaching tool, to place equal emphasis on visual communication as on written or linguistic features in content.

Media Connection: If you compare TV and newspaper texts, you will note that they are looking remarkably alike these days, because one has influenced the other. That is, newspapers have become far more visual than linguistic, and television now more written text scrolling on the top and bottom of the screen.

Narrative in Newspaper Writing

Traditionally, narrative has been regarded as a form of storytelling. Narrative can also be regarded as a particular way of presenting events or thoughts and feelings. In newspaper writing, narratives are a means by which to depict a series of events or an incident. In his ground-breaking work on the language of a black community in New York, William Labov explored patterns across different narratives within a community. Labov claimed that a fully formed narrative shows the following structure:

1. Abstract: a brief summary of the whole story
2. Orientation: the time, place, people, situation
3. Complicating action: the content or events of the narrative
4. Evaluation: an indication of the point of the narrative
5. Result: the termination of the series of events
6. Coda: a summing up that signals the end of the narrative.

Students should be able to identify these key aspects of a newspaper's narrative and be able to critically frame their role in the narrative.

Audience

Audience has a strong impact on newspaper content. Simply put, newspapers decide to whom they will target, and they write to that audience, to its interests, its values, its likes and dislikes, its visual dispositions, and its turns of phrase and discourse. There are certain assumptions people make, although not necessarily spoken, about newspaper readerships: The *National Post* in Canada is generally read by conservative-leaning professionals with an eye to financial information; and *The Herald Tribune* is read by international travelers who want an overall picture of global news and events. There are of course variations in readership, but broadly, characteristics can be ascribed to readers of specific newspapers.

Common Device, Different Medium

Find evidence of journalists writing to a particular audience by looking at an article in terms of the following:

- headlines
- syntax
- visuals
- figurative language
- perspective
- overall commentaries (in favor of or against).

Compare the article to an item in another genre, such as a news program on television, and examine how they use similar devices in a different medium. Have students brainstorm other examples of common devices in a different medium.

Language

Newspapers guide reader interpretations of events in the manner in which they are written or in which they use visuals to depict events. Newspapers are artifacts of our culture. Asian newspapers are different from North American newspapers, which are different still from British papers. Differences among papers reveal key aspects of a culture, its values, its habits of mind, and turns of phrase. In this way, language functions on a series of levels and it is important for our students to understand language in this way—as multi-voiced and governed by multiple identities. Texts operate on a graphophonic level (sounds and visual aspects of words) and a semantic-level (ideas). Language—particularly language in mass media texts like magazines and newspapers—carries cultural values and ideas. Representation is a key aspect of journalism, and how one represents groups reflects on the values of a newspaper and ultimately speaks to its target audience. A powerful tool in journalistic writing is choice of words. Students should be encouraged to think critically about how language is used to depict a certain group or to depict people in a particular situation. Once they begin to deconstruct journalistic voices, they will appreciate how these voices influence public opinion.

Newspaper Memories

When I think of newspapers, I cannot help but remember a story about my dad. He grew up during the Great Depression and his family did not have much money. Rather than using rags or cloths to clean windows, his parents used discarded newspapers. The image of my dad using newspapers to clean windows remains firmly in my mind. Like Isabel, I have a tie to newspapers—they served an intellectual, recreational, and practical function in our family that sits with me.

Constructing a Journalistic Voice

Ask junior-age students to be journalists and write an article about a current event. To do so, they need to inhabit the role of a journalist:

- establish a stance on the topic

- adopt a voice
- represent people in a certain light
- use particular words with particular visuals
- have an audience in mind.

In this way, you can assess their ability to deconstruct the audience and build their narrative and visuals around this target audience.

Rap and Hip-Hop Culture

by Marika Autrand

Marika Autrand is in the process of becoming an English teacher with a keen interest in youth culture. In her pursuit to speak to the interests of her high school students, Marika highlights the following skills:
• Understanding of poetic and figurative language
• Awareness of how music can form cultures and identities
• Examining how music reflects societal changes

One way of building hip-hop into the curriculum is to have students look at the Harlem Renaissance and the growth of hip-hop to see that it is a culture in and of itself, with clothing, fashion, attitude, music, books, and movies associated with it. In an age with the Internet, online communication, instant messaging, DVDs, etc., there are so many forces competing for students' attention that appealing to students' interests motivates them to succeed. Young people are tied into receiving and extending information orally.

Misconceptions and generalizations around rap often characterize it as a genre that deals primarily with drugs, sex, money, and murder. For this reason, the thought of incorporating rap into lessons may not only be shocking, but also terrifying to many secondary English teachers. Educators must move past these generalizations about rap and come to a more accurate and unbiased understanding of it, since rap is a genre of music that many secondary students engage with regularly. For some students, rap is relevant to them because they like it and listen to it out-of-school. For others, the hip-hop style and culture play a part in shaping their lives and emerging identities. Regardless of the degree to which students are affected by this genre, rap's emergence into mainstream music and culture proves more and more that teachers should be aware of its presence in the lives of their students. Beyond that, English educators can use this out-of-school literacy within the context of their classrooms as a tool not only for engagement, but also for critical analysis.

When incorporating rap into lessons, educators should be careful not to limit the value of the genre by treating it as merely an enticing hook into a lesson focused on other material. Rather, teachers should validate rap as a genre with a rich linguistic and cultural history that can be addressed in the classroom. The intended meaning of a rap can be constructed and shaped in relation to cultural contexts, history, prejudices, societal and power hierarchies, and feelings of community. All of these devices and ideas work together in different ways in the work of different rap artists, and it is important to consider a variety of raps when critically analyzing this genre.

Media Connection: Incorporating hip-hop poetry is a great way of inciting interest in poetic language. Have students share their knowledge of what they listen to and enjoy outside of school. In critically analyzing this genre, one finds that rappers, like poets, carefully choose the language they use and how they use it. Also like poets, they use sound devices—including rhyme, rhythm, and alliteration—in conjunction with figurative devices as they convey meaning.

Analyzing Rap

Look online to find rap lyrics, or ask your students to bring them in. Check with administration about rules on content, and make sure you set clear guidelines with your students regarding acceptable language and content. In addition to reading the lyrics, allow your students to listen to some raps. As they explore this genre, challenge them to think critically about rap by posing the following questions:

1. How would you describe rap music? How is it different from other types of music?
2. How is rap similar to and different from genres of poetry and spoken-word poetry? Why are these similarities and differences significant? What do they tell us about these genres?
3. What subject matter is addressed in rap? What themes do you find?
4. What meaning and messages do you think the speaker wants to convey?
5. How does the language combine with the music to convey this meaning?
6. How does hearing an audible voice in rap convey meaning differently from reading "voice" in written texts that are not performed? Within the cultural context of our contemporary society, why is an audible voice significant to this genre?

Rap as Multimodal

The last few questions of the activity above reflect how rap is a multimodal medium; it engages its listeners in a variety of ways. English educators may first be inclined to examine the oral and written modes of rap—what is said (rapped) along with the actual written text of the lyrics. These aspects of rap are integral to discussions that critically frame this genre, and they are ways of thinking about texts that students in English classrooms are accustomed to. Importance also lies beyond these linguistic modes, and students should consider how sound—including music and rhythm—works together with the words of the rap to convey meaning. Examining the visual mode is also important when critically framing rap in the classroom, since many raps have music videos that students have access to and engage with both on TV and on the Internet. This consideration of multimodality can provide a focused entry point into larger issues in the rap.

Rap and Identity Formation

With students, examine the following:

1. How are voice and identity important to the piece?
2. Does the voice transcend the identity of the rap and speak from the perspective of a larger group, beyond the individual? How does this happen in the rap and why do you think it happens?
3. How is the self addressed? How are others characterized?
4. Who belongs to dominant groups in society and who belongs to marginalized groups? Where is the speaker positioned in these hierarchies and how does s/he position the listener?
5. Are power relations or prejudices between different groups addressed? If so, how do they challenge or reinforce societal "norms"? What does this mean to you?

Voice and Identity

Marika Autrand accesses her students' home literacies by incorporating rap and hip-hop into lessons, centring her unit thematically around the ideas of voice and identity.

- She begins with a focus on written poetry from the period of the 1950s to the end of the 20th century. Picking up from there, she teaches spoken-word poetry from the end of the 20th century and into the 21st. Students recognize how the art and craft of spoken-word poetry relate to written poetry, and how performance poets may blend the genres of spoken-word poetry and rap by incorporating rhythms or music into their pieces.
- The transition into lessons on rap is fluid. When discussing rap, Marika challenges her students to think critically about the pieces as artistic achievements, to examine how and why certain poetic conventions may be used or ignored, and which elements of rap separate it from the other genres covered in the unit.
- Throughout the unit, students are asked to compare and contrast the works of different writers and artists. Students are encouraged to examine how similarities and differences between works speak to larger ideas and questions about pieces.
- Since the thematic focus of the unit is identity, Marika asks her students to think about how identity plays out in the pieces and to explore their own emerging identities, taking culture, history, family, interests, and prejudices into account.

The material covered in the unit—particularly rap—forms a bridge between classroom instruction and the individual identities and home literacies of students.

Rap and Identity

One of the reasons home literacies are engaging for students is because of their relevance to the lives of the students. As literacy teachers, we have to remember not only to use relevant texts like raps, but also to create discourse around these texts that focuses on issues that, like the texts themselves, are engaging and meaningful to students. In the preceding activity, the ideas of voice and identity serve as a thematic focus for the unit on rap. These themes—and many other themes addressed in rap—are not gender biased and therefore can be relevant and meaningful to all students. As rap is incorporated into lesson planning, one must be mindful of potential biases—gender and others—so as not to unintentionally privilege some students while disadvantaging others.

Composing Rap

At the end of a mini-unit or unit on rap, ask students to compose their own rap. When creating the assignment, consider whether or not it would be helpful to your students if you set specific guidelines as to how many verses, choruses, and refrains are required. Ask students to first think about the ways that speakers and identities in the texts you have studied have been shaped through societies, cultures, history, communities, prejudices, power relations, and personal pride. Following reflection on these issues, ask students to reveal the voice and identity in their own raps by considering these same issues. The final product can be presented through writing, recording, or performance.

Video Games

Whether we like it or not, video games are to children today what novels were to readers fifty years ago. Most video games carry with them elaborate fantasy worlds with complex characters, dramatic settings, and enticing narratives that can be put to use in your literacy program. Video games range from games played on brand platforms to games played on the computer. There are many different genres of video games.

When we speak of video games, we cannot avoid the issue of violence in them and the amount of time spent on them. Some video games are more violent than others; like texts in any medium, video games sit on a continuum in terms of the degree of violence they exhibit. What we cannot and should not do is ignore them or discount them. Children will continue to use them and continue to be interested and motivated by them. Teachers need to work with children and access the skills that they use when they play with them.

There is of course also an equity issue for those students who do not have access to video games. It can be said with some certainty that students with fewer media trappings in the home still have some access to video-game-like technologies, such as game cards or games through the Internet. Yet another criticism of video game use is that it is a solitary enterprise, and that students spend endless time engaged in game worlds. The time factor is a reality, which is all the more reason to draw on skills of use; however, there have been findings to show that students game in groups. That is, playing video games is much more an interpersonal, social act (Delpit, 2003) than has been assumed. What is more, research also tells us that gamers' learning transfers to situations that use different task and different stimuli.

With this in mind, we need to understand the nature of computer narratives as literacy teachers to build on them in our teaching. There are similar criteria at work with video games as there are with novels. Are characters believable? Are settings appealing? Is the dialogue complex? What types of actions take place? What rewards and obstacles are inherent to the narrative? Admittedly, video games hone different sorts of skills, but skills that are equally valuable. One set of such skills are problem-solving skills. For example, an age-old game like Tetris, with its configuration of geometric shapes, activates our visual systems to find patterns. Tetris players have been known to dream about the game in order to figure out how to get to the next level. Specifically, the game draws on our skills of recognizing parallel and perpendicular lines.

Teaching Strategy

Creating Video Games out of Movies

by John DeLaurentis

For his Grade 12 English classroom, John DeLaurentis designed a lesson using his students' textual knowledge of video games. Most video games involve problem-solving, character identification, and the importance of strategizing. John has frequently noticed that students read manuals that accompany games. Drawing on students' knowledge of gaming alongside their use of the Internet, John created a lesson plan that would use these kinds of skills in the classroom.

John asked students to create on paper or on the computer a video game based on the Fire Swamp scene in the 1987 movie *The Princess Bride*. To complete the assignment, students needed to include the following elements:

- the dangers users will encounter while they play
- strategies and solutions to subvert danger
- background music for the game
- action figures who exist in the game
- adventure texts that may be drawn upon to inspire ideas for the games journeys
- names and descriptions of creatures users encounter
- a detailed description of the setting of the game

Upon completing the assignment, students showed an ability to solve problems, to develop settings, and consolidated an understanding of identity creation. They had integrated multimodal skills and used one genre—film genre—to create another genre—a video game. This assignment is an effective way to bring students' existing knowledge base from their home environment into the classroom and use it to engage them in textual meaning-making.

A System of Rewards

In his book, *Everything Bad is Good For You,* Steven Johnson discusses the game world at length. What he highlights is how important rewards are to players. Johnson discusses how game interface revolves around keeping players notified of potential rewards available to them. Tetris, for example, uses "the fuzzy world of visual reality to a core set of intersecting shapes" (Johnson, 2005) that increase in complexity as you move up levels. Most video games, however, present fictional worlds that users need to understand and exist in to move through. There are rewards within these fictional worlds, often moving into another level of reality with accompanying weapons or tools.

Profile of a Meaning-Maker

by Tony Balazs

Oliver is a master at creating Cheat Sheets, notes on video game strategies to use or the best moves to get you to another level. What is more, Oliver is a reader and will actually use a flashlight in bed to finish a novel. In fact, I cannot buy books quickly enough for him. In school, Oliver has exhibited a strong capacity for words and for the spelling of words, which I can trace back to his keyboarding skills and a strong awareness of how words look and of the tactile act of keyboarding them in.

Overt Instruction Activity

Creating Strategy/Cheat Sheets

While playing video games, you will see boys or girls making notes to track moves that have worked while they navigate their way through a game. This form of intertext works as a support for themselves and other users. To access this skill in your teaching, ask students to keep a strategy sheet in their reading of different kinds of texts—print and electronic.

Strong readers have a repository of strategies they draw on when they encounter new content or new texts (Tovani, 2000). The Strategy Sheet takes this concept to other genres. Have students write out how they navigate texts; what helps them in their comprehension; and generally what kinds of strategies they use as they move their way through texts. Encourage students to do this as homework with all media that they use and enjoy.

What Computer Games Teach Our Students
- Games teach our students to understand identity formation.
- Games teach how to connect different sign systems, such as words, symbols, artifacts, etc.
- Games promote problem-solving skills.
- Games demonstrate how students learn from non-verbal cues.
- Games allow students to transfer abilities learned while doing one task (e.g., typing text into a keyboard) while doing another.
(Gee, 2003)

Choice in Meaning-Making

Video games stretch literacy skills by building choice into the meaning-making process. A video game such as Sim City is well-known for the capacity to have you create your own story with settings, characters, and story trajectories of your own choosing. You can create any kind of community you want: urban settings or farming communities, set in school or in a park. Characters can be a variety of ages and at various stages. The game allows children to think about creating a story world and what that entails. Investment in a story becomes that much greater when a child contrives the plot, imagines settings, and casts characters.

Game Genres and Skills

Computer games rely heavily on patterns inherent within them. Returning to Tetris as an example: you anticipate where shapes fit and place them accordingly. The game develops a particular part of the brain that sorts patterns and mathematical principles. You can use Tetris to teach geometry and principles of calculus. In Tetris you quickly fit shapes together into interlocking shape patterns (Gee, 2003). Yet every problem is different; that is, the configuration of pieces changes over time.

Media Connection: Many video games are developed with comics in mind. Playing video games often brings together the skills of being able to read narratives (in the rules and onscreen) with having computer literacy and visual literacy. Compare and contrast the genres of comics and video games in your teaching. Ask students as a homework assignment to move from a print story or favorite comic and adapt it to a video game. This kind of assignment accesses their understanding of two out-of-school texts at once.

Action Games

Tetris is popular because of the pattern recognition component to the game. In action games like Full Spectrum Warrior, the player controls two squads of four soldiers each, using buttons on the controls to give orders to the soldiers. Such games demand that you step into identities and find ways to "think, act, and value like a professional" (Gee, 2005). The player has to decipher professional military practice. As the manual says, the soldiers "understand how to operate in a hostile, highly populated environment" and the player needs to master this skill. Although certainly parents could quibble with the fact that it is military

If you do not feel comfortable working within a video game genre, ask students to bring a freeze frame to class. For those students who do not like video games, ask them to go to the library and print out an animated text from the Internet.

practice, it is quite a feat to learn a foreign discourse with its own practices, values, and attitudes, and master all of them.

In Gee's work on video games, he cites recent research on the mind that contends, "humans, when they are thinking and operating at their best, see the world in terms of the affordances for actions they want to take" (2005). Video games quite naturally compel children, adolescents, teenagers, and adults to hone the skills of finding the best possible way of completing an action in a timely and effective manner. Gee extends the notion of seeing and action to seeing and knowing, "to know something is to be able to imagine—to see in the theatre of one's mind—what difference this makes to what the world might otherwise have looked like" (2005). He talks about combining what we learn in the real world with what we have gleaned and learned from texts and other media. Our students, perhaps more than at any other time, have honed this capacity to move between and among imagined worlds, to decipher the affordances of each one, and to best take advantage of these affordances. We need to account for this in our literacy teaching.

Strategy Games

There are strategy games in which players create and command civilizations, building them up from primitive stages to more and more advanced stages "by collecting resources, building buildings, settling new land and building whole new cities, engaging in research, fighting wars, and engaging in diplomacy" (Gee, 2005). Strategy games give players a god-like status: "the player feels like a god who uses people, groups, objects, time, and space as tools or resources to carry out both small and grand strategies in competition with other civilizations" (Gee, 2005).

A video game like The Sims can also give you god-like status, with its capacity for players to construct worlds how they see fit. You build a world, a home, and relationships however you like. The act of constructing a world and a living space to correspond with that world actively engages players in identity formation. Whether it is Tetris or The Sims, video games build worlds, and users have to understand and work with the logic of these worlds. How different is this skill from reading books and becoming enconsced in the characters and settings?

Situated Practice Activity

Analyzing and Strategizing Video Games

Analyze a scene in a book juxtaposed with a freeze frame of a popular video game, such as Castlevania or Runescape. With students, closely examine the visual depiction of characters, the use of setting, the gestures and movements used by characters within the game. Then look at the book passage and ask students to visualize what the scene would look like. What did they find easier? What did they visualize? What were some of the affordances and constraints (strengths and weaknesses of two texts)?

Assessment Frame

Create a Virtual World and Game It

Ask your students to devise a video game concept and then build a narrative around it. Students write it on their own as a writing sample. It does not have to be an action video game, but can fall into any genre: supernatural, comical, pattern-based, adventures in a mall.

The key aspect of the assignment is to see how students create a world and, importantly, imbue a logic into the world. Video games need an inherent logic that leads players from one level to the next with many obstacles along the way. To complete the assignment, they need to include the following features:

- Context/Theme (e.g., an apothecary's studio as a site for visitors and outside adventures with twists and turns)
- Characters (e.g., a warlock, a princess, a peasant)
- Obstacles (e.g., tiered world in which you can go to higher worlds or lower worlds by taking certain actions).
- Supports (e.g., the apothecary will provide potions and remedies to get you out of situations)

The assignment will draw on video game skills and access such literacy skills as prediction, problem-solving, prior knowledge, and identity formation.

Collector Cards

by Brenda Stein Dzaldov

Brenda Stein Dzaldov is a teacher of some years and is completing her Ph.D. in the areas of multimodality and literacy education. In this chapter, she highlights the following skills:

• Understanding phonetic patterns
• Sorting and summarizing information
• Writing skills that emerge from card use
• Developing a meta-awareness of letters and words
• Appreciating multimodality in cards

"In grade six, [Toronto Maple Leafs defenceman] Bryan McCabe wrote in a school assignment that he wanted to be a hockey player. Unfortunately his teacher wouldn't accept the report because playing hockey "wasn't a real job'."
—Paul Romanuk

Literacy Moment

Hockey is Real... Hockey Cards as Text

I grew up in a family with one sister and parents who weren't very interested in hockey; consequently, neither was I. However, now that I am the mother of three (two sons, aged nine and seven, and an 11-year-old daughter), I have become very aware of how important hockey is in the lives of many young Canadian children. I have also become acutely aware of how much literacy is intertwined with hockey and sports in general. The first thing my sons do when they come downstairs for breakfast in the morning is check the sports section of the newspaper. They read the headlines, debugging this genre that communicates with headlines such as "Habs off the Mark" or "Sens lose a heart-breaker." The boys check the scores of the previous day's games and read and discuss the game statistics. They always check how many goals and assists their favorite players scored. They don't read any other parts of the newspaper. Perhaps most interestingly, they read this text with a passion I don't observe for any of the other texts they read. The boys spend enormous amounts of time reading, trading, and discussing hockey cards. They are able to pronounce even the most difficult names (e.g., Roy pronounced "Wah," or LeCavalier pronounced "Likavelyay"), and they have recognized these names on hockey cards with relative ease since age five or six. One of the most noticeable things to me: the fact that these names are NOT phonetically regular. However, using background knowledge gained from other media—TV, radio, oral discussion with others—they are able to identify, remember, and decode these names easily. They have also learned the names and histories of a number of retired players (Guy Lafleur, Bobby Orr, Phil Esposito), and have memorized volumes of statistics about those players. I have observed the same phenomenon in their friends, who trade, read, and talk about hockey cards for large amounts of their recreational time.

Given the amount of time and the incredible amount of literacy learning that occurs with these cards, I became interested in how to use this medium to teach academic skills.

> The nature of the print text being read affects so strongly the potential of the reader to make any significant meaning. What we read, whether as males or as females, is determined by our life experiences, sometimes by our constructed gender, by what we bring to the print, by our familiarity with the words and the style, by the expectations of the genre, by the social frames of the event, and, of course by the content. (Booth, 2002)

Media Connection: Yu-Gi-Oh© cards are popular with children, tweens, and even adolescents. There are rituals and practices surrounding the use of them, including dueling. The vocabulary of the information on each card is quite advanced, and reading them a skill you will want to access in your teaching—just like the use of hockey cards.

Character: Yugi

Enemy: Maximillion Pegasus

Story: Yugi's grandfather gives him an Egyptian puzzle. When the puzzle is put together, it fills Yugi with magical powers and he becomes Yami Yugi.

Superhero quality: Ancient magical powers from his puzzle.

Mission: To stop villains who want to use the power of the Millennium Items for evil. The Millennium Items are ancient magical items made in Egypt 3000 years ago. Maximillion Pegasus has the Millenium Eye, one of the Millenium Items. Yugi has the Millenium Puzzle, which he uses for good.

Using the Elements of Cards

There are many different types of hockey cards, each with a different visual layout, different fonts and scripts used to name the players and the teams, and numerical statistics organized in a chart form using abbreviations (e.g., GP = games played, A = assists). Many cards include a description of the player of between 50 and 100 words.

Children are able to search for and locate a great deal of complex information from these cards, and they are able to do so in a willing way where the same skills would be considered boring practice if using another medium. The motivational aspect of using a text to which students can relate is obvious: "Boys like to read newspapers, magazines, comic books, baseball cards and instruction manuals—materials that are often not available in the classroom" (Moloney, 2002). Michael Smith and Jeffrey Wilhelm (2002) suggest providing boys "with a variety of texts, including text that provides 'exportable knowledge'—that is, information boys can use in conversation, such as headlines, box scores, jokes and 'cool parts' of books or movies."

Using hockey cards along with other texts that engage the interests of boys is a way of scaffolding the learning of disengaged or struggling readers as well. There are a number of activities that can teach important academic skills as they incorporate hockey cards as a classroom text.

Critical Framing Activity

Crack the Code of Cards

The learner as "code user" (Freebody & Luke, 1990) has an opportunity to recognize and use the features and structures of texts, including graphics and other visuals, to break the "code" of the text. In this activity, students collect various types of texts related to hockey (newspaper game statistics, various types of hockey cards) and use the texts to debug the non-fiction text features of the samples:

- abbreviations
- text organization
- tables
- graphics
- information gained from pictures
- symbols (e.g., team symbols, league symbols, ™, ©, ®)
- captions
- fonts (signatures vs. various types of print)

Multimodality in Sports Cards
- **Visual:** player positions, facial expressions of players, placement of print, layout of cards, colour and numbers on uniforms, charts, tables.
- **Written:** team names, use of color in text, variety of fonts, symbols, lists of awards won, abbreviations, heading and subheadings.

The Sports Fanatic

by Jessica Rosevear

In Jessica Rosevear's English class, she works with Robert, who loves football and basically all sports. Robert devotes much of his time to sports: playing sports, reading about sports, and applying sports to schoolwork. He likes to read magazines and books about sports, such as the *ESPN* magazine and *The Colour Orange* by Russell Martin. In his words, "I play a lot of sports. I love watching sports, and reading sports in the newspaper, like stats about players and schedules." As part of his high school's varsity football team, Robert reads the play book that describes the team's different plays and scouting reports. In his Sports and Entertainment Marketing class, Robert films commercials that relate to his sports interest. His latest creation is a commercial for Nike Shox™, a basketball sneaker. For the commercials, Robert writes scripts, films his friends acting them out, and then edits the films with iMovie©, a film editing program available through the school. Although Robert does not get excited about *Macbeth* or *Of Mice and Men*, his love of sports engages him endlessly and having a teacher mine those interests certainly paid off for Robert.

Create a K-W-L Chart

Since research and report writing can often be a long, arduous process, using engaging texts and topics may propel students through the research. When students are assigned report writing, have them research a famous hockey player using the Reading and Analyzing Non-Fiction (RAN) Strategy (Stead, 2005) in which the students' prior knowledge is valued and confirmed. In the RAN strategy, the first part is to access prior knowledge. In contrast to the familiar K–W–L chart, the RAN strategy allows students to either discard or confirm prior knowledge during research, while adding new, relevant information and valuing questions that are raised based on new information gathered. See the RAN Organizer on page 115. Among other sources, such as newspapers and texts that give autobiographical information, hockey cards can be a useful tool for research, providing much new information that is specifically gathered from an engaging non-fiction text.

Sorting

My husband and I bought each of our boys a binder and some plastic sheets, with space for nine cards on each sheet. We suggested some ways to sort the cards (e.g., by team or alphabetically by player). Eventually, they chose to sort the cards in their own ways. Many of their friends carry around similar binders of cards, and they sort the cards using many different methods.

Sorting Hockey Cards

Add hockey cards and card sheets to a sorting centre and have students sort the hockey cards by different characteristics including:

- alphabetically by player
- alphabetically by team
- with the same team cards together

- by type of card (e.g., Parkhurst, Topps, MVP)
- by player position
- by increasing or decreasing number of goals scored
- rookies or all-stars

Links to the Known

Although many players' names are not phonetically regular, the fact that children can remember the names upon sight can be linked to some other, more commonly spelled words. Just as we encourage literacy learners to link the known to the new, so we also can use this "tool" to link known names to word work for students.

Situated Practice

Word Work with Hockey Cards

Have students look for high-frequency words and word patterns in the names of the hockey players ; for example, "all" in "Hextall" or the "er" ending in Alexander Ovetchkin.

Assessment Frame

Using a Graphic Organizer With Cards

Have students chart the various features of non-fiction text using a three-column chart (see Features of Text page 116) for three types of text; e.g., collector cards, a web page, a newspaper page. Text could include hockey cards, sections of the newspaper, and web pages such as www.nhl.com/kids.

RAN Organizer

What I Think I Know	Confirmation	Misconception	New Information	Questions

(adapted from Brenda Stein Dzaldov)

Features of Text

	Text 1	Text 2	Text 3
Print Features			
Graphic Aids			
Organizational Aids			
Illustrations			

Print Features include font, bold print, colored print, bullets, titles, headings, subheadings, italics, labels and captions

Graphic Aids include diagrams, sketches, graphs, figures, maps, charts, tables, cross-sections, timelines, overlays

Organizational Aids include table of contents, index, glossary, preface, pronunciation guide, appendix

Illustrations include colored photographs, colored drawings, black-and-white photos, black-and-white drawings, labeled drawings, enlarged photos, paintings in different media

(created by Brenda Stein Dzaldov)

Magazines: Words and Images

Literacy Moment

Magazines and Magna Doodle

by Lisa Murphy

Some of my earliest memories are of my dad's place littered with books, newspapers, and magazines, half-folded, mid-read, clearly in use. My mom was also a book-a-week gal, so it's no surprise that by eight or nine, I was reading until the wee hours of the night. (I put a hat over my light so I wouldn't get caught.)

Today, my children are picking up the reading bug. Sometimes when my partner or I read a newspaper or a magazine my three-year-old son, Rowan, will point out a word and ask what it is. Other times, he'll see a word on the cover of what we're reading and spell it out on his MagnaDoodle. (He can write the alphabet upper and lower case, as well as spell words such as "Mommy," "Daddy," and "Florida" from memory. But he's not so good on the monkey bars.) Thirteen-month-old Maggie, on the other hand, prefers to grab the newspaper or magazine from our hands and crumple it or rip off the cover. Ah, the sacrifices we make for literacy.

I have known Lisa—the editor of a national Canadian magazine—for many years and many a time caught her with her nose in a magazine, lingering over its photographs, content, and pearls of wisdom. Magazines are often considered a low-brow form of entertainment, but in fact they are visually and linguistically complex, and carry skills and messages about language and how language works with visuals. Importantly, whether it is a car, computer, or teen magazine, our students spend a lot of time reading them. Magazines inhabit our homes and allow us to escape into other worlds. Just as we need to understand the landscape of blogs and collector cards, so too we need to know about the genre of magazines to access the kinds of skills that they bring out.

Magazines are issued at regular intervals—weekly or monthly—and focus on particular audiences. The content of magazines distinguishes one from another. Magazine genres cover a broad spectrum, from fashion to hobbies to computing to child-rearing. Magazine covers are selling tools. They help us to distinguish one magazine from another. Visual images, layout, and graphology are used in order to create an identity. Magazine covers are the face of a text. The title of the magazine plays a large part in shaping the reader's expectations.

Media Connection: The clearest connection between magazines and other kinds of texts is when the magazine is targeted directly at users of other media. From TV and movie fan magazines, to magazines devoted to music or video games, the vast array of magazines published means that there is significant overlap with the other genres studied here.

Comparing Front Covers

Collect some magazine front covers and bring them to class. Have students analyze them and describe in detail the ideal reader of the publication.

- Do the covers present head and shoulder photographs?
- Are models looking away or directly into the camera? What facial expressions do they have?
- Does the verbal text interact with images?

Elements of Magazines

Sentence Functions

Sentences can vary within the content of magazines, but they generally fall into four types:

- **Exclamatives:** for expressing surprise, alarm, or a strong opinion; are accompanied by an exclamation point; e.g., *Lose Weight in Days?!*
- **Imperatives:** for making requests or giving orders; e.g., *Get out of the sun!*
- **Declaratives:** for making a statement or assertion; e.g., *Television helps with literacy*
- **Interrogatives:** for asking questions; e.g., *Are you fed up with wrinkles?*

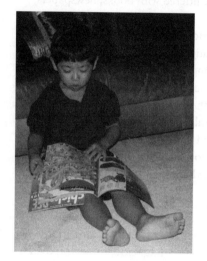

At times, magazine writers will introduce problems and offer immediate solutions. Magazines often offer advice and frequently simulate conversations to lessen the distance between magazine writers and their readers; for example, *Stressed out? Here is the answer.* At times, a topic is introduced, followed quickly by a reassurance.

In titles and within texts, writers use literary devices, such as alliteration, assonance, or rhyme, to catch reader attention:

- Alliteration occurs when initial consonants are repeated in adjacent words; e.g., *Smooth, Silky, Supple Skin*
- Assonance occurs when the same vowel sound is repeated in adjacent words; e.g., *Sun Fun*
- Homphones are words that are spelled differently but have the same sound; e.g., *Rough Ruffing: Train Your Dog to Bark Selectively*
- Intertextuality, making reference to other texts, incites interest in an article. Intertextuality allows writers to make relationships between often unrelated matters; e.g., *Stern's Justice: It Is Swift, But Is It Fair?*

Collectively, these devices serve as hooks to grab reader attention and as literary devices in a very different context from poetry or prose, they can be incorporated into language lessons.

The Composition of Texts

We often read magazines in an unpredictable way, leafing through them until we find a topic of particular interest. Tables of contents lead readers to topics that might be of particular interest. The contents page has a set agenda, which remains constant although features change from issue to issue, and illustrate

the range of genres included in magazines. Caldas-Coulthard (1996) found that magazines have a fixed structure:

1. *Reportage*: reporting on an event or an issue
2. *Profile*: featuring a person
3. *Emotional*: a writer reports about an emotional issue
4. *Society*: looking at social life
5. *Designer profile*: focus on fashion
6. *Life stories*: mini-biographies
7. *Review section*: books, music, films, etc.
8. *Editorial*: an author's opinion about an issue, event, news item, etc.
9. *Horoscopes*: predictions of people's future based on zodiac signs.
11. *Advertisements*: promoting certain items or commodities.
12. *Reader's Letters*: provides a forum for readers to interact with the magazine producers.

Transformed Practice Activity

Analyzing the Problem Page

Magazines can problematize aspects of life, and offer solutions that often involve the purchase of products. Students need an awareness of these kinds of pages and how to read them critically. Most magazines, particularly women's magazines, have a problem page that invites readers to write in with their emotional or physical dilemmas and problems.

How can we analyze the language and visuals in problem pages? Problem pages often follow the same pattern:

1. *setting the scene*: which language marks time, place, and other circumstances (e.g., describing a specific place where an event takes place)

2. *complication*: language and tense define the episode (e.g., you have a disagreement with a friend)

3. *resolution*: the denouement or final resolution; the moral when the point of the story is explained and analyzed.

Magazine Layout

The position of information on a page conveys meaning. In our culture we read from left to right, and from top to bottom of the page. The prime position for important information is the top left-hand corner (Kress & Van Leeuwen, 1996). However, Kress and Van Leeuwen found that "in women's magazines, the right pages were dominated by large, salient photographs from which the gaze of one or more women engages the gaze of the viewer" (1996). It is worth mentioning that the reason why the left-hand page has the most prominent text and large, attractive pictures appear on the right-hand top of the page has to do with how readers usually flip through a magazine—holding it in the left hand while riffling the pages with the right. This means that if whatever is at the top right of the right-hand page is big and attention-grabbing, it will leave the biggest impression. What is more, magazine advertisements placed in this position are the most expensive. Kress and Van Leeuwen concluded that there is a complementarity and continuous movement from left to right and that the right was the place for key or new information. Meanwhile, the left was reserved for information that was already known by the reader.

Three principles of composition:
- *Information Value*: the placement of elements from left to right, top to bottom, centre and margin, can give specific information value.
- *Salience*: the elements are placed to attract the reader's attention to different degrees; for example, foreground or background, contrasts in colour, etc.
- *Framing*: the presence or absence of framing devices, which connect or disconnect elements showing unity or disunity.

Critical Framing Activity

Locating Magazine Genres

Have students sort genres of stories within a wide variety of magazines, from *Time* to *Cosmopolitan*. Ask students to analyze

- structure
- voice
- images
- layout
- perspective
- position in magazine
- headings
- conclusion.

As an assignment, ask students to choose a magazine genre, focus on a topic, and write in the genre.

Situated Practice Activity

Writing Horoscopes

Ask your students to write their own horoscopes. To help them begin, provide them with the first line:

The Moon meets Jupiter in a mysterious alignment, so you will be in a mood for…

Have them keep in mind the following questions:

- What will your predictions for the month be?
- What kind of language will you use?
- What kind of voice does the horoscope have?
- How does your horoscope compare with ones in other magazines?
- Do you ever read your horoscope?
- Do you believe their predictions?

Magazines and Identity

The Editorial

Magazines often feature a letter from the editor. The purpose of the editorial is to introduce the magazine's contents, but it also gives text producers the opportunity to address their readers directly. The "reader synthesized" is the target audience, someone who shares the same views, attitudes, and values as the magazine producers/writers. The editor's letter has a standard style and serves as a compendium of the whole issue.

Constructing Identities in Magazines

Magazines speak to particular readers at particular stages in their lives. The notion that identities can be constructed in language is important for our students to understand and appreciate. In Linda McLoughlin's book, *The Language of Magazines*, she discusses the concept of presenting ideal-reader images. McLoughlin signals magazines as writing for femininities and masculinities: "by turning femininity into a verb, it highlights the active process whereby women readily engage in various practices which are needed to make them appear appropriately feminine" (McLoughlin, 2000). It is important to note that femininity is culturally specific. McLoughlin claims that magazine producers similarly speak to male audiences through language and visuals. Magazines place hooks in texts in order to appeal to certain readers over another.

Magazine writers address readers directly by using pronouns such as "you" and "your," as though the reader is known to her or to him. In writing, you can position yourself to speak to particular kinds of people at particular moments. One way for students to identify the audience and goals of a narrative is by looking for the following:

- the agent (Who is the target audience?)
- the process (What words are used?)
- the goal (What are they trying to do or say?)

All students read magazines at one time or another. Young children like to cut them up and make collages with them, and we can foster early concepts about print by having them look at photographs and images on the page. Adolescents and teenagers enjoy magazines because they feature people and things in their social worlds. Magazine genres are excellent tools for looking in detail at language, figurative devices and conventions, and the visual communication or multimodality of texts. The glossy formats of magazines disguise complex structures and complex, carefully crafted language.

Assessment Frame

Creating Magazines in Literature Circles

As a form of a literature circle, ask groups of five junior-grade students to choose the kind of the magazine that they will produce. Once they have decided, choose roles: two writers, one editor, one graphic artist, and one project manager (who will handle schedules, tasks, commissioning advertisers, meeting with team members, and generally oversee a timely completion of the project). The groups will have two weeks to create a magazine of 10 to15 pages, with all of the required features; e.g., cover, table of contents, lead editorial, articles, images, horoscopes, letters to the editor. The assignment will serve as a culminating activity at the end of a unit. There will be a peer evaluation component in the form of the rubric on page 122, with key areas identified (e.g., fulfillment of tasks; effectiveness of work; cooperating with other team members, etc.).

Peer Evaluation of Magazine Creation

	Showed a high degree of competence	Showed a moderate degree of confidence	Showed a satisfactory degree of confidence	Showed a limited degree of confidence
Fulfillment of tasks				
Effectiveness of work				
Cooperating with other team members				
Understanding of magazine image and mission				

Blogs: Collaborating Online

by Erica C. Boling

Erica Boling is an Assistant Professor of Literacy Education at Rutgers University Graduate School of Education who looks at ways of meaningfully infusing technology and information literacy into teaching and learning. In her chapter, she highlights the following skills:
• Choosing visual templates to match personal tastes and identities
• Using blogs to support teaching and as a way to communicate with parents
• Forging and forming communities in your classroom
• Teaching about anonymity and dangers on the web
• Steps in creating a blog

Imagine a collaborative, online space where students practise critical reading skills, synthesize information across various texts, and share ideas with others from around the world. Imagine a collaborative, online space where students participate in constructive learning environments that extend beyond the boundaries of classroom walls and provide real audiences for their written work. Imagine having access to an online tool that can be used to support multi-sensory learning and students' various learning styles. This powerful tool, which is easily accessible to anyone who has a computer and Internet connection, is called a weblog or blog. Personal blogs have traveled from the home and have entered politics, the business world, and news media. In addition, blogs are increasingly entering our schools and being used to support teaching and learning.

Media Connection: While the connection between blogs and messaging or texting online seems obvious, blogging in many ways shares more aspects with traditional paper publishing. The planning required, the cooperation involved, the variety of elements that can be included, and the more permanent nature of the product take blogs far beyond simpler types of online communication.

Blogs are essentially interactive web sites that allow people to create personal web pages with the same ease as creating a word-processing document. Blogs provide free, instant publishing to the Internet, allowing individuals to create and share text, pictures, graphics, videos, and other multimedia within a matter of minutes. Blogs, like web sites, allow individuals to link other resources and web sites to their own personal blogs. Unlike traditional web sites, however, they allow individuals or groups to create an online space where people can post comments and engage in online conversations (Richardson, 2006). Comments written by visitors to the site are usually posted in chronological order and can be stamped with the date and time they were posted. Blogs are different from online discussion boards and other types of online forums, because only the author can post entries that are shown on the front page of the blog. By having control over the site, the author, or blog administrator, can control who has permission to comment on the site. He or she also has the power to delete messages, control whether a message can be viewed by the public, and add (or delete) other authors and administrators to the site.

Literacy Moment

Baghdad Burning

In August 2003, a young Iraqi blogger began reporting her experiences as a civilian observer in Baghdad. Calling herself Riverbend, she offered eyewitness accounts of daily life in a war-torn city and managed to garner a worldwide audience for her fresh analysis of what was going on in Iraq. Riverbend's blog, Baghdad Burning, has been written into a book by James Ridgeway, in which he recounts how this girl described her family and the fate of Iraqi women.

For individuals who would like an easy way to publish to the Internet, blogs are the way to go. Most programs provide users with a choice of free, professional-looking templates for their sites, allowing users to decorate the site with images, colors, and graphics with a simple click of the mouse. Some of the newer programs even provide interactive calendars for individual blog sites. They might also include programs that document when and how many times a site has been viewed, providing charts and graphs that document incoming visitors. Some programs allow authors of the site to label and categorize individual postings, making it possible to conduct keyword searches through multiple blog entries that were created over a period of time.

While conducting research that investigated individuals' knowledge, skills, and beliefs towards the role of technology in literacy education, I discovered that teacher candidates and practising teachers often saw blogs as simply online journals or diaries, where individuals reveal very personal thoughts, pouring out their heart and soul to a public audience (Boling, 2006). It is true that many blogs are used in a diary-like manner; however, it is important to know that there is more to blogs than a free flow of thoughts and images. In fact, some of the greatest benefits of using blogs in the classroom come from using them in ways that are not personal. When considering how to integrate blogs into classroom instruction and how to use blogs safely, it is useful to consider the ways in which they have been used in business, politics, and news media.

Creating Communities Through Blogs

In business, project managers are using blogs "to direct and coordinate complex projects, e.g., giving directions but at the same time inviting updates and commentary" (Dearstyne, 2005). Additionally, technical experts have used them for the development or design of projects and for managing and sharing content. In this way, blogs are versatile and make information instantly available and easy to retrieve (Dearstyne, 2005).

For teachers, blogs can be used for sharing ideas, information, policies, and resources with parents and students. A blog might be used to post the latest school news, classroom events, weekly schedules, and homework assignments. Teachers can use blogs to communicate with parents and students to keep them updated on important classroom assignments and events. By creating links from their class blog to other educational sites, teachers can provide both parents and students with homework help, tips for using comprehension strategies, and access to interactive web sites that allow students to practise various skills. Blogs can be used to link readers to dictionary web sites, online thesauri, and web sites that provide online activities that support reading, writing, and vocabulary development. There are web sites that provide both online tutorials and practice. Additionally, students can use blogs while working on collaborative class projects to socially construct meaning as they share, critique, revise, and comment upon the various texts, graphics, sounds, and images that might appear on individual blog sites.

Weblog Hosting
- Blogger — http://www.blogger.com/start
- Xanga — http://www.xanga.com/Default.aspx?
- LiveJournal — http://www.livejournal.com/
- Edublogs — http://edublogs.org/
- 21 Publish — http://www.21publish.com/
- TeacherHosting — http://teacherhosting.com
- Weblogs Compendium — http://www.lights.com/weblogs/hosting.html

Resources that Can Be Linked to Blogs
- International Reading Association's Parent Resources (http://www.reading.org/resources/tools/parent.html) — Provides links to various parent brochures that can be downloaded from the Internet
- Reading is Fundamental (RIF) Parent Resources (http://www.rif.org/parents/) — Resources and information for motivating students to read. All ages are covered
- Cyber Kids (http://www.cyberkids.com/) — Online magazine written by kids for kids ages 7–11
- Starfall.com (http://www.starfall.com/) — A free learn-to-read web site that provides online activities and tutorials for children

Blogs Mediate Identities

During the devastation brought about by Hurricane Katrina in New Orleans, families turned to blogs as a way to post messages to loved ones letting them know they were alive and where they could be found. Sometimes journalists posted these messages for families after hearing their stories from actual sites of devastation. Individuals posted messages and pictures of missing loved ones, including their pets.

In a similar way, blogs can bring together communities of students who share common interests. Blogs can be created by and for sports fans, animal lovers, science-club members, and poetry- or book-club groups. Students can use blogs to engage in literacy practices that incorporate critical reading skills. They can post entries to keep readers updated on current events, their favorite sports star, or the latest breakthroughs in science.

In addition to summarizing, critiquing, and reacting to information that they have found elsewhere, students can create links between their summaries, critiques, and opinions to texts and multimedia found on the Internet. When responding to blog entries, others can read, post comments, and react to the entries. This can spark ongoing conversations or debates. In this way, students can use blogs as spaces to communicate and share ideas and different perspectives with other students around the world. Individuals' comments might extend beyond traditional texts to include links and postings that incorporate art, music, graphics, or even digital video.

Blogs can also be used to promote student activism. For example, a teacher might use blogs to give students voice and power by having them collaborate with a local animal shelter and create postings that introduce dogs and cats in need of homes. By posting online pictures and descriptive narratives of the animals, students can learn about the power of persuasion and how to effectively use images and words so that people will want to provide a home to animals in the shelter. In terms of design and available designs, students can add in their own flair and sense of aesthetic by choosing photographs, fonts, and color schemes that match their identities. In this way, blogs can mediate identities.

Critical Framing Activity

Analyzing Blogs

Provide a link on your class blog to The Pacific Northwest Tree Octopus (http://zapatopi.net/treeoctopus/) or Dog Island (http://www.thedogisland.com/) web sites. Teach students how to critically evaluate a web site to determine its author, purpose, and validity. Have students post comments to your class blog indicating why the web site is or is not reliable and trustworthy. (Ideas for this activity came from the Information Literacy Materials found at http://www.novemberlearning.com/.)

Creating Your Own Blog

By visiting blog sites that have been created by other teachers and students, educators will begin to develop ideas for how to use them in their own classrooms. In addition to visiting blogs, it is useful to take the time to explore and try out the various free blog programs that are available on the Internet (see list in margin of page 124). For those who are new to blogs, it would be best to begin by exploring a simple program such as Blogger (http://www.blogger.com/start) and then to explore new programs after becoming familiar with some of the basic blog functions.

While testing various blog programs, you can compare the different types of tools and user controls provided by each program. Blog administrative controls are often found on the blog "dashboard." Some programs allow the blog administrator to create user groups and control whether registered group members or anybody in the general public can post a message on the blog. You will want to maintain some control over who can and cannot post on a site. Templates control the overall appearance of the site and reveal what additional tools might be added to the blog.

Once a teacher becomes familiar with one or more blog programs, it is time to decide the purposes for using blogs in the classroom and the educational goals that one hopes to achieve. Part of our job as educators requires us to teach students about the importance of never posting personal information online. You will need to set clear expectations and procedures with students when creating individual and class blogs.

It is good to keep in mind the following questions:

- How will blogs be managed?
- Who will post blog entries and manage the publishing of these entries?
- Will students have their own blogs? If yes, how will the teacher monitor students' uses of blogs?
- Who will be given responsibility for controlling what is or is not made public on each blog?
- Will the teacher view blog entries as drafts before they are made public?
- How will the teacher communicate expectations for the appropriate use of blogs?

You may want to introduce parents and school administrators to the ways in which they can use blogs, and to explain how they can monitor and control the information that is posted online. Parents need to be assured that their children's identity will be protected and that blogs will be used safely. Once teachers inform parents, administrators, and students about safe and effective uses of blogs, it is time to go "live" and make blogs public. Once this occurs, more authentic and meaningful learning experiences can be created in the classroom.

Teaching Strategy
....

A Class Blog

by Garth Ferrante

During class discussions in my inner-city college classroom—where students traditionally interact with both instructor and text—I noticed that there were very few outspoken individuals, some who would comment if asked, and still those who seemed to have little to say about any text we covered. After a professional development seminar on the incorporation of technology in the higher education classroom, I began building my own professional weblog (or "blog" as it is popularly known). My express purpose in providing this digital forum was to compel all of my students to participate, not just the garrulous, or those naturally inclined to the verbal mode.

For students, the blog works as a traditional discussion proxy—and as a text itself over time—for several reasons: students feel less intimidated because the physical immediacy of giving an on-the-spot response is removed; students are more likely to reflect on what they wish to say and be more candid and substantive in their comments because of this additional "holding" time; students are more likely to understand the writing process (particularly the revising, editing, and publishing sub-processes) and internalize what many students are usually resistant to; students want their peers to read "the best" of them, so are usually more thoughtful and discriminating in their writing; students are more likely to suss out issues, information, and meanings of a deeper, hidden, implied, related, and/or peripheral nature when given appropriate guidelines for responding; students create, by semester's end, a digital portfolio that serves as an actualization of their body of work; students have the opportunity to discover what everyone thinks of the spotlighted topic/text/concept, not just the instructor and, in so doing, are more apt to form relationships, which also complement the in-class atmosphere.

For educators, the benefits are myriad: in creating posts that students respond to, one can set a specific task that "leads" students to complex concepts, or builds on prior experiences or background knowledge; one can create task-, course-, or curricula-based sets of protocols for responding to posts; because instructors create the posts that students respond to, they regulate what kind of language is used specific to blog events, how often students respond, how many comments they make, whether blog events happen at home or in class, and how many guidelines students work within when responding to posts; one can "track" students' thought process and address issues of faulty logic or misinformation.

Assessment Frame

Blogs and Identity

Ask students to describe in prose and, if they like, with visuals, how they would design a blog – what visuals would they use? Where would they place them? Why these visual over others? What kind of written text do you feature? Who do you think will visit your blog? Who do you hope visits your blog?

Movies as More than Entertainment

Movie Viewing as an Intergenerational Practice

Movies loomed large in our family. In particular, my brother Don loves watching movies at home, and the tradition has been carried over to his own children. Theo, my nephew, adores movies and can watch them endlessly. From *The Incredibles* to *A Bug's Life*, he can often be seen absorbed in moving pictures. Characters in his favorite movies come alive in his play, and he contrives costumes to step into role.

Movies are created to entertain us. Like magazines, video games, and TV, watching DVDs or going to movies take up much of our students' time. Movies derive their capacity to entertain from several factors: the plot or story; actors in the movie; action; emotions; special effects and visual appeal; the sound-track, etc. Narrative is a key motif in movies as a process of telling a story. Different genres of film use different kinds of narratives to tell a story. There is a basic narrative structure to most films or movies:

1. The exposition, or establishment of the setting (Who is involved? Where are they?)
2. The problem, or situation that needs to be resolved
3. The complication, or problem that is not easily solved
4. The crisis, or point at which decisions or actions are made
5. The climax, or what happens when those decisions are made
6. The denouement, or when things return back to normal.

Films can scaffold your teaching of the stories, novels, plays, or short stories that your class is studying. It is important to emphasize that movies are a different medium from literature, with their own ways of presenting ideas, and that students use the affordances or particularities of the medium to best use. For example, students can look in particular at cinematic effects in a movie juxtaposed against how the same ideas are presented in a book. Cinematic elements can vary from one film genre to the next (e.g., fantasy films vs. suspense movies). When you incorporate movies into your literacy program, consider the following elements in a movie version of a story:

- What is the setting like? How does the director present setting? Is it key to the plot?
- How actors express themselves: with emotion or without emotion; quickly or slowly; do they have a notable accent, and is it part of the plot?
- Do facial expressions play a role?
- Positioning of characters in scene: at eye-level or face-to-face; above or below; looking up or looking down; etc.

- What are actors doing while speaking or listening (e.g., driving a car? holding a gun?)
- Lighting of the scene: is it bright or dark?
- What kinds of activities are taking place? Do they play a role in the plot?
- Are colors important in the movie?
- What kind of music is playing in the background?

Movies allow you to escape to other worlds. Fictional movies recount stories that have not happened in real life, such as *The Lord of the Rings*, and non-fiction movies recount events that have happened in real life, such as *Hotel Rwanda*. A biographical movie about the life of a real person like Ray Charles is non-fiction. Movies can be based around events like the Vietnam War. Even when a movie is non-fiction, directors will take liberties with a story, based on their vision of how it took place or on their attempt to make it more appealing or interesting to the audience.

Movies as a Segue to History

Judith Gorman gives tours at the Royal Ontario Museum in Toronto, and for years she has used film as a hook to incite student interest in historical exhibits. She took me on a tour of all of the exhibits and we discussed each one in light of films that tell the stories of the emperors or warriors or rulers. We moved from the story of Dionysus and choruses to Elizabethan England and discussed *Shakespeare in Love* and how its story resonated with historical accounts of Elizabethan life. Each statue came alive with the fusion of story and accompanying movie. For example, when I asked Judith if students asked a lot about gladiators when the Russell Crowe movie *Gladiator* came out, she said:

> Well, they would ask, did he exist? I would tell them that he didn't. They want to know why and I would tell them that someone in his position at that point in history would not be able to hold that kind of position. Also, Commodus did not murder his brother. They took some liberties with the story, but it was entertaining. For example, the statues were white in the movie and they should have been painted. Someone was eating tomatoes in the movie and that would not have been possible back then. One Gladiator had spikey hair and that is a contemporary look and would not have been popular back then. Students are fascinated by this level of detail and it makes history come alive when you can relate them to contemporary films.

Situated Practice Activity

Movies and Museums

Take a field trip to the museum and find a film that deals with periods of history on exhibit. Watch the film once for the story, and then ask students to take detailed notes on setting, props, costumes, characters, etc. Organize and give a tour that investigates what is true in the movie and what is not.

Media Connection: Increasingly, movies spawn a host of related, licensed products, from books to bedspreads to video games. Clark Wakabayashi creates books about Disney animated movies such as *The Lion King*, *Tarzan*, and *Chicken Little*.

I really enjoy working with Disney. This is because when we create a book about how a movie such as *Chicken Little* is made, we get to see the animation studio. We talk to the creators, artists, and the animators about every stage of their work. Then we decide what kind of book we want to make. If the book is based on a film, we interview the people involved in the making of the film. From these interviews, we write about interesting aspects of the story and the production. Then we look at lots of different artwork created by the animators and artists and also at the final images from the scenes in the film. We choose pictures we like and we begin to create the book, playing with different ideas for design, art, and color, and putting them together with the words to produce layout designs of each page of the book.

The best books are the ones I create all on my own, such as Disney's *Brother Bear* and *The Wild*. For these I handled the entire projects myself, including the writing, the design, and overseeing the manufacturing of the book. To make a book about an animated film is not always easy, but in the end, the book will be a success if the pictures and the words work together to tell an interesting and unique story.

My Dad is a well-known photographer, so I have always thought about visuals and how they work. I decided to go into visual book publishing because it was a natural choice for me. I love creating books with great pictures!

Types of Movies

Animated Movies

Animated films have become popular with our students. Many animated cartoons seen on television today originated as short films shown in movie theatres. Increasingly, movie stars are taking on voice parts in animated features, such as Ellen Degeneres as Dory in *Finding Nemo*. In David Buckingham's book, *Small Screens*, Paul Wells talks about how several animated films and television shows model cultural difference or otherness in their stories, citing the example of *The Simpsons*. Wells' analysis goes as far back as *The Flintstones* as an early rendition of a culture. Fred, Barney, Wilma, and Betty represent blue-collar families in search of the good life.

Overt Instruction Activity
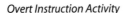

Creating a Soundtrack for a Film

Soundtracks have become a key piece in making movies. Some of the songs in a soundtrack are part of the movie story; however, some songs are never heard in the movie. The soundtrack is then being used to create synergy. To foster an awareness of how songs match moods, characters, and even settings in a story, have students compile their own soundtrack. Remind them that they need to sequence their songs to parallel the plot of the movie, and that the beginning and concluding songs are key. Have them choose 10 songs and create a CD insert with visuals.

Niche Movies

Over the past decade, movie producers have identified target audiences and produced movies with them in mind. For example, the "tween" population has been identified as a viable market for movies. Tweens range in age from 8 to 14. Hollywood studios have produced a surfeit of tween-minded movies in the past few years. *Harry Potter* was a popular tween hit, as was the modestly budgeted *Spy Kids*, which scooped up $113 million. Tweens also flocked to *Shrek, Ice Age, Big Fat Liar, Snow Dogs, Legally Blonde,* and *Princess Diaries.* Research shows that the tween population can see a film several times in a row. Specific themes tend to emerge in tween movies including

- transformations and supernatural happenings
- revenge and rescue fantasies
- the classic, family and friends.

Tweens are still innocent enough to appreciate these themes without subversive topics being introduced.

Girl power features prominently in movies and what goes along with them—fashion, gadgets, and ancillary materials (knapsacks, T-shirts, etc.) in general: "In this marriage of marketing and message, then, a seamless fit emerges where advertising for products, freedom to consumer, and self-transformation are fused in an overall 'feel good' film" (Tally, 2005). As teachers, we need to have our students think critically about all aspects of the films they view, so that they appreciate stereotypes, commodification, and and other important issues.

Critical Framing Activity

Shakespeare and Movies

When studying Shakespeare with senior students, show a film version of a Shakespearean play first to understand the story. Then work through the text and revisit the film with the following questions in mind:

- Does the movie aptly and accurately depict the story?
- How did you find the language?
- Were there any scenes missing? If so, what scenes and why do you think they were missing?
- What characters stood out? Was it due to the actor playing the character or Shakespeare's creation of the character?
- Which did you prefer as a medium?

Assessment Frame

Adapting Books to Film

Have a class discussion how movies often derive from adaptations of novels, plays, short stories, and biographies. Provide examples, such as *Portrait of a Lady* and *Lord of the Rings.* Ask students to think of a book that has been adapted to film. Brainstorm what you need to think of to adapt a book to film:

- how to depict settings; what actors will befit characters
- what scenes will have to be changed or cut to adapt the story to a film version
- how to deal with set design and costumes, particularly for period pieces.

Ask students to get into groups of two or three, and have them take a book, short story, or play and adapt it to film. Ask groups to create visuals of costumes and sets, and have them use sticky notes in the texts just as actual film editors do. Assess how they:

- think through characters and how actors will take on particular characters (and why they chose them).
- choose a particular location
- make decisions about scenes (why did they keep certain ones and not others?)
- choose sets

Have groups present their adaptations to the class, and include a peer assessment component.

Zines: A Voice on Issues

by Mary P. Sheridan-Rabideau

Mary P. Sheridan-Rabideau is an Assistant Professor of English at Rutgers University, and has devoted much of her recent research to exploring and theorizing zines. Her chapter highlights the following skills:

• Encouraging children, youth, and adults to address social issues and be social activists

• Drawing on students' understanding of design, available design, and redesign

• Appreciating the use of figurative language to transmit a message in a genre

When students in my Literacy in the New Media Age handed in their project draft, I was intrigued. In this mockup for a zine, their first edition of "Shoujo: The Power to Revolutionize the World," students focused on *The Revolutionary Girl, Utena*, a popular Japanimation book and TV series that followed the more publicized Pokemon® phenomenon. As a reworking of students' individual research papers, this collaboratively-written zine offered a glossary of terms, a history of *manga* and *shoujo* (Japanese *anime* directed at girls), an analysis of imagery, a series of actual and spoof ads, and several zine articles that had been transformed from students' academic research essays (e.g., the meanings of feminism in Japan; the challenges to a US adaptation of this series; the media effects on children; the commercialization of youth culture).

The cover of their zine offered the enticing tag:

> We are the chick; the world is our egg.
> If we don't break the world's shell,
> We will die without truly being born.
> Smash the world's shell,
> For the Revolution of the World.

Below this were nine animated face-shots. The different shapes and colors of the girls' hair, eyes, and mouths, as well as their choice of jewelry and other accoutrements, all signified how readers informed in *shoujo* visual culture should make sense of this editorial team. Through text and graphic, students sought to educate and persuade others to share their passion for *shoujo* and to explore a variety of issues about reading and writing practices, visual culture, cross-cultural assessments of girlhood, and a host of other issues.

The Zine Philosophy

In some ways, zines (rhyming with "teens" not "nines") and school seem antithetical. Meant to shock as well as inform, zines generally address personal, political, and pop cultural issues. Their irreverent and even defiant tone rebukes authority figures who limit what youth can discuss, challenges a commercialized youth culture that limits what options seem readily available, and undermines capitalistic structures that limit who has access to distribution networks and therefore publication possibilities.

Media Connection: Despite the original relationship between zines and TV (see page 77), zines now share more with genres that mediate identity and activisim, like blogs.

The 1990s zines boom was sparked by a resurgence of Do-It-Yourself philosophy that encouraged youth to create their own spaces, largely on their own terms. Because of this, I caution against a too-easy adoption of zines into the classroom. When teachers assign what was originally meant to challenge adult authority, the disrupting and playful potential of zines can be drained away. Despite these reservations, I believe that if zines are invited (and not required) and assessed as zines (and not as academic essays), then zines can foster spaces where youth create meaning—and themselves as meaningful—within and beyond the classroom.

One reason I use zines is to encourage students to understand that through their writing they can actively participate in public conversations that matter to them. If students imagine themselves as authors in public, textual conversations, they become genuinely invested in thinking about who will read their zines and what will persuade these audiences. These rhetorical concerns often lead to material ones where students think about what is needed to create and distribute zines. Therefore, exploring zines' rhetorical and material conventions can help students participate in public discussions that previously seemed closed to them.

Another reason I use zines is that they provide an occasion to address questions about multimodality. Zines blur the boundaries of text and graphics (and sound/film if electronic "e-zines") and ask students to consider which individual and combined modes will best make their arguments. This work cracks open conventions, giving students a fresh opportunity both to investigate why certain modes are favored and to design something new that might better meet their needs.

Addressing the rhetorical constructions, material conditions, and multimodal aspects of writing are issues we address everyday in our classrooms. Zines provide yet another possibility, an imagined third space, for students and teachers to understand these complex relationships surrounding literate activities.

Overt Instruction Activity

A Guided Assignment

In a guided assignment, students can re-tell a classroom text as a contemporary zine. On one level, this re-telling can help students achieve traditional goals, such as learning to summarize or to make meaningful connections between academic and non-academic audiences. On another level, students can reformulate these teacher-initiated inquiries by privileging what students find interesting. Students and teachers examine these student-driven texts to investigate what arguments can be made, by whom, in what contexts, and through what modes.

Transformed Practice Activity

An Open-ended Assignment

The open-ended assignment is more in line with the DIY spirit since it gives students greater control over the zine. In this assignment, I ask students to find ways to make their academic research essays accessible and meaningful to those outside the classroom. Zines are one possibility that students often take up. For example in a Rhetoric of Activism class, one student wrote a zine motivating his peers to challenge local efforts to gentrify campus town. A second student warned others about the dangers of the sugar sweetener Splenda,™ so she dropped off her zine at the local coffee shop. A third sought to encourage young African-American women to perform breast self-examines and enticed sorority sisters to publicize her project by placing their photo in her zine. In each of these projects, students gained a deeper understanding of the rhetorical and material problems they needed to solve if people beyond family and teachers were to read their writing.

The Mechanics of Zines

Zines can be any shape or size, but frequently they are folded sheets of 8 -1/2" x 11" paper that have been turned landscape and stapled along the middle crease. Images and graphics bleed into or can be superimposed onto text. The text itself can vary, and is often displayed on a slant, in various fonts, or with atypical characters and other stylized formatting. Since zines are about writers creating their own message, having students thoughtfully determine their own design conventions is central to the project.

Assessment Frame

Creating a Rubric and Assessing Writing

I work with students to create a rubric about what makes "good" writing. If zines can ever mediate a possible third space, students need the power to shape that space. Consequently, students are given great latitude in determining the criteria. To get to that point, we discussion:

- What tone is appropriate?
- How will their credibility be established (evidence, sentence structure, grammatical)?
- Who will choose to read their zines and how will students capture their attention? Answers to these questions need not conform to academic conventions, but students should justify their choices. When students decide for themselves the criteria for "good" writing, they see that "clarity" and "argument" and even "writing" are situated terms, open for negotiation. Students also learn that they can be part of that negotiation.

Throughout this process, I help students assess how well they are meeting their rubric through a "feasibility" test. Why would someone want to read writing that has misspellings or is grammatically confusing? Is everyone really interested in stem-cell research or redevelopment of green space in a particular community? If not, how and from whom can you generate that interest? These genuine questions ask students to reflect on their writing and to determine if their rhetorical strategies will be effective.

At the end of their project, I ask students to turn into me both their zines and a one page single-spaced rhetorical analysis (e.g., Who is their audience and what visual and textual strategies would this audience find persuasive? How did their research paper change as they created their zine, and why?). This assignment allows students to maintain control over their writing project while simultaneously prods them to develop a meta-language about and awareness of their writing.

Concluding Thoughts: Meeting Students Halfway

If literacy was a predictable, natural capacity for everyone, there would be no need to write a book like this. If our students followed an ideal trajectory—learning letters, putting letters together, developing phonological awareness, then decoding text, then reading phrases, then learning vocabulary, then comprehending increasingly more difficult texts—our jobs would be easier; not as interesting or rewarding, but easier. However, literacy is far from predictable and is as variable as we are. The point of the book is that this is not a bad thing to be changed, but instead, literacy is tied to who we are and what we like. As seen time and time again in the book, there are so many stories of literacy that inform our reading, listening, speaking, writing, and visually communicating. The patchwork of stories in the book serve as compelling evidence of the variability of literacy. As many strategies as we try, they seem to fall short in inspiring students to read.

For many struggling readers, it is not a lack of ability to develop literacy, but instead an issue of disengagement. For whatever reason, children, adolescents, and adults disengage from reading and writing and fall back in their literacy. We know from research and practice that the longer we allow literacy learners to fall behind, the longer it will take them to be proficient readers, writers, and meaning-makers. As I embark on a study, going into homes and schools in New Jersey, I recall a father expressing his deep concern for his son who did not enjoy reading and certainly could not be convinced to write, but who could spend hours reading comic books. As parents and teachers, it may not be a picture that we like, but it clearly is one that we need to accept and work with to think about how our children and students think and to respect what they love.

The book is about meeting students halfway. It is about what many educators already do, which is to put aside fears, lack of knowledge, and even feeling overwhelmed by curriculum and assessment to look at our students and their worlds.

Afterword

by Kate Pahl

It was a pleasure to read these accounts of family literacy practices, elegantly framed by Jennifer Rowsell. What is exciting about this book is the way it theorizes family literacy practices as always *in process*, constantly moving, and subject to complex crossings. The sites where family literacy takes place are found to be multiple. As children travel between sites—such as home, school, and playspaces—and experience those crossings, their narratives and literacy practices travel with them. Children and parents share the same spaces, and their literacy practices are shared and co-constructed. Family literacy practices weave in and out of school, home, and community settings, crossed by intergenerational practices and voices. Literacy, as produced within families, is created with siblings, parents, grandparents, and relatives (Gregory, Long and Volk, 2004). Many families speak more than one language, and these home languages are vital in keeping family relationships alive, often across diasporas, as children write letters to aunts and uncles in different parts of the globe (Kenner, 2004). Each family carries with it its own ways of doing and being in the world, and these practices and ways of being all form the *habitus* that informs family practices (Bourdieu, 1990; Pahl, 2005). In the process of understanding that traces of the habitus can be found sedimented in children's texts, the enormously important role of families and the cultural resources they bring to schooling can be grasped.

In my work looking at children's texts across home and school, I have drawn on the work of Merchant in seeing how children's texts can be related to "transient identities"; that is, children's identities that are in process and created through popular cultural texts, such as Barbie, and more anchored identities built up through the habitus of the household and intergenerational traditions, such as the Islamic ritual of Muharram (Merchant, 2005; Pahl, 2006b). What makes family literacy practices so fascinating is that they weave in and out of these different identities, changing and developing as children's experiences, with those of their parents, change and develop. They then resurface in school. Rather than talk about "schooled" literacy practices, classroom literacy can be seen as hybrid, crossed with different voices (Maybin, e-mail communication 24/3/06). In order to understand these hybrid textual spaces, I draw on the notion of "small stories" to describe where family stories surface in classroom texts and discursive practices (Georgakopoulou & Baynham, 2006). Small stories are fragments of stories—they might connect to other stories, told at different times and in different places. They can be identified within classroom discourse and also within children's texts. By identifying small stories, the day-to-day talk from family experiences can be listened to. May, a five-year-old child, drew a plan of her home and described to me the different aspects of her plan (Pahl, 2006b):

Kate: What gave you the idea?

May: My mum was drawing the plans.

Kate: Why was she doing a plan?

May: I don't know. She was doing a plan because she wanted t' house to be nice.

Kate: Yeah.

May: We are getting our kitchen made.

Kate: Is she doing an extension?

May: (louder) We haven't got no builders. Our builders have gone to a different (unclear)

Kate: Oh no!

May: So me dad's got to do it all by hisself!

May embeds the small story of her household's builder crisis within the larger description of her plan.

Within classroom discourses can often be found evidence of "seepage" (Marsh, in press) between domains, as children draw on cultural resources from outside school. Family literacy practices can be supported to become more visible in schools, permeating curricula and spreading across the school domain (Maybin, 2005; Marsh, in press). Ways of joining up home and school are numerous, and the value of this book is that it describes many of them and provides practical and inspirational ideas about how to take family literacy provision forward.

This book recognizes that family literacy is multiple in that it involves many generations; multiple in that multiple modes and multiple languages are involved when families make meaning. Families bring creativity to these multiple literacy practices. Families tell stories, create texts and artifacts, and give children space when they listen to them and support their meaning making. Family literacy can be honored in schools and out of schools as something growing, resourceful, meaningful, and strong. By building on families' strengths, as Zentella has suggested, we honor our families (Zentella, 2005). By honoring our families, we honor the cultures that surround and permeate our schools and give parents, teachers, and children a voice. Parents and children can enjoy together the multiple meanings of literacy. This book celebrates these meanings and takes forward the multi-sited and multimodal nature of family literacy practices in the 21st century.

Acknowledgments

In particular, I wish to thank the following people:

- Kate Pahl, for being my friend and collaborator.
- Kat Mototsune for her editorial wisdom.
- Mary Macchiusi, for her encouraging advice and guidance.
- Dorothy Strickland, for her gracious and thoughtful foreword.
- Lauren Amato, Yvon Appleby, Sandy Arbuck, Marika Autrand, Clive Beck, Erica Boling, Kathy Broad, Anne Burke, Louis Chen, John DeLaurentis, Marianna Diiorio, Brenda Stein Dsaldov, Hilary Inwood, Suzanne Kaplan, Catherine Compton Lilly, Nydia Flores Ferrán, Victoria Purcell-Gates, Lesley Mandel Morrow, Margaret Mackey, Jessica Rosevear, Isabel Pedersen, Mary Rabideau-Sheridan, Larry Swartz, Pippa Stein, Mary Lynn Tessaro, and Clark Wakabayashi, for their varied, textured, and enriched accounts of literacy—texts, practices, and family moments.
- Paris Campbell, for his inspired artwork.
- My Colleagues at Rutgers Graduate School of Education and OISE/University of Toronto, for their support.
- David Booth, Clare Kosnik, Melanie Kuhn, and Brian Street, for being my mentors.
- Lois Gatt, Lisa Murphy, Nathalie Laniado, Isabel Pedersen, Katherine Skippon, Larry Swartz, and Helen Tsotsos, for their friendships.
- Rowsell and Webster/Wanklyn families for their continued support.
- In memory of Sunny and Murray, for being a great Mum and Dad.
- Fred, Madeleine, and Kierra, for their love, of course.

Bibliography

Auerbach, E. (1995) "Which Way for Family Literacy: Intervention or Empowerment?" in L. Morrow (ed.) *Family Literacy: Connections in Schools and Communities*, Newark, DE: IRA.

Barrs, M. (1999). "Texts and Subtexts" n Barrs and Pidgeon's *Boys and Reading*. London, UK: Centre for Language in Primary Education.

Barton, D & Hamilton, M (1998) Local Literacies: *Reading and Writing in One Community*. London, UK: Routledge.

Bastiani, J. (2000). "'I Know It Works! … Actually Proving it is the Problem!':
Examining the Contribution of Parents to Pupil Progress and School Effectiveness" in S. Wolfendale and J. Bastiani (eds) *The Contribution of Parents to School Effectiveness*, pp. 19–36. London, UK: David Fulton.

Bearne, E. (2003). "Rethinking literacy: communication, representation and text." *Reading, Literacy and Language*. Volume 37, Number 3, November 2003. Norwich: Blackwell Publishing. pp. 98–103.

Beck, C., & Kosnik, C. (2006). *Innovations in Teacher Education: A social constructivist approach*. Albany, NY: SUNY Press.

Bennet, K.K., Weigel D. J., & Martin, S.S. (2002) "Children's acquisition of early literacy skills: examining family contributions" *Early Childhood Research Quarterly* 17, pp. 295–317.

Bloom, D. "Targeting those Twicky Teenagers." *Variety*, April 29, 2002.

Boethel, M. (2003). *Diversity: School, family & community connections*. Austin, TX: National Center for Family and Community Connections with Schools, Southwest Educational Development Laboratory.

Boling, E. C. (2006). "Teaching Literacy in the 21st Century: How can we best prepare teachers for integrating technology?" Paper presented at the annual Meeting of the American Educational Research Association (AERA). San Francisco, CA.

Bolter, Jay David & Grusin, Richard (1999). *Remediation: Understanding New Media*. Cambridge, MA: MIT Press.

Booth, D. (2002). *Even Hockey Players Read*. Markham, ON: Pembroke.

Bourdieu, P. (1990) trans, Nice, R., *The Logic of Practice*. Cambridge, MA: Polity Press.

Briggs, R. (1950). *The Bear*. London, UK: Random House.

Britto, P., Brooks-Gunn, J., & Griffin, T. (2006). "Maternal reading and teaching patterns: Associations with school readiness in low-income African American families" *Reading Research Quarterly*. Newark, DE: International Reading Association.

Broad, K, Diiorio, M., Rowsell, J., & Tessaro (2006). *The Home-School Divide: A Family Literacy Initiative*. Report produced for OISE/University of Toronto.

Bruno, L. (2005, October 24). "Principal Curbs Kids' Internet Activity" *Asbury Park Press*. Retrieved March 1, 2006 from http://www.app.com/apps/pbcs.dll/article?AID=/20051024/NEWS03/510240319/1007.

Burke, A. and Rowsell, J. (2006). "From Screen to Print: Publishing Multiliteracies Pedagogy" *The Learning Journal*, Volume 1, No. 20. Victoria, AU: Common Ground Publishers.

Bush, V. (1945). "As We May Think" *Atlantic Monthly*.

Cazden, C. (1989). "Richmond Road: A multilingual/multicultural primary school in Auckland, New Zealand" *Language and Education*. 3, 143–166.

Comber, B. and Nixon, H. (2005). "Children Reread and Rewrite Their Local Neighbourhoods: Critical Literacies and Identity Work." *Literacy Moves On: Popular Culture, New Technologies, and Critical Literacy in the Elementary Classroom*. Portsmouth, NH; Heinemann.

Comber, B. (2006). Presentation at Special Forum on Travel Notes From the New Literacy Studies. March 19, 2006

Cope, B. and Kalantzis, M. (eds.). (2000). *Multiliteracies: Literacy Learning and the Design of Social Futures*. London, UK: Routledge.

Dearstyne, B. (2005). "Blogs: The new information revolution?" *The Information Management Journal*, (Sept./Oct.), 38–44.

Delpit, L. (2003). "Educators as 'Seed People' Growing a New Future" *Educational Researcher*, Volume 7, No. 32, pp. 14–21.

Delpit, L. (1995). *Other People's Children: Cultural Conflict in the Classroom*. New York, NY: The New Press.

Desforges, C. & Abouchaar, A. (2003). *The impact of parental involvement, parental support, and family education on pupil achievement and adjustment: A literature review*. London, UK: National Literacy Trust.

Dora the Explorer http://www.nickjr.com/home/shows/ dora/index.jhtml

Douglas, M. (1991) "The Idea of a Home: A Kind of Space" *Social Research*. 58 (1): 287–307.

Dyson, A. Hass. (2005). Foreword to Evan, J. (ed) *Literacy Moves On*. Portsmouth, NH: Heinemann.

Dyson, A.H. (1993). *Social Worlds of Children Learning to Write in Urban Primary School*. New York, NY: Teachers College Press.

Dyson, A.H. (1997). *Writing Superheroes: Contemporary Childhood, Popular Culture, and Classroom Literacy*. New York, NY: Teachers College Press.

Dyson, A.Haas. (1993) *Social Worlds of Children Learning to Write in an Urban Primary School*. New York, NY: Teachers College Press.

Dyson, A.Haas.(2001) "Where are the childhoods in childhood literacy? An exploration in outer (school) space" *Journal of Early Childhood Literacy*. Vol. 1, Number 1 April 2001.

Epstein, J.L., Simon, B.S., & Salinas, K.C. (1995) "Involving parents in homework in the middle grades" *Research Bulletin*. No. 18.

Evans, J. (ed) (2005). *Literacy Moves On*. Portsmouth, NH: Heinemann.

Farr, M. & Guerra, J.C. (1995). "Literacy in the community: A study of Mexicano familias in Chicago" *Discourse Processes 19*. 7–19.

Feiler, A. (2005). "Linking home and school literacy in an inner city reception class." *Journal of Early Childhood Literacy*. Vol 5(2) 131–149. London, UK: Sage.

Freebody, P. & Luke, A. (1990). "Literacies programs: Debates and demands in cultural context" *Prospect: Australian Journal of TESOL*, 5(3), 7–16.

Fountas, I.C. & Pinnell, G.S. (2001). *Guiding Readers and Writers*. Portsmouth, NH. Heinemann.

Gee, J.P. (2003). *What Video Games Have to Teach Us About Learning and Literacy*. New York, NY: Palgrave-Macmillan.

Gee, J.P. (2005). *Why Video Games Are Good For the Soul*. Victoria, AU: Common Ground Publishers.

Georgakopoulou, A. and Baynham, M (2006) "'Big' stories and 'small' stories: reflections on methodological/theoretical issues in narrative research" BAAL Linguistic Ethnography Seminar. Marsh 2006. Milton Keynes.

Gilbert, K. & Appleby, Y. (2005). "'Sometimes I tell them from my old family': Bi-lingual family language, literacy and numeracy learning" Report written for the National Research and Development Centre for Adult Literacy and Numeracy. Lancaster, UK: University of Lancaster.

Gillen, J. (2003). *The Language of Children.* London, UK: Routledge.

Google "Company Overview" 2005, 16 March 2006 http://www.google.com/
intl/en/corporate/index.html

Google Earth http://earth.google.com/index.html

Greene, Maxine (1995). *Releasing the Imagination: Essays on Education, the Arts and Social Change.* New York, NY: Teachers College Press.

Gregory, E. (2001). "Sisters and Brothers as Language and Literacy Teachers: Synergy Between Siblings Playing and Working Together" *Journal of Early Childhood Literacy* 1 (3): 301–22.

Gregory, E., Long, S., & Volk, D. (eds) (2004) *Many Pathways to Literacy: Young children learning with siblings, grandparents, peers and communities.* London, UK: RoutledgeFalmer.

Gregory, E. (1996). *Making Sense of a New World.* London, UK: Paul Chapman.

Halliday, M.A.K. (1994). *An Introducion to Functional Grammar.* London, UK: Arnold.

Hannon, P. (1995) *Literacy, Home and School: Research and Practice in Teaching Literacy with Parents.* London, UK: Falmer Press.

Hart, B. & Risley, T.R. (1995). *Meaningful differences in the everyday experience of of young American children.* Baltimore, MD: Brookes.

Heath S. B. (1983). *Ways with Words: Language, Life and Work in Communities Homes and Classrooms.* Cambridge, MA: Cambridge University Press.

Holland, D. (1998). *Identity and Agency in Cultural Worlds.* Cambridge, MA.: Harvard University Press.

Hull, G. & Schultz, K. (2002). *School's Out! Bridging Out-of-School Literacies with Classroom Practice.* New York, NY: Teachers College Press.

Johnson, M. (1987) *The Body in the Mind.* Chicago, IL: U of Chicago Press.

Johnson, S. (2005). *Everything Bad Is Good For You: How Popular Culture Is Actually Making Us Smarter.* London, UK: Penguin Books.

Kamil, M. (2003). *Adolescent Literacy.* Department of Education Report.

King and Hornberger, N. (2005) "Literacies in Families and Communities" in *International Handbook of Educational Policy(Part 2)* Sascia, N., Cummins, A., Datnow, Leithwood, K., & Livingstone D. (eds) Dordrecht, Netherlands: Springer.

kooky kitchen http://pollypocket.everythinggirl.com/house/ kitchen/kitchen.aspx#

Kenner, C. (2004). *Becoming Biliterate: Young Children Learning Different Writing Systems.* Staffordshire, UK: Trentham Books.

Kosnik, C., & Beck, C. (2005). "The impact of a preservice teacher education program on language arts teaching practices" in C. Kosnik, C. Beck, A. Freese, & A. Samaras (eds.), *Making a difference in teacher education through self-study: Studies of personal, professional, and program renewal.* Dordrecht, Netherlands: Springer.

Kosnik, C. & Beck, C. (2003)." The contribution of faculty to community building in a teacher education program: A student teacher perspective" *Teacher Education Quarterly,* 30(3), 99–114.

Kress, G (1997). *Before Writing: Rethinking Paths to Literacy.* London, UK: Routledge.

Kress, Gunther (1998) "Visual And Verbal Modes Of Representation In Electronically Mediated Communication: The Potentials Of New Forms Of Text" 53–79 in *From Page to Screen: Taking Literacy into the Electronic Era* Ilana Snyder (ed), London, UK: Routledge.

Kress, G. (1995). *Writing the Future.* London, UK: Institute of Education Publication.

Kress, G. & Van Leeuwen, T. (1996). *Reading Images: The Grammar of Visual Design.* London, UK: Routledge.

Landow, George P. (1997). *Hypertext 2.0: The Convergence of Contemporary Critical Theory and Technology.* Baltimore, MD: The Johns Hopkins University Press.

LeCourt, D. (2004). *Identity matters: Schooling the student body in academic discourse.* Albany, NY: SUNY Press.

Lenhart, A., Rainie, L, & Lewis, O. (2001). "Teenage life online: The rise of the instant-message generation and the Internet's impact on friendships and family relationships" *Pew & Internet American Life*. Retrieved March, 2003 from http://www.pewinternet.org.

Lotherington, H. (2004). "What four skills? Redefining language and literacy skills in the digital era" *TESL Canada Journal*, 22 (1), 64–78.

Luke, A. and Freebody, P. (1997). "Shaping the social practices of reading" 185–225 in S. Muspratt, A. Luke, and P. Freebody (eds.), *Constructing critical literacies: Teaching and learning textual practice*. Cresskill, NJ: Hampton.

Luke, C. (1999). "Media and Cultural studies in Australia" *Journal of Adolescent and Adult Literacy*, 42, 622–626.

Luke, A. and Carrington, V. (2002). "Globalization, literacy, curriculum practice" 231–250 in R. Fisher, M. Lewis, and G. Brooks (eds). *Raising Standards in Literacy*. London, UK: Routledge/Falmer.

Marsh, J. & Millard, E. (2000). *Literacy and Popular Culture: Using Children's Culture in the Classroom*. London, UK: Paul Chapman.

Marsh, J. (in press). "Popular Culture in the Language Arts Curriculum" in J. Flood, S.B. Heath, and D. Lapp (eds) *Handbook on Research in Teaching Through the Communicative and Visual Arts, Volume 2*. New York, NY: Macmillan/ IRA.

Marshall, J. and Werndly, A. (2002). *The Language of Television*. London, UK: Routledge.

Maybin, J. (2005) *Children's Voices*. London, UK, and New York, NY: Palgrave Macmillan.

McLoughlin, L. (2000). *The Language of Magazines*. London, UK: Routledge.

Meek, M. (1971). *On Being Literate*. London, UK: The Bodley Head

Merchant, G. (2005). "Electric Involvement: Identity performance in children's informal digital writing" *Discourse: studies in the cultural politics of education*. Vol 26. No 3, 3301–314

Merchant, G. (2003). "Email me your thoughts: digital communication and narrative writing." *Reading, Literacy and Language*. Volume 37, Number 3, November 2003, pp. 104–110.

Moll, L.C., Amanti, C., Neff, D. and Gonzalez, N. (1992). "Funds of Knowledge for Teaching: Using a Qualitative Approach to Connect Homes and Classrooms" *Theory into Practice* 31 (2): 32–141.

Moloney, J. (2002). "Ideas for getting boys to read" www.home.gil.com.au/`cbcqid/moloney/books7.htm.

Moss, G. (1999). "Text in Context: Mapping Out the Gender Differentiation of the Reading Curriculum" in *Pedagogy, Culture, and Society*. Volume 7, No. 3. pp. 507–522.

Moss, G. (2001). "To work or play? Junior age non-fiction as objects of design" *Reading*, Volume 35, Number 3.

NHL hockey for kids http://www.nhl.com/kids/index.html

Oakley, A. (1994). "Women and children first and last: parallels and differences between children's and women's studies," in B. Mayall (ed.). *Children's Childhoods Observed and Experienced*. London, UK: Falmer Press.

Ormerod, F. & Ivanic, R. (2002). "Materiality in children's meaning-making practices" *Visual Communication* 1(1), 65–91.

Ontario Ministry of Education (2004). *Literacy for Learning: The report of the expert panel on literacy in grades 4 to 6 in Ontario*.

OWL Online http://www.owlkids.com

Pahl, K. (2005) "Narratives, artifacts and cultural identities: an ethnographic study of communicative practices in homes" *Linguistics and Education* (15) 4, 339 –358.

Pahl, K. (2006a) "An inventory of traces: children's photographs of their toys in three London homes" *Visual Communication* (5) 1, 95–114.

Pahl, K. (2006b) "Identity in children's texts: a story of crossings in a creative project" Paper presented as part of the AERA Symposium 2006 DIVISION G, Travel Notes from the New Literacy Studies: Instances of Practice. AERA San Francisco April 2006.

Pahl, K (2002). "Ephemera Mess and Miscellaneous Piles: Texts and Practices in Families" *Journal of Early Childhood Literacy* Vol. 2 No 1, April 2002.

Pahl, K. (1999). *Transformations: Meaning Making In Nursery Education.* London, UK: Trentham Books.

Pahl, K. & Rowsell, J. (2005). *Literacy and Education: Understanding New Literacy Studies in the Classroom.* London, UK: Paul Chapman.

Pahl, K. & Rowsell, J. (2006). *Travel Notes from the New Literacy Studies: Instances of Practice.* Clevedon, UK: Multilingual Matters.

Preece, Jennifer, Rogers, Yvonne, & Sharp, Helen. (2002) *Interaction Design: Beyond Human-Computer Interaction,* New York, NY: John Wiley & Sons.

QCA (Qualifications and Curriculum Authority) (2004). *More than words: Multimodal texts in the classroom.* Royston, UK: United Kingdom Literacy Association (UKLA).

Randall, N. (2002). *Lingo online: A report on the language of the keyboard generation.* Retrieved May, 2004 from http://arts.uwaterloo.ca/~nrandall/LingoOnline-finalreport.pdf

Randall, Neil & Pedersen, Isabel. (2000). "Metaphors of the Physical: Why the Internet Coheres." *Internet Research 1.0: The State of the Interdiscipline. The First Conference of the Association of Internet Researchers.* University of Kansas Lawrence, Kansas, September 14–17, 2000.

Reah, D. (1998). *The Language of Newspapers.* London, UK: Routledge.

Reese, L. & Gallimore, R. (2000). Immigrant Latinos' cultural model of literacy.

Richardson, Will. (2006). "The Educator's Guide to the Read/Write Web" *Educational Leadership,* (Dec. 2005/Jan. 2006), 24–27.

Ridgeway, J. (2005). *Baghdad Burning: Girl Blog From Iraq.* New York, NY: The Feminist Press.

Romanuk, P. (2005). *Hockey Superstars.* Markham, ON: Scholastic.

Rowsell, J. (2006). "Improvising on Artistic Habitus" in *Literacy Education and Bourdieu.* A. Luke and J. Albright (eds) Rahway, NJ: Erlbaum.

Rowsell, J. & Rajaratnam, D. (2005). "There is No Place Like Home: A Teacher Education Perspective on Literacies Across Educational Contexts." *Literacies Across Educational Contexts.* Brian Street (ed). Philadelphia, PA: Caslon Publishing.

Safford, K. & Barrs, M. (2006). *Many Routes to Meaning.* London, UK: Centre for Literacy in Primary Education.

Saraceni, M. (2003). *The Language of Comics.* London, UK: Routledge.

Sims, M. (2002). *Designing Family Support Programs: building children, family and community resilience.* Victoria, AU: Common Ground Publishing.

Selfridge, Benjamin & Peter. (2004). *A Kid's Guide to Creating Web Pages.* Chicago, IL: Zephyr Press.

Smith, M. & Wilhelm, J. (2002). *Reading don't fix no Chevys: Literacy in the lives of young men.* Portsmouth, NH: Heinemann.

Sponge Bob Square Pants Videogame: Battle for Bikini Bottom (2003). Produced by Viacom International. Created by Stephen Hillenburg.

Sports Illustrated for Kids http://www.sikids.com

Starks, D (1994). Planned vs. Unplanned Discourse: Oral Narrative vs. Conversation

Stead, T. (2005) *Reality Checks.* Portland, ME: Steinhouse.

Street, B. (1995) *Social Literacies: Critical perspectives on Literacy in Development, Ethnography and Education.* London, UK: Longman.

Tally, P. (2005). "Re-imagining Girlhood: Hollywood and the Tween Girl Film Market" in C. Mitchell & J. Reid-Walsh, *Seven Going on Seventeen.* New York, NY: Peter Lang.

Taylor (1991). *Learning Denied.* Portsmouth, NH: Heinemann

Teletubbies http://pbskids.org/teletubbies/everywhere.html

Teele, S. (2004). *Overcoming Barricades to Reading.* Thousand Oaks, CA: Corwin.

Tovani, C. (2000). *I Read It, But I Don't Get It: Comprehension Strategies for Adolescent Readers.* Portland, ME: Stenhouse Publishers.

Turkle, S. (1995). *Life On The Screen: Identity In The Age Of The Internet.* New York, NY: Simon & Schuster.

Vasquez, V. M. (2004). *Negotiating Critical Literacies With Young Children.* Mahwah, NJ: Lawrences Erlbaum.

Vygotski, L. (1978). *Mind in Society.* Cambridge, MA: Harvard University Press.

Wells, P. (2002). "Tell Me about Your Id, When You was a Kid, yah?" in D. Buckingham *Small Screens.* London, UK: Leicester University Press.

Wenger, E. (1992). *Communities of Practice: Learning, Meaning, and Identity.* Cambridge, MA: Cambridge University Press.

Williams, A. & Gregory, E. (2001). "Siblings Bridging Literacies in Multilingual Contexts" *Journal of Research in Reading* 24 (3): 248–65.

Winnicott, D. (1971). *Playing and Reality.* Middlesex, UK: Penguin.

Yahooligans http://yahooligans.yahoo.com

Zentella, A. C. (ed) (2005) *Building on Strength: Language and Literacy in Latino Families and Communities*, Language & Literacy Series. New York, NY: Teachers' College Press.

Glossary

Affordance: the ability to use materials that enhance a text; e.g., adding animation or a video to a blog

Artifact: an object that is important to an individual and tied to a context or place, often with sets of practices associated with it; e.g., a three-dimensional figurine belonging to a child

Bilingualism: having the capacity to speak two languages; e.g., Arabic and English.

Blogs, or Weblogs: web spaces that present identities and have personal or professional messages.

Constraint: an aspect of a text that holds it back from being functional; e.g., having too few visuals and too much written text, or vice versa. Constraints can shift from one context to the next (i.e., in school, more written text in essays is better; however, too much written text in an electronic text is neither appealing to the eye nor what we are accustomed to).

Critical Literacy: a framework that peels back language and visual elements to look at underlying meanings and assumptions; e.g., analyzing two different newspapers and their interpretation of the same event

Crossing: leaving one context and entering a new one; e.g., leaving school and entering home

Cultural Capital: The benefits that we bring to situations and events; e.g., when children who come from different cultures and have two languages bring these skills to school

Cultural Resources: artifacts, texts, practices, and linguistic systems that we have that can inform our meaning-making

Discourse: language in a social context; e.g., the language of English educators (Gee, 1996).

Domains: spaces or contexts where meaning-making takes place; e.g., school, home

Ethnography: the detailed recording of a particular culture or context that requires a researcher to stand away and draw near at the same time; e.g., trying to observe your classroom with fresh eyes

Family Literacy: activities that involve parents and children in literacy; for the purposes of this book, it is bringing family literacy as a philosophy into school

Funds of Knowledge: the cultural resources and competencies that we bring to other settings; e.g., home stories built into children's writing and drawings

Genre Theory: categories for different kinds of texts in a variety of media; e.g., how rap is a genre of music and perhaps poetry

Global: networks and entities that exist outside of the local; e.g., international publishing corporations with multiple communicational satellites

Globalization: changes in our social, political, technological, economic, and cultural landscape due to innovation and changes in society

Hybridity: different texts operating in the same frame; e.g., using hypertext while visiting an institutional web site

Identity: a way of describing people, their backgrounds, and their funds of knowledge

Ideology: ideas that are embedded in the things we do, say, write, and depict visually; e.g., the use of photographs in magazines to depict an emotion like anger or seduction.

Lifeworlds: figurative and actual spaces in which children make meaning; e.g., a child might spend a lot of time in cyberspace surfing the Internet or playing video games

Literacies: different kinds and styles of meaning-making based on our variable experiences, backgrounds, cultures, etc.; e.g., we have a literacy in quilt-making or in newspaper writing

Literacy: making meaning in multiple modalities; e.g., reading a picture book, reading an academic article

Literacy Event: any interaction with print or other modalities; e.g., creating a unit.

Literacy Practice: patterns of activity around literacy; e.g., having a literature circle with students

Local: contexts that are nearby; e.g., a community centre.

Materiality: how the materials we use in our making and reading of texts affects its content and design

Meaning-making: any oral, visual, linguistic/written, tactile, spoken understanding that takes place with texts of all kinds. There is a deliberate use of the term in the book to signal a broadening of the terms *reading* and *writing*; e.g., meaning that is derived from a child in the making of pictures and three-dimensional figures

Mode: the aspects of a text from which we make meaning; e.g., using the color red to signal love in a Valentine card

Multiple Literacies: many linguistic systems existing within a common space; e.g., students with languages other than the primary language in your classroom.

Multiliteracies: pedagogy and practice that is based on the screen and our students' understanding of multimodality in their meaning-making; e.g., an activity about non-fiction text that involves creating a web site for a company and how icons, symbols, written text, images, and photographs send a particular message

Multimodality: deriving meaning from the mixing and melding together of different modes; e.g., deriving meaning from a movie, i.e., the combination of moving pictures, color, dialogue, and narration

Narrative: choosing a particular way of telling or writing a text; e.g., writing descriptions of scenes in a graphic story

New Literacy Studies: a field of literacy education that views literacy as taking place everywhere all of the time, guided by social context and practices that take place in that context; e.g., the language and practices of skateboarding

Out-of-School Literacy Practices: any meaning-making that takes place outside of school; e.g., a group of adolescents playing a video game

Pedagogy: frameworks and habits of mind in teaching that guide our instruction; e.g., thinking about inclusivity in our planning and assessment

Schooled Literacy: a view of literacy that is tied to schooling; e.g., having students get into groups to read and respond to texts based on a set of questions developed by a teacher

Sedimenting Identity into Texts: a process whereby individuals use their own experience, prior knowledge, and background and embed it in texts that they create; e.g., how young children bring family narratives and family artifacts into their artwork or multimodal texts

Sign: a combination of meaning and form; e.g., a yield sign on the roadside

Site: a place or context that carries its own set of ideologies and practices; e.g., a grocery store

Social Practice: ways of being and doing that are informed by contexts; e.g., recycling bins and how to separate recyclable items

Space: an environment, real or imagined, that conjures up pictures in the mind; e.g., your kitchen.

Synaesthesia: our immediate response when we respond to a mode; e.g., seeing colors when we read a word

Syncretic Literacy: two cultural practices that come together during a literacy practice; e.g., reading a math textbook at the diningroom table

Text: any object from which we make meaning; e.g., a chair that is made in a particular style for a particular purpose and to be used in a particular place or context

Third Space: where we draw on discourses, texts, and practices from other domains to make meaning; e.g., making the classroom a third space by building on texts students use outside of school

Visual Communication: ways of expressing meaning through multiple modes to send across a certain message; e.g., advertisements that use photographs to send a certain message

Zines: online magazine-style web spaces that present ideas and topics, and elicit responses

Index